INTERCULTURAL EDUCATION IN THE EUROPEAN CONTEXT

Research in Migration and Ethnic Relations Series

Series Editor:
Maykel Verkuyten, ERCOMER
Utrecht University

The Research in Migration and Ethnic Relations series has been at the forefront of research in the field for ten years. The series has built an international reputation for cutting edge theoretical work, for comparative research especially on Europe and for nationally-based studies with broader relevance to international issues. Published in association with the European Research Centre on Migration and Ethnic Relations (ERCOMER), Utrecht University, it draws contributions from the best international scholars in the field, offering an interdisciplinary perspective on some of the key issues of the contemporary world.

Also in series

Suspect Families
DNA Analysis, Family Reunification and Immigration Policies
Edited by Torsten Heinemann, Ilpo Helén, Thomas Lemke,
Ursula Naue and Martin G. Weiss
ISBN 978 1 4724 2424 2

Diasporas and Homeland Conflicts
A Comparative Perspective
Bahar Baser
ISBN 978 1 4724 2562 1

Full series list at back of book

**EUROPEAN RESEARCH CENTRE
ON MIGRATION & ETHNIC RELATIONS**

Intercultural Education in the European Context
Theories, Experiences, Challenges

Edited by

MARCO CATARCI
Roma Tre University, Italy

MASSIMILIANO FIORUCCI
Roma Tre University, Italy

ASHGATE

Published by
Ashgate Publishing Limited
Wey Court East
Union Road
Farnham
Surrey, GU9 7PT
England

Ashgate Publishing Company
110 Cherry Street
Suite 3-1
Burlington, VT 05401-3818
USA

www.ashgate.com

British Library Cataloguing in Publication Data
A catalogue record for this book is available from the British Library

The Library of Congress has cataloged the printed edition as follows:
Catarci, Marco.
 Intercultural education in the European context : theories, experiences, challenges / by Marco Catarci and Massimiliano Fiorucci.
   pages cm. – (Research in migration and ethnic relations series)
 Includes bibliographical references and index.
 ISBN 978-1-4724-5162-0 (hardback) – ISBN 978-1-4724-5163-7 (ebook) –
ISBN 978-1-4724-5164-4 (epub) 1. Multicultural education–Europe. I. Fiorucci,
Massimiliano. II. Title.
 LC1099.5.E85C38 2015
 370.116–dc23

2014029210

ISBN   9781472451620 (hbk)
ISBN   9781472451637 (ebk – PDF)
ISBN   9781472451644 (ebk – ePUB)

Printed in the United Kingdom by Henry Ling Limited,
at the Dorset Press, Dorchester, DT1 1HD

Contents

List of Figures and Tables

Figures

Tables

Notes on Contributors

Hana Alhadi is a Master's graduate on the Migration and Ethnic Studies Programme at the University of Amsterdam. Her personal background as a European Slovenian and Middle Eastern Yemeni gives her a particular perspective on intercultural education. Her research interests lie in addressing intercultural experiences, intercultural dialogue and policy implementation of intercultural education at the European to the Dutch district level.

Lidia Cabrera Pérez holds a PhD in Educational Science. She is a tenured lecturer in research methods and diagnostic studies in education at the University of La Laguna, Spain, where she teaches the Master of Psychopedagogy course on assessment and evaluation in education. She is also on the staff of the doctoral programme in education as research at the university. Her focus is on dropouts and failure in higher education, and intercultural education, and she has published extensively on these topics. Dr Cabrera Pérez has also participated in different projects at the Universities of Lisbon, Amsterdam, Massachusetts-Boston and at the Instituto Politécnico (Costa Rica).

Marco Catarci is Associate Professor of Social and Intercultural Education in the Department of Education, Roma Tre University. He holds a PhD in Education and collaborates with the Research Centre on Intercultural and Development Education at Roma Tre. He is a member of the PhD School in Educational Research and Theory, and has been a member of the Board of the Italian Society for Pedagogy and of the Italian National University Council. He has taken part in many national and European research projects in the field of education, and has presented several papers at international conferences. His major research interests include intercultural education, cultural mediation and inclusion of refugees, and he is the author of books, articles and research reports on these topics.

Giovanni Cicero Catanese holds a PhD in Intercultural Education (University of Messina). His research focuses on the bilingual education of deaf children through sign language, and he has completed an analysis of educational initiatives in linguistic contexts with a high concentration of immigrants. He is the author of several publications on these issues and since 2004 has cooperated with the Institut für Interkulturelle Pädagogik im Elementarbereich (IPE) of Mainz (Germany), where he has developed a European Language Portfolio for young children. Since 2009, he has been a lecturer (*Lehrbeauftragter*) in several German universities

(Cologne, Hildesheim, Karlsruhe), where he teaches courses on issues of intercultural education and plurilingualism in kindergartens and primary schools.

Otto Filtzinger has been professor at the University of Applied Sciences in Koblenz for group work in social services and intercultural community work, and was a co-founder of the European Centre for Community Education (ECCE). Until 2012 he taught comparative sciences of education and intercultural pedagogy at the Free University of Bolzano (Italy) but is currently Director of IPE-Mainz Institut für Interkulturelle Pädagogik im Elementarbereich e.V. (Institute for Intercultural Pedagogy in the Elementary Education Sector). He works in continuing education, and is the author of German- and Italian-language publications addressing intercultural pedagogy, intercultural opening of institutions, intercultural dimensions in educational institutions for qualified pedagogic personnel and early multilinguism.

Massimiliano Fiorucci is Associate Professor of Social and Intercultural Education in the Department of Education, Roma Tre University. He holds a PhD in Education and coordinates the Research Centre on Intercultural and Development Education at Roma Tre. He is a member of the PhD School in Educational Research and Theory and has been member of the Board of the Italian Society for Pedagogy. His research interests include intercultural education, lifelong learning and cultural mediation. He has been a principal investigator on these topics and in many other research projects; has lectured and hosted conferences at various European universities; and has published books, articles and research reports.

Guadalupe Francia is Associate Professor of Education at Uppsala University (Sweden), and a specialist in the Network of Experts on Social Aspect of Education and Training for the EU Commission (NESET). Her research interests are: education policies and education reforms; comparative education research; equity research; children's rights; equality standards and assessment claims; free choice and diversity; social and cultural justice; and intertextuality in the analysis of educational policies and reforms.

Jagdish S. Gundara is Professor Emeritus of Education at the Institute of Education, University of London. He has held important positions in several international institutes, including: UNESCO – International Studies and Teacher Education at the School of Culture, International Centre for Intercultural Education; the International Broadcasting Trust (IBT), and Board member until 2012; the Commission for Racial Equal; and the Evens Foundation Intercultural Education Jury. He is the author of *Interculturalism, Education and Inclusion* (2000), co-editor of *Intercultural Social Policy in Europe* (Ashgate, 2000) and has published extensively in the fields of human rights and education in multicultural studies.

George P. Markou is Professor of Education in the Department of Philosophy, Education and Psychology at the University of Athens. He has studied pedagogy, psychology, sociology and philosophy both there and at the Free University of Berlin. He has participated as an expert in several research projects developed by the Council of Europe, UNESCO and the European Union. He has worked in the Ministry of Education as Secretary of Primary and Secondary Education, and has represented Greece on several educational committees at European level. He was president of the Institute for the Education of Greeks Abroad and Intercultural Education (IPODE) from 2000 to 2004 and is the founding president of the Centre for Intercultural Studies of the University of Athens, a position he has held since 1995. His major professional interests are related to the scientific/research fields of comparative education, educational policy and intercultural education.

Martha Montero-Sieburth is a research fellow at the University of Amsterdam Institute for Migration and Ethnic Studies (IMES) and a lecturer at the Graduate School of Social Sciences at Amsterdam University College. She is also Professor Emerita of the University of Massachusetts-Boston, where she served until 2007. She holds an EdD in Instructional Development and Administration, with a focus on bilingual education (Boston University) and is a Postdoctoral Fellow in International Education (Harvard). Dr Montero-Sieburth is a multicultural, international, cross-cultural, comparative education and intercultural educator whose research and publications in the US have been directed at Latino and Mexican communities in New England. She has researched indigenous populations and issues of bilingualism in Latin America; in Europe she has studied Latin Americans in Spain, second-generation Dutch-Turkish high school students in the Netherlands and, most recently, Mexicans in the Netherlands in collaboration with Dr Lidia Cabrera Pérez. She has written more than 150 articles and has co-edited *Latinos in a Changing Society* (with Edwin Melendez, 2007); *Making Invisible Latino Adolescents Visible: A Critical Approach to Latino Diversity* (with Francisco Villarruel, 1999); and *The Struggle of a New Paradigm: Qualitative Research in Latin America* (with Gary L. Anderson, 1998).

Christos Parthenis is lecturer in Educational Research (Theory and Practice of multicultural Education) at the University of Athens. He holds a PhD from the National and Kapodistrian University of Athens and an MSc in Science and Research from Gothenburg University, Sweden. For many years he has participated as an expert in the Programme *The Education of Returning Greek and Foreign Immigrant Children*, and more precisely, for the years 1997–2000, 2002–2004, 2006–2008. Since 2013, he has been Academic Supervisor of the programme *Education of Roma Children* developed by the European Union in collaboration with the University of Athens and specifically, the Research Centre for Education in Athens. He is the author of various scholarly publications including two books: *Theory and Practice: Macro- and Micro Approaches to Intercultural Education in the Context of Applied Education* (2013) and *Epistemological Principles of*

Intercultural Education (2008), in Greek language, while he has presented several papers at international conferences.

Teresa Pozo Llorente holds a PhD in Educational Science and is tenured Lecturer in Research Methods and Diagnostics in Education at the University of Granada. She is part of an institutional research group which focuses on the social, environmental and institutional evaluation. Currently, she works in programme evaluation and social and intercultural education. Her research focus is qualitative research methods and evaluation research. She is the author of various scientific publications and contributions to international conferences, and participates as a researcher and collaborator in numerous projects, ranging from regional and national to international events. She has lectured and attended several conferences at various universities in Europe (Hamburg, Rome, Florence), Latin America (Cienfuegos, Ciego de Avila, Santo Domingo) and the USA (Massachusetts-Boston).

Martine A. Preteceille is Professor Emerita at 'Paris 8' University and Paris III Sorbonne. She is also a professor at New York University and a member of the Conseil Scientifique de la Recherche et de la Technologie du Ministère de l'enseignement (CSRT). She has published numerous books and articles on intercultural education and communication, and carried out expert missions for UNESCO, the OECD and the Council of Europe. Among her publications are: *Vers une pédagogie interculturelle* (1986, 2004); *L'éducation interculturelle* (1999, 4th edn 2013); *Education et communication interculturelle* (1996, 2001); *Diagonales de la communication interculturelle* (ed., 1999); *Former et éduquer en contexte hétérogène. Pour un humanisme du divers* (2003); and *Les métamorphoses de l'identité* (ed., 2006).

Jordi Vallespir Soler obtained a PhD in Educational Science in 1987. Currently he is a tenured lecturer in the Department of Applied Pedagogy and Educational Psychology at the Universitat de les Illes Balears, and is also principal researcher for the Intercultural Education Research Group. He is the author of various scientific publications related to multicultural education, as well as a contributor to numerous international conferences. He also lectures and presents at various Spanish and international universities (Rome, Berlin, Sao Paulo, Sibiu, Los Angeles) and is currently conducting intervarsity studies.

Preface

This volume focuses on a comparative analysis of the intercultural theories and practices which were developed in the European context in the main 'old immigration countries' (the United Kingdom, France and Germany), the 'new immigration countries' (Italy, Spain and Greece) and some Northern European countries (the Netherlands and Sweden) in which specific approaches to intercultural education have been established.

The study has been carried out by a network of scholars and researchers active in the field of intercultural education in several European countries: Italy, the UK, France, Germany, Spain, Greece, the Netherlands and Sweden. The contributors have carried out their analyses in these countries using the following joint research questions:

- What are the main features of the presence of immigrants and/or groups with different cultural backgrounds in the country?
- What are the main features of the presence of immigrant students and/or students with different cultural backgrounds in the school?
- What are the most important issues raised by scientific research about the presence of immigrant students and/or students with different cultural backgrounds in the school?
- What are the most relevant educational practices and strategies that have been adopted to address these problems in the school?
- What is one example of best practice in the school with reference to its educational context?
- In conclusion, what are the major strengths and weaknesses of the intercultural education approach adopted in the country?

In assuming that specific meanings are related to the cultural, social, economic and political characteristics of each national context, these questions represent a solid foundation for a rewarding debate among the researchers involved in the study. The study's methodological framework relates particularly to comparative research. It must be highlighted that the study of education in a globalised context unavoidably invites comparisons. According to David Phillips and Michele Schweisfurth (2014: 3), 'we are all comparativists now'. Comparative inquiry is commonly adopted in all fields of education in order to take into account the complexities of educational processes and view them in a more global context.

In general, cross-national comparative research aims to observe social phenomena across nations in order to develop explanations of similarities or differences; to attempt to predict their consequences; and to acquire a better understanding of the processes being analysed (Hantrais, 2007: 3). In this sense, the wide-ranging nature of the field of comparative methods sets up a 'liberating' involvement for the scholars, who can work with both their own ideas and those of other people. The strength of this approach lies in it not being a real discipline, but rather a 'context'. In fact, the factor which brings together scholars who adopt comparative methodologies in order to deal with a wide range of topics that demand specific expertise is the common attempt to compare multidimensional subjects.

The ability to develop ways of making comparisons is an essential aspect of intellectual inquiry which is indispensable in the process of decision-making in a field such as education. Such an approach provides a global description of the various forms of education; determines the relationships and interactions between the different aspects of education; and defines the essential conditions required for educational change. In other words, a comparative approach involves the pursuit of a wide range of aims. It can examine alternative means of provision; offer yardsticks by which to judge the performance of educational systems; predict possible outcomes of actions by looking at experiences in other countries; and provide a body of descriptive data in order to view diverse educational practices in a wider context. It can contribute to the development of a theoretical framework in which analyses of educational factors provide data for politicians' and administrators' decisions, and can also play an important supportive role in the development of any educational reform and foster co-operation and mutual understanding between nations. As a scholarly activity it is also of intrinsic intellectual interest (Phillips, 2000: 298).

From a methodological point of view, in comparative inquiries a range of research methods into several aspects of education are adopted. The methods are:

- descriptive (of phenomena or conditions and of relations between variables);
- analytical (of roles and the specification of cause-and-effect relations or of relations and consequences);
- evaluative (of the merits and value of programmes or techniques of decision making);
- exploratory (generating new hypotheses or questions); and
- predictive (exploring relationships and functions with the potential for in-depth research) (Phillips and Schweisfurth, 2014: 103).

According to Robert Cowen, a comparative approach allows the researcher to 'read globally' by applying appropriate levels of academic attention and providing an interpretation of conditions in various parts of the world which are being raised to visibility. The approach also involves shifting paradigms in relation to political and economic modifications and to the researcher's trains of thought (Cowen, 2009: 337–8). In this sense, the classic problem of comparative education is made up of three essential moments: *transfer*; *translation* of educational ideas, principles, policies and practices; and the *transformation* of educational phenomena in a new place (Cowen, 2009: 339).

It must be observed that, with regard to the complexity of the international scenario, the study of the 'transfer' – concerning the movement of and educational idea in a supra-, trans- or inter-national space – has become increasingly relevant, when:

- transfer is the movement of an educational idea or practice in a supra-national or trans-national or inter-national space, creating a 'space-gate' moment, with its politics of attraction;
- translation is the shape-shifting of educational institutions or the reinterpretation of educational ideas which routinely occurs during a transfer in space – the 'chameleon process'; and
- transformations are metamorphoses which the compression of social and economic power within education in the new context is imposed on the initial translation – that is, a range of transformations which cover both the indigenisation and the extinction of the translated form (Cowen, 2006: 566).

In this sense, comparative approaches aim at both 'improvement' and 'knowledge' in the field of education, underlining the close interweaving of comparative studies and international dynamics and the complexity of the cultural relations of power (Palomba, 2011: 39).

Thus, the analyses provided in this book focus on the characteristics of the presence of immigrants and of students from different cultural backgrounds; on the major issues raised by the educational research; on the practices and approaches developed; and on their strengths and weaknesses. In examining these topics, the study will provide a wide framework involving several perspectives and practices of intercultural education as adopted in the European context, so highlighting the contribution of education to the development of a fair, democratic and pluralistic Europe.

In conclusion, acknowledgment must be given to all the scholars who took part in the study, each of whom have offered, from a particular point of view, a unique contribution to the overall analysis, as part of a tangible intercultural perspective.

MARCO CATARCI AND MASSIMILIANO FIORUCCI
Roma Tre University

References

Cowen, R. (2006). Acting comparatively upon the educational world: Puzzles and possibilities. *Oxford Review of Education*, 32, 561–73.

Cowen, R. (2009). *Editorial Introduction: The National, the International, and the Global*. In Cowen, R. and Kazamias, A.M. (eds). *International Handbook of Comparative Education*. Dordrecht: Springer.

Hantrais, L. (2007). Contextualization in cross-national comparative research. In Hantrais, L. and Mangen, S. (eds). *Cross-National Research Methodology and Practice*. Oxford: Routledge.

Palomba, D. (2011). Comparative studies in education: An historical-critical introduction. *Journal of Educational Cultural and Psychological Studies*, 4, 29–45.

Phillips, D. (2000). Learning from elsewhere in education. *Comparative Education*, 36, 297–307.

Phillips, D. and Schweisfurth, M. (2014). *Comparative and International Education: An Introduction to Theory, Method, and Practice*. 2nd edn. London: Bloomsbury.

Chapter 1

Interculturalism in Education across Europe

Marco Catarci

> Ideas, cultures, and histories cannot seriously be understood or studied without their force, or more precisely their configurations of power, also being studied.
>
> (Said, 1978: 5)

Interculturalism and its many implications for the education system is among the important issues that will decisively shape the dynamics and features of oncoming European society. In particular, the question of an education system able to assure equal opportunities to all students regardless of their social or cultural background and to develop intercultural awareness and skills on behalf of the entire school population will be a fundamental testing ground for an increasingly multicultural Europe. This will require a strong capacity of ensuring high-quality education for all its members, minimising disparities and avoiding polarisation in outcomes.

Indeed education, in the several forms of its study, analysis and application, is strictly related to the project of a society that will be built through such engagement. Highlighting the importance of taking this into account, Freire explained:

> The pedagogy which we defend, conceived in a significant area of the Third World, is itself a utopian pedagogy. By this very fact it is full of hope, for to be utopian is not to be merely idealistic or impractical but rather to engage in denunciation and annunciation. Our pedagogy cannot do without a vision of man and of the world. It formulates a scientific humanist conception which finds its expression in a dialogical praxis in which the teachers and learners together, in the act of analyzing a dehumanizing reality, denounce it while announcing its transformation in the name of the liberation of man. (Freire, 1970: 20)

Throughout the world, national education systems are currently facing several major challenges:

- adjust learning processes, curriculum content and school management to learner's backgrounds;
- stress democratic citizenship and respect for human rights and address issues related to discrimination and exclusion;
- emphasise sustainable development as the desired social outcome of education;
- plan special measures to reach vulnerable and marginalised groups; and
- improve school and educational environments (UNESCO, 2009: 98–100).

In this sense, Cushner, McClelland and Safford suggest that 'it is worth thinking about our changing circumstances and the impact these changes are having on the way we live, work, play, govern ourselves, worship, and learn' (Cushner et al., 2012: 7). Indeed, processes like international integration of the world, demographic and migration trends, technology and changing attitudes among generations provide on the whole a rationale for better cross-cultural awareness.

Without doubt, although a source of difficulties and problems, the multicultural dimension of current society represents first of all a hard fact that calls for urgent reflection at the political, social and educational levels to address the numerous challenges derived from it.

Multiculturalism and Interculturalism

Two major terms have been at the centre of the scientific debate on how to manage cultural diversity in the education system and in society in the last 50 years: 'multiculturalism' and 'interculturalism'. It must be observed that a semantic analysis of these expressions does not highlight merely formal considerations, as these terms carry implicit theories and settings in formal and non-formal education systems in national contexts, or even different approaches within the same national context. For both expressions – multiculturalism and interculturalism – different definitions provided by the scientific literature will be examined, along with their cruces and their current developments.

The first term, multiculturalism, first appeared in the 1960s and 1970s in Canada and in Australia, and then in Britain and the USA. It came to be associated with diversity and how the state dealt with different religious and cultural groups in order to provide equal opportunity, individual freedom and group recognition (Barn, 2012: 103).

Specifically, in 1971 Canada was the first country to adopt multiculturalism as an official policy, affirming the value and dignity of all citizens regardless of their cultural origins, language or religious affiliation; confirming the status of Canada's two official languages; and highlighting that cross-cultural understanding and mutual respect can develop common attitudes.

Banks has defined 'multicultural education' as 'a movement designed to change schools, colleges, and universities so that students from diverse racial, ethnic, cultural, language, social, class, and religious groups will experience equal educational opportunity' (Banks, 2008b: 393). Furthermore, it also supports students from all groups to develop democratic attitudes needed to function effectively in culturally diverse communities (Banks, 2008b: 393).

Ultimately, a multicultural approach is also aimed at changing the structure of educational institutions to assure equal chances to achieve academically in school (Banks, 1993: 4). In this sense, Banks traces this perspective back to the civil rights movement of the 1960s in the United States, remembering that in that period African American people started an unprecedented quest for their rights, and highlighting a strong connection between multicultural education and the major goals of promoting equity in educational outcomes across diverse populations of students and educational equality for all students.

In this perspective, students must be considered as change agents, overcoming their traditional roles of reproducing the social structure, enabling them to acquire knowledge useful for social action and change (Banks, 2001: 239–40). Among essential dimensions of multicultural education are:

- *content integration*, assuring the use of content from a variety of cultures in education;
- *knowledge construction*, deconstructing the implicit cultural assumptions in the construction of knowledge;
- an *equity pedagogy*, aimed at promoting educational achievement of students from diverse socio-cultural background; and
- an *empowering school culture*, addressed to increase political, social and educational strength of students from diverse socio-cultural background (Banks, 1993: 20–23).

According to Grant, the notion of multiculturalism is both a philosophical concept and an educational process, which assumes that 'equality' and 'equity' do not coincide, as equal access does not necessarily guarantee fairness. Therefore, providing knowledge about the history, culture and contributions of the diverse groups in society, multicultural education:

> prepares all students to work actively toward structural equality in the organizations, and informs all subject areas and other aspect of the curriculum. … Like all good educational strategies, it helps students to develop positive self-concepts and to discover who they are, particularly in terms of their multiple group memberships. (Grant, 1997: 171)

In particular, Lynch proposes a definition of culture as a network of values, conceptions, methods of thinking and communicating, customs and sentiments adopted as a socio-ecological coping mechanism and as an active capital of non-material, socio-historical character by individuals, groups and nations. Within this framework, prejudice, discrimination and stereotyping are functions not only of personality but also of societal and institutional structure and power distribution (Lynch, 1983: 33).

Other definitions of multicultural education in scientific literature highlight its assumption that gender, ethnic and cultural diversity of a pluralistic society should be reflected in all of its institutionalised structures – but particularly in schools (Chu, 1997: 182); and its application in policies and practices that recognise, accept and affirm human differences and similarities related not only to culture but also to gender, disability, class and sexual preference (Armbruster and Ahn, 2003: 229).

However, in the course of time, the practice of the notion of multicultural education has also highlighted several critical issues. In particular, multiculturalism has been criticised for not offering a critical enough perspective; or, in other words, for not being more anti-racist in its analysis (Thayer-Bacon et al., 2003: 229).

Steinberg and Kincheloe remark also that – becoming more related with the politics of education, and not just as a further content area subject – such an approach needs a deep analysis of multiculturalism as a discipline unto itself, traditionally constructed adding pieces of information about 'other' people while primarily discussing dominant culture (Steinberg and Kincheloe, 2009: 3). Furthermore, a critical approach to multiculturalism calls for a better understanding of how social, cultural, political and economic structures shape each person and establish how that person is perceived, as 'in an educational context, critical multiculturalism names the power wielders who contribute to the structuring of knowledge, values, and identity' (Steinberg and Kincheloe, 2009: 5).

Finally, concerning the current developments of the notion of multiculturalism, Banks calls for an evolution of such a notion within the framework of 'citizenship education', not to be meant in the traditional assimilationist acceptation of educating students to reach the mythical conception of a 'good citizen' regardless of their cultural background, but rather to provide opportunities of maintaining aspects of their community cultures while participating effectively in the shared national culture (Banks, 2008a: 319).

Moving to the notion of interculturalism, in his professorial lecture on the right to education for all, Gundara remarks that education will always be directed to the full development of human personality; to the strengthening of respect for human rights and fundamental freedoms; and to the promotion of understanding, tolerance and friendship among all nations, cultural and religious groups, for the maintenance of peace. This actually constitutes 'a good definition for intercultural education but it remains far from a reality' (Gundara, 2003: 2).

In this perspective, 'intercultural' identifies a dynamic process of positive interaction between various identity groups of a society, calling for an inherent interdependence beyond static descriptions and recognition of differences (Smith, 2003: 185). Such a notion originates from the attempt to address the issues of cultural pluralism as a counter to assimilation, and aims to promote understanding among different groups while seeking to value the contributions of minority groups in mainstream society (Woyshner, 2003: 186). In this sense, education is aimed not only at migrants to enhance their integration, but also at members of the majority culture to acquire less prejudiced behaviours (Golz, 2005: 7).

The United Nations Educational, Scientific and Cultural Organization (UNESCO) has defined interculturalism as a 'dynamic' concept which 'refers to evolving relations between cultural groups. Interculturality presupposes multiculturalism and results from *intercultural* exchange and dialogue on the local, regional, national or international level' (UNESCO, 2006: 17). Three basic principles on intercultural education stem from this definition:

1. Intercultural education respects the cultural identity of the learner through the provision of culturally appropriate and responsive quality education for all.
2. Intercultural education provides every learner with the cultural knowledge, attitudes and skills necessary to achieve full participation in society.
3. Intercultural education provides all learners with cultural knowledge, attitudes and skills that enable them to contribute to respect, understanding and solidarity among individuals, ethnic, social, cultural and religious groups and nations (UNESCO, 2006: 32).

Spotting some problems of intercultural education, Gundara draws attention to a current major challenge: addressing educational inequity. In fact, in a context of continuous social change, intercultural education should contribute to addressing the many forms of exclusion and marginalisation, rethinking policies such as affirmative action so that they do not exacerbate differences, and developing policies that include disadvantages from all communities (Gundara, 2003: 9).

In the European countries a broad spectrum of interculturalism has been developed, shaped by national histories, contemporary educational politics and migration experiences: former colonial experiences, guest workers, societies with growing cultural diversity, eastern countries asserting new national, political, and cultural identities (Holm and Zilliacus, 2009: 17).

Concerning the critical issues of interculturalism, it has been claimed that there is a need for an approach able to analyse the distribution of power in intercultural relations. Giroux and Shannon remark that this approach consists of an:

> engage[ment] in cultural work locating politics in the in-between space of representations, audience and text, engaging also cultural politics as an experience of learning as the outcome of diverse struggles, giving importance to understanding theory as the grounded basis for intervening into context. (Giroux and Shannon, 1997: 1–2)

In this perspective, the current development of interculturalism is strictly related to its capacity of providing equity in education. Figueroa remarks that:

> educational inequality is related both as cause and effect to inequality in the society at large, of which it is part and parcel. It cannot be accounted for simply in individual terms, and least of all simply in terms of real or supposed individual characteristics, perceptions, frames of reference and behaviour of the majority population. (Figueroa, 1991: 193)

Hence, the notion of 'educational equality' could be substituted by one of 'educational equity', which implies maintaining personal particularity and respecting individual abilities and ambitions, aiming at a smoother integration into society, allowing everyone to adequately develop skills and to improve chances for successful integration, and also strengthening social cohesion and connectivity (Zmas, 2010: 144–5).

A further relevant development of the intercultural perspective has been pointed out by Philipson, Rannut and Skutnabb-Kangas, which draws attention to the current question of the maintenance of linguistic and cultural diversity as well as biodiversity. Defending linguistic human rights means, at an individual level, that everyone can identify positively with their mother tongue; have that identification respected by others; and have the right to learn their mother tongue and to use it as well as to learn at least one of the official languages of one's country of residence. As a result, bilingual teachers should be increasingly widespread (Philipson et al., 1995: 2).

Grant and Portera (2011) have widely discussed the different implications of multicultural and intercultural approaches, highlighting settings in theory and practice, and in methodological and political categories. Meanwhile Grant and Brueck remark that:

> although born of different times and space, both Multicultural Education and Intercultural Education are continuing to develop as important responses to, engagements with and preparations for contemporary life. Each can assist in developing an understanding and ethical negotiations of the complex world in which we interact. (Grant and Brueck, 2011: 3)

In this regard, as far as the European context is concerned, this difference can be summarised by the words of Gundara, who suggests 'that the term "multicultural" is better used as a descriptive term. The term "intercultural" is a more appropriate term for discussing programmes, policies and practices' (Gundara, 2003: 5). Also, Allemann-Ghionda remarks:

> In multicultural education, the prefix 'multi' describes the multiplicity of different cultures which live on the same territory and/or are taught in the same institution, for example in school or in higher education. In intercultural education the prefix 'inter' underlines the interactive aspect. (Allemann-Ghionda, 2009: 135)

In other words, with regard to the European context, the term 'intercultural' stresses the process of interaction, whereas 'multicultural' is seen as a less dynamic concept and as describing a situation related to diversity of cultures (Holm and Zilliacus, 2009: 11).

Thus, although criticised because it is often used uncritically to 'celebrate' cultures – and therefore unable to make understandable issues of power and oppression and historically embedded in a 'deficit' model – the notion of a 'multicultural' society appears to adapt to describe a broad range of diversity within a society from which arises the need of an 'intercultural' education providing students with the means to understand such a context (Gundara, 1986: 11).

In this sense, since positive qualities in terms of encouraging communication and recognising dynamic identities usually associated with interculturalism are also important features of multiculturalism, it must be remarked that the first should be considered not as an updated version of the second, but instead as complementary to it (Meer and Modood, 2011: 18).

Finally, it must be observed that, in the European context, the concept of interculturalism can now be found in several education programmes (Meer and Modood, 2011: 3), suggesting the use of 'interculturalism' in Europe to identify an interactive dialogic perspective, generating synthesis and social cohesion.

The Cultural Side of Fortress Europe

In the European political debate, the multicultural perspective has been often accused of cultural relativism and of fostering separate societies. Actually:

> a strange dimension of this broad rejection is that multiculturalism has never really existed in the shape alleged by its critics. […] The idea of 'multiculturalism', bound up in a mesh of associations with race, nation, culture, belongings and legitimacy, has become pronounced as a lightening conductor for more profound political problems. (Titley, 2011: 163)

Furthermore, the roots of such a criticism can be found particularly in problems and issues specifically related to the history and the culture of each specific country (Silj, 2010: 9).

Europe is a region of great cultural and geographical diversity, with 23 official languages in the European Union (EU) and more than 60 indigenous regional or minority language communities. In this perspective, 'while most of the European nations have been built on the platform of their language of identity, the European Union can only build on a platform of linguistic diversity' (Maalouf, 2008: 5). Besides, as Europe is a contested region in terms of its borders and constituent countries, it is the definition of 'Europe' in itself that is problematic. Where does Europe begin, where does it end and who are the Europeans? Who belongs and who is excluded from being a European? (Gundara, 2000c: 47).

According to Lynch, the aetiology of cultural pluralism in Europe can be identified in three major contextual influences:

1. the early patchwork settlement of Europe by different linguistic groups, attested by the fact that, when they emerged, no nation-state in Europe was monolingual;
2. the later equally varied religious overlay, confirmed by the fact that the Reformation superimposed on the linguistic, cultural and political maps of Europe a plane of cultural complexity; and

3. the post-Second World War economic boom which drew migrant workers first from colonies, former colonies and Southern Europe and then from around the globe (Lynch, 1986: 125–6).

As a result, cultural diversity is really inborn with the idea of Europe and, in this sense, 'cultural multiplicity is a European characteristic worth preserving' (Wulf, 2002: 23). Hence, in a context that has never been culturally homogeneous, the perspective of interculturalism can represent an essential tool to address marginalisation and enhance social cohesion (Barn, 2012: 101).

Such a constitutive role of cultural pluralism has been also acknowledged in several documents, first of all in the *Ventotene Manifesto* 'for a Free and United Europe', written in 1941 by Altiero Spinelli, Ernesto Rossi and Eugenio Colorni, in which the idea of a federation of European states is presented as a means to prevent cultural conflicts:

> The multiple problems which poison international life on the continent have proved to be insoluble: tracing boundaries through areas inhabited by mixed populations, defence of alien minorities, seaports for landlocked countries, the Balkan Question, the Irish problem, and so on. All these matters would find easy solutions in the European Federation, just as corresponding problems, suffered by the small States which became part of a vaster national unity, lost their harshness as they were transformed into problems regarding relationship between various provinces. (Spinelli et al., 1941)

An analogous reference to pluralism and interculturalism is incorporated in the text of the *European Convention on Human Rights*, signed in Rome on 4 November 1950, where Article 14 states that:

> The enjoyment of the rights and freedoms set forth in this Convention shall be secured without discrimination on any ground such as sex, race, colour, language, religion, political or other opinion, national or social origin, association with a national minority, property, birth or other status. (Council of Europe, 1950)

All these perspectives have been merged in the recent 'White Paper on Intercultural Dialogue', formulated by the Council of Europe to provide policy makers and practitioners with specific guidelines for the promotion of intercultural dialogue, defined as follows:

> Intercultural dialogue is understood as a process that comprises an open and respectful exchange of views between individuals and groups with different ethnic, cultural, religious and linguistic backgrounds and heritage, on the basis of mutual understanding and respect. It requires the freedom and ability to express oneself, as well as the willingness and capacity to listen to the views of others. Intercultural dialogue contributes to political, social, cultural and economic

integration and the cohesion of culturally diverse societies. It fosters equality, human dignity and a sense of common purpose. It aims to develop a deeper understanding of diverse worldviews and practices, to increase co-operation and participation (or the freedom to make choices), to allow personal growth and transformation, and to promote tolerance and respect for the other. (Council of Europe, 2008: 17)

It has been observed that while seeking to become increasingly fortified economically, politically and territorially, Europe is also becoming more culturally diversified, developing a perspective of 'interculturalism' which places its focus on being a new model of the management of diversity (Barn, 2012: 104). In this context, one of the main critical issues for a European intercultural perspective is that the idea of inclusion that came along with a process of expansion of the EU occurs in an undeniable contradiction with many processes of exclusion taking place both internally among vulnerable groups within the member states and externally among immigrants pushing at Europe's borders.

Regarding the first aspect, Woodward and Kohli note that inclusion in the European process does not necessarily lead to expansion of internal social inclusions, because where the material well-being of a country has been raised, differences may have been paradoxically exacerbated:

> Many of the processes of inclusion have thus been accompanied by exclusion and creation of new borders of resources, rights and identities. Within the expanding physical space of 'Europe' there is greater awareness of economic, cultural and ethnic heterogeneity than ever before and a higher mobility of people from an increasingly global pool. One consequence of greater contact and awareness may be backlashing border building ... (Woodward and Kohli, 2001: 1)

Jacobs and Gundara have also drawn attention to this risk, underlining that 'nationalism, in its various modern guises, is seemingly still intent on creating racially and ethnically *pure* states, apparently oblivious to both the lessons of history and the impracticalities of the arithmetic, let alone the moral repugnance of their exclusivist agendas' (Jacobs and Gundara, 2000: 3). In this sense, an equitable intercultural public and social policy needs to address the problem of institutionalised exclusion and racism within public and social systems. In fact, as most European societies have historically been and still are very diverse, it is essential to develop inclusive intercultural policies to ensure that all groups have citizenship rights in the perspective of a critical interculturalism based on intellectual foundations and firmly in the core functioning of institutions. In this framework, the risk of discrimination still remains very high (Gundara, 2000b, 2000c, 2012).

With regard to the processes of exclusion taking place at the borders of the EU, it has been remarked that Europe has become increasingly entrenched over the years and, referring to this condition, the expression 'Fortress Europe' has been used to point out, with a negative connotation, that Europe tends to close itself off from a political and economic point of view.

Underscoring that boundaries define some as members and others as aliens, in a context where state sovereignty is becoming frayed and national citizenship much less clear, Benhabib formulates a proposal of moral universalism and cosmopolitan federalism, advocating 'porous' boundaries recognising the admittance rights of refugees and asylum seekers and the regulatory rights of democracy:

> I believe that the best way to approach political membership at the dawn of a new century is by accepting the challenge of conflicting moral visions and political commitments suggested by one of the slogans of the Immigrant Workers' Freedom Ride: *No human is illegal.* (Benhabib, 2004: 221, emphasis added)

However, the notion of Fortress Europe can actually have not only a political or economic connotation but also a fundamental cultural meaning, identifying dynamics functional to political and economic aspects. In particular, it must be remarked that although citizens of the European community originate from several diverse cultures, educational systems in member states are still devised as if they were meant for citizens with one national culture. In other words, 'education remains tied to a hegemonic canon, shut up in a cultural prison which recognises only its own Eurocentered tradition or, if it does recognise those outside it, interprets them according to its own values' (Gundara, 2000a: 116).

In this regard, examining how the European identity has been constructed in different historical phases appears crucial. Ross explains the role of some critical moments in triggering the construction of a European identity.

- Firstly, in about 490–480 BCE the Persian Wars produced a dramatic shift of attitude towards others, above all easterners, and of the use of the term 'barbarian', so far meaning foreigner or not speaking Greek and then used with intent of vilification.
- The second event is related to the onset of the Middle Ages and the reformulation of the European identity caused by the split of the Roman Empire; and the Alans, Goths, Huns and Visigoths opposing Romans for several decades. The thesis that in sacking Rome in 410 then moving through France, Spain and along the North African coast, these populations destroyed Roman and European culture, heralding 'the dark ages', has been seriously challenged by historians such as Jacques Le Goffe (2005), who instead points out an essential continuity of the economy of the Roman Mediterranean after the barbarian invasions. The subsequent Islamic expansion into North Africa, the eastern Mediterranean and Spain in the seventh and early eighth centuries broke economic connections to Europe. The new empire of the west led to a major reorientation of European identity on itself. Finally, leading to a new strong empire explicitly allied

to the papacy, the empire of Charlemagne encouraged the formation of a common European identity.
- The third critical event corresponds to the fall of Constantinople in 1453 at the hands of the Ottomans. The shift from a theocratic world-view to an anthropocentric view in the Renaissance – exemplified by the work of Erasmus and Copernicus and by geographical explorations – led to the discovery of new 'others'. In this period, the final stage of the Reconquista, with the expulsion of the Moors from Spain after 800 years of settlement, represented a new violent radicalism of identity. Also, the rise of the autonomous nation-state gave European identity a nationalistic streak, producing cultural imperialism, colonialism and nationalism (Ross, 2008: 27–40).

As a result, the critical issue of 'Eurocentrism' emerges, along with its related but more general notion of 'ethnocentrism'. The latter term was firstly formulated by Summer (1906), referring to the tendency to identify with one's own group and to evaluate out-groups and their members according to those standards (Gudykusnt and Kim, 2003: 13), and identifies a way of thinking firmly centred in the self, assuming our own world as central (Houghton, 2012: 28).

Conversely, Eurocentrism means more specifically 'centered on Europe and Europeans' (Smith, 1997: 117). Such an attitude includes several beliefs: the inherent superiority of all European things (i.e., European cultures, perspectives, values, behaviours); that these various aspects of European culture are valid universal norms to judge non-European contexts; and even that non-European cultures are inferior and should be denigrated and dominated (Smith, 1997: 117).

Amin unveils the essential contradictions of Eurocentrism, which 'has replaced rational explanations of history with partial pseudo-theories, patched together and even self-contradictory at times. […] The Eurocentric distortion that makes the dominant capitalist culture negates the universalist ambition on which that culture claims to be found' (Amin, 1989: 104).

Particularly after 1492, with the continual Europeanisation of the globe, Eurocentrism became crystallised as a global project, building its counterpart in 'the other' and 'the Oriental' (Gundara, 2000a: 117). In this regard, in the eighteenth and nineteenth centuries Europeans developed a historiography which distanced Greece from the Egyptians and Phoenicians, constructing a 'pure' childhood of Europe which denies learning acquired by Africans and Semites (Bernal, 1987). This has deep educational implications, because knowledge systems confront dual challenges as European integration takes shape: '[as] a result of the imperial enterprise not only is Europe in the world but the world is in Europe' (Gundara, 2002: 75–6).

Highlighting the need to tackle Eurocentrism within broader public policies ensuring the legitimacy of 'belongingness' of different groups, Gundara observes that the relevance of intercultural education cannot be viewed only as a mere consequence of those who have recently emigrated to Europe, but must be related to the long and complex legacy of a multicultural European past, avoiding that 'education remains trapped in the tramlines of nationalist tautology' (Gundara, 2002: 77). In this sense:

> All children have a right to know and understand their own personal 'story'. This is an important enough issue because when children do not have access to their parents, family or community history they may become obsessed by it. Young people not only need access to these stories, but also need to be able to read them critically. This entails young people being able to analyse critically historical information, facts and documents. These histographic skills would be invaluable to young people in evaluating 'stories' and 'histories'. (Gundara, 2002: 80)

Thus, an effective antidote to Eurocentric settings and radicalisation of identities can be found in critical thinking, as formulated by the strand of 'critical pedagogy' informed by the writings of (among others) Antonio Gramsci, the Frankfurt School, cultural studies and, particularly, Paulo Freire's *Pedagogy of the Oppressed* (1970), which proposed the corpus of analyses of domination as 'a relation of power that subjects enter into and is forged in the historical process' (Leonardo, 2005: 39).

The importance of critical thinking was also affirmed by Dewey, who remarks that 'the essence of critical thinking is suspended judgment; and the essence of this suspense is inquiry to determine the nature of the problem before proceeding to attempt at its solution' (Dewey, 1997: 74).

In a perspective of 'critical race theory', originated in the Civil Rights movement in the USA – and particularly in the famous case of school desegregation litigation, *Brown vs. Board of Education* (1954), in which the Supreme Court declared state laws establishing separate public schools for black and white students unconstitutional (Peters, 2005: vii) – a 'critical' approach can contribute to an analysis of how social systems really work and how ideology or history conceals the processes which oppress people (Gillborn, 2004: 44–5). Indeed, such an approach is deeply committed to the promotion of emancipatory possibilities – through an effort of critical analysis at a societal, institutional or local classroom level – of how relations of power mediate in education policy, processes and practices (Wallace, 2008: 143).

In a paper presented at the Virginia Women's Studies Association conference, Peggy McIntosh clarifies the educational implication of power structures in cultural and social systems:

> I think whites are carefully taught not to recognize white privilege, as males are taught not to recognize male privilege [...]. My schooling gave me no training in seeing myself as an oppressor, as an unfairly advantaged person, or as a participant in a damaged culture. I was taught to see myself as an individual whose moral state depended in her individual moral will [...]. Whether through the curriculum or in the newspaper, the television, the economic system, or the general look

of people in the streets, I received daily signals and indications that my people counted and that others *either didn't exist or must be trying, not very successfully, to be like people of my race*. I was given cultural permission not to hear voices of people of other races or a tepid cultural tolerance for hearing or acting on such voices […]. I was taught to recognize racism only in individual acts of meanness by members of my group, never in invisible systems conferring racial dominance on my group from birth. (McIntosh, 1998: 94, 96, 100–101, 104)

Such an approach stems from the classic reflection on 'Orientalism', which has illustrated devices and processes of culturally constructing others. In his well-known analysis, Edward Said describes the style of thought based upon an ontological and epistemological distinction between 'the Orient' and 'the Occident' named 'Orientalism', highlighting that the Orient is the source of European civilisations and languages, its cultural 'contestant' and one of its most recurring images of the 'Other', which helped define Europe as its contrasting image. In other words, 'The Orient is an integral part of European material civilization and culture' (Said, 1978: 1–2). Adopting Foucault's methodology of 'Archaeology of Knowledge', Said describes Orientalism as follows:

> Taking the late eighteenth century as a very roughly defined starting point Orientalism can be discussed and analyzed as the corporate institution for dealing with the Orient – dealing with it by making statements about it, authorizing views of it, describing it, by teaching it, settling it, ruling over it: in short, Orientalism as a Western style for dominating, restructuring, and having authority over the Orient […]. Without examining Orientalism as a discourse one cannot possibly understand the enormously systematic discipline by which European culture was able to manage – and even produce – the Orient politically, sociologically, militarily, ideologically, scientifically, and imaginatively during the post-Enlightenment period. (Said, 1978: 3)

Hence, European culture gained in strength and identity by setting itself off against the Orient as a sort of surrogate. As a result, Orientalism has been shaped as a body of theory and practice through a considerable investment for many generations, originating a real system of knowledge and a widely accepted grid for filtering the Orient into Western perception and flourishing in the general culture (Said, 1978). Such a system of knowledge has built a precise idea of Europe as:

> a collective notion identifying *us* Europeans as against all *those* non-Europeans, and indeed it can be argued that the major component in European culture is precisely what made that culture hegemonic both in and outside Europe: the idea of European identity as a superior one in comparison with all the non-European peoples and cultures. (Said, 1978: 7)

In conclusion, a relevant aspect of the issue of cultural pluralism is that difference is also culturally and socially shaped. The 'Orient' or 'the Other' is a constituted entity, and 'the notion that there are geographical spaces with indigenous, radically *different* inhabitants who can be defined on the basis of some religion, culture, or racial essence proper to the geographical space is equally a highly debatable idea' (Said, 1978: 322).

Immigrant and Immigrant Student Populations in the European Union

Addressing the issue of the management of cultural diversity in education in Europe requires taking into account that growing cultural diversity in European societies has its roots not only in immigration but also in several further processes such as emigration, internal migration, the historical presence of cultural minorities and the legacy of a colonial past.

Nevertheless, social, political and economic participation by migrants is undoubtedly a relevant aspect of the issue of social cohesion in the European context, and their 'integration' is not at all a 'separate' issue but a matter of coexistence pertaining to all the citizens (Council of Europe, 2011: 16–17). The question of how to promote social cohesion has become one of the key policy challenges in a world changed by globalisation. How education impacts, at the societal level, social cohesion is a key question revealing the intimate connection between education and social cohesion (Green and Preston, 2006: 21–4).

The Commission of the European Communities (2004: 9) remarks that immigration plays a vital role in the economic and social development of the European Union, in a framework of an ageing and shrinking working-age population. In this perspective, the Council of the European Union set out common basic principles for an immigrant integration policy, remarking that integration is a dynamic two-way process of mutual accommodation in which efforts in education are crucial both to prepare immigrants to be successful and active participants in society and to enhance frequent interaction between immigrants and member state citizens, with specific attention to shared forums, intercultural dialogue, education about immigrants and immigrant cultures (Council of Europe, 2011: 23).

As is known, migration is the consequence of a combination of economic, political and social factors, both in countries of origin (push factors) and in countries of destination (pull factors). Considering non-national persons (those who are not citizens of their country of residence), today there are around 32.5 million immigrants in the European Union, representing 6.5 per cent of its population – a considerably increased presence from the mid-1980s onwards. In absolute terms, more than three-quarters (77.4 per cent) of non-nationals live in five countries: Germany (7.1 million), Spain (5.7 million), the United Kingdom (4.4 million), Italy (4.2 million) and France (3.8 million) (Eurostat, 2012).

Concerning the continent of origin of third-country nationals living in the European Union, the largest proportion (36.5 per cent) – corresponding to 7.2

million people – are citizens of a European country outside the EU. Among these, more than half are citizens of Turkey, Albania or Ukraine. The second biggest group is from Africa (25.2 per cent) and, among these, more than half are from North Africa. This is followed by Asia (20.9 per cent), with a strong presence from southern or eastern Asia, in particular India or China; the Americas (16.4 per cent), with the largest share from Ecuador, Brazil and Colombia; and Oceania (0.9 per cent) (Eurostat, 2012).

Since the Second World War there have been three main migration flows to Western Europe:

1. Primary labour migration occurred between the 1950s and the oil price rises of 1973–74 driven by the needs of Western European economic reconstruction, with a peak in the 1960s. This was the object of a misplaced assumption that this migration was temporary.
2. Secondary/family migration took place between the mid-1970s and the end of the Cold War in 1989–90, when restrictions on labour migration led not to the end of immigration, but rather to the entry of highly skilled immigrants and to migration for the purpose of family reunion.
3. Finally, a '"third wave" of migration developed in the aftermath of the end of the Cold War in 1989–90 with a particularly noticeable increase in asylum seeking migration and migration defined by state policies as illegal' (Geddes, 2003: 17–18).

In this sense, it must be remarked that the categories 'voluntary labour migrant' and 'forced refugee' are defined by the receiving states and can be redefined by them.

Scientific literature has highlighted a distinction between 'older' immigration countries (like the UK, France and Germany), in which migration is linked to former colonies or to post-World War II economic reconstruction, and 'newer' immigration countries in South, Central and Eastern Europe (among them Greece, Italy, Portugal and Spain) with relatively new experience of migration and with high levels of economic informality and less structured or irregular immigration (Geddes, 2003: 16).

With a shift from an expansive notion of citizenship in the imperial experience (the 1948 British Nationality Act formally gave all subjects of the Crown in Britain and its empire the right to move to Britain) to a restriction on large-scale labour migration especially between 1962 and 1971 and culminating in the 1981 British Nationality Act, in Britain 'race relations' policies – focused on race and supposed racial differences – have centred on the strict control of immigration coupled with anti-discrimination laws and positive action to address inequalities, which conferred social and political meaning on 'race relations' (Geddes, 2003: 30–31). However, restrictive legislation did not prevent the increase in numbers of asylum seekers in the 1990s.

The influence of communitarian thinking has allowed great emphasis on the moral relevance of communities and the rights and responsibilities of individuals within them. This was evident also in the conclusion of the 1997 report produced by the Commission on the Future of Multi-Ethnic Britain, which proposed a vision of the UK as a 'community of communities' (Geddes, 2003: 40).

Basically, Britain took North America as a policy model in managing post-war immigration: UK legislation of the 1960s reflected the US debate on civil rights, while in the 1970s ideas of race consciousness, prevalent in the US, had a great impact. Finally, it must be observed that UK responses to immigration have been related to domestic concerns, detached from the effects of European integration, maintaining its own form of 'race-related' immigrant integration policy (Geddes, 2003: 50).

Moving to France, it must be highlighted that in this context there has been a long history of encouraging labour migration from neighbouring or nearby countries (organised until the 1970s by the private sector), and a long debate on immigration and nationality emerged in the context of decolonisation in the 1950s and 1960s. A French republican model of national integration has combined universalist and assimilationist state strategies, with a strong emphasis on universalism as enshrined in the Rights of Man of 1789; unitarism in the one and indivisible republic laity; separation of church and state; and assimilation with an obligation for foreigners to acquire French traits (Geddes, 2003: 57).

In Germany, post-war recruitment of 'guestworkers' was impressive, but the country has lacked a system for the regulation of immigration or the integration of migrant newcomers, denying immigration until the end of the 1990s. Social provisions for guestworkers were provided for a long period of time only in accordance with their temporary presence. In contrast to France, Germany was conceived as a community of descendants, and turned to a *jus soli* system only in 1991, when Germany turned the page on the guestworker period, ending the divergence between the French and the German models (Geddes, 2003: 80–90).

In highly organised welfare states like Sweden and the Netherlands, multiculturalism and integration are related to the background conditions of corporatist decision-making and the welfare state (Sweden) and 'pillarisation' (Netherlands). Post-colonial ties and labour recruitment agreements structured post-war migration to the Netherlands, while Sweden was not a large-scale recruiter of migrant workers until the 1960s. Both Sweden and the Netherlands moved after the 1980s from their own versions of identity-affirming multicultural policies to approaches that emphasised language training and education as ways of enhancing full immigrant participation in these societies (Geddes, 2003: 102–3). The Netherlands has moved from a minorities policy to an integration policy, with more emphasis on socio-economic integration, policies promoting equal opportunities and some actions of cultural assimilation – focusing on individuals instead of groups. The Swedish response to immigration was characterised by the swift recognition of permanent immigration and the social democratic welfare state (Geddes, 2003: 113–19).

With regard to southern European countries (Greece, Italy, Portugal and Spain), it must be observed that they have only become destination countries for migrants since the 1980s, with shared features of economic informality and irregular migration (Geddes, 2003: 149–52).

In each of these contexts the immigrant population has several educational needs, which usually concern, initially, lack of adequate knowledge of the local language and, at the same time, difficulty in successful social and cultural adaptation. Thus, the crucial question becomes whether the national educational systems in Europe can function as a 'pivotal mechanism' for the social inclusion of students with immigrant backgrounds (Zmas, 2010: 135).

It must be remarked that in this context immigrant conflict – with clashes in the double forms of 'immigrant–native' conflict and 'immigrant–state' conflict – is a crucial 'social fact' which occurs with the interaction of two main variables: economic scarcity (a situation in which there is a shortage of 'goods'); and immigrant electoral power (related to the ability of an immigrant group to claim valuable 'goods' and their political power) (Dancygier, 2010: 21–34).

Since the Treaty of Amsterdam (1999), the European Union has progressively adopted an effective policy for asylum and immigration, aimed at governing the entry and residence of immigrants and asylum seekers in member states. In 1999 the Tampere European Council stated that issues of asylum and migration call for the development of a common EU policy, including elements like the partnership with countries of origin; a common European asylum system; fair treatment of third-country nationals; management of migration flows; and granting migrants rights and obligations comparable to those of EU citizens and aimed at enhancing non-discrimination in economic, social and cultural life and developing measures against racism and xenophobia (European Union, 1999).

Furthermore, in setting the objective of becoming the most competitive and dynamic knowledge-based economy in the world – capable of sustainable economic growth with more and better jobs and greater social cohesion – with the conclusions of the Lisbon Summit in 2000 the European Union has identified in the integration of immigrants as an important dimension of such a policy and the education system as an essential context in which integration can occur.

At the Thessaloniki European Council in 2003 it was stated also that EU policy for integration of third-country citizens should cover factors such as education and language training; and again the integration of immigrants has been referred to as a priority during several other European Council agendas.

With regard to immigrant students, on the whole European legislation confers entitlement to education under the same conditions as those applicable to nationals. However, it contains no specific provisions regarding children irregularly present in EU territory or positive measures for the assistance of immigrant children. Article 14 of the Charter of Fundamental Rights states that 'everyone has the right to education and to have access to vocational and continuing training. This right includes the possibility to receive free compulsory education' (European Union, 2000: 11).

However, the first legislative measure of the European Community concerning the education of the children of migrant workers dates back to 1977 when a

Council Directive (77/486/EC) stated that children of immigrants from member states should receive education adapted to their special needs as well as tuition devoted to their mother tongue and culture of origin. In the same year, the European Convention on the Legal Status of Migrant Workers conferred this right, declaring that the host state had to promote the teaching of the national language as well as teaching in the migrants' mother tongue, and sought to ensure that migrant children were granted scholarships on the same terms as those applicable to nationals.

Afterwards, a resolution and three recommendations were passed by the Council of Europe between 1983 and 1989, broadening the responsibility to include immigrant children from non-member countries. Further European directives (2000/43/EC, 2003/9/EC and 2003/109/CE) have defined immigrant children as minors who are nationals of third countries (whether or not they are accompanied) and have stated that those with the status of long-term residents must receive the same treatment as nationals as far as education is concerned, including the award of study grants. However, member states may limit such an essential principle of equal treatment by requiring proof of appropriate language proficiency for access to education (Eurydice, 2004: 12).

Intercultural Education and Social Equity

It must be remembered that when we refer to 'immigrant students' this is a very wide expression. It includes children with different biographical experiences (such as those born in another country within or outside Europe or whose parents or grandparents were born in another country) and in various situations (newly arrived children, migrant children, children of immigrant background of second or third generation). For this reason it is particularly important to differentiate immigrant students in relation to their particular biographical experiences, social and cultural backgrounds, and specific needs. But it must be observed that in several EU countries immigrant students are not representative of the overall cultural heterogeneity, as in many countries only newly arrived students are included in national statistics, without considering cultural minorities or second- and third-generation immigration.

As the issue of integration of immigrant students is strictly related to the question of the inclusion of their families, features of national education systems and national strategies adopted to address migrant marginalisation play an essential role.

It must be observed that today, in the European context, immigrant students still appear to be disadvantaged in terms of enrolment in type of school, duration of attending school, achievement, dropout rates and types of school diploma attained (Park and Sandefur, 2010). However, their educational achievement is generally comparatively higher in countries with lower levels of economic inequality, high investments in child care and well-developed systems of preschool education, with late selection of students to different ability tracks (Heckmann, 2008: 6).

Addressing the challenge of the presence of students from a migrant background in weak socio-economic positions, a Green Paper by the Commission of the European Communities underlines that there is consistent evidence that many of them have lower levels of educational attainment than their peers (Commission of the European Communities, 2008: 4–5). The most important cause of low educational achievement is represented by unfavourable socio-economic conditions. Indeed, such a factor is generally strongly correlated with school performance. Among the factors that must be taken into account are:

- the loss of value of knowledge and native language experienced by migrant families;
- lack of proficiency in the language of instruction, which cannot be reinforced at home and hinders the relation between school and family;
- expectations and self-esteem, which are crucial to avoid the transmission of disadvantage to the next generation;
- role models and supportive behaviours in the socio-economic position of the community (Commission of the European Communities, 2008: 8).

However, understanding reasons for immigrant students' low performance compels moving to the 'macro level' of educational concerns, dealing with political, economic and cultural aspects which are in interaction with education, taking into account, for instance, measures taken against socio-economic inequalities or immigration policies (Zmas, 2010: 143).

As a result, in analysing the wide range of factors that play a role in determining educational disadvantage of migrant students the following aspects must be taken into account:

- the structural features of education systems, such as school choice, tracking, selection mechanisms and resource inequalities;
- features of school at an individual level, including teacher expectations, classroom environments and school organisation;
- individual student characteristics, such as socio-cultural background and language proficiency (Nusche, 2010: 179).

In this framework, non-school factors (e.g., family background or parenting practices) are also important determinants of migrant students' educational success.

Furthermore, even the 15 'old' member states of the European Union are still characterised by large differences in levels of education, and in organisation and funding of the education system (Dolton et al., 2009: 21). In this context, school achievement of minorities is increasingly becoming a relevant issue for the effectiveness of educational systems, and in such an issue an intercultural approach aimed at educational process is crucial.

The Organisation for Economic Cooperation and Development (OECD) observed that although in many countries education has expanded over recent decades, inequalities in outcomes continue to hinder social mobility in several contexts. This issue is fundamental for the overall system, as those without skills to fully participate in society may not realise their potential and are likely to generate higher long-term social and financial costs – with regard to health, income support, child welfare and security (OECD, 2010: 52).

OECD data show that high-performing school systems provide high-quality education to all students, regardless of their background or school attended. These systems tend to have large proportions of students performing at the highest levels of reading proficiency and relatively few students at the lower proficiency levels (OECD, 2010: 13).

Where longstanding policies to favour skilled migration are carried out, the average achievement level of native children of immigrants is about the same as that of other natives, while more generally native-born children of immigrants tend to perform better than their immigrant counterparts of the same age. Finally, in most European countries significant gaps are registered between children of natives and the native-born children of immigrants (Liebig and Widmaier, 2010: 24).

As achievement gaps between immigrant and native students are largely explained by language barriers and socio-economic differences, policies targeting more broadly less socio-economically advantaged students could be relevant factors of education equality (OECD, 2010: 37). In particular, school performance of immigrant students is examined by the OECD Programme for International Student Assessment (PISA), which aims to evaluate education systems worldwide by assessing 15-year-olds' competencies in reading, mathematics and science.

On the basis of the information reported by students on the country of origin of both their parents, the PISA survey highlights that immigrant students represent more than 5 per cent of the student population in 25 of the 34 OECD countries (OECD, 2012b: 26). Across them, 10 per cent of the students assessed by PISA have an immigrant background, but this group represents 40 per cent of students in Luxembourg; around 24 per cent in Switzerland; 15–20 per cent in Germany and Austria; 10–15 per cent in Belgium, France, the Netherlands, Sweden and the UK; and below the 10 per cent OECD average in Spain, Greece, Italy and Finland. With regard to school performances of immigrant students, PISA survey data show the following essential aspects:

- First of all, immigrant students generally underperform in PISA, but the performance gap between them and non-immigrant students varies noticeably across countries, even after adjusting for socio-economic differences. There are only a few OECD countries where reading outcomes are similar to those of non-immigrant students. This happens not only in countries which have practised selective immigration policies for many years (like Australia, Canada and New Zealand), but also in several countries in which there have been significant improvements since 2000, such as Belgium, Germany and Switzerland. PISA results suggest also that the older a child is at arrival, the less well he or she does in reading (OECD, 2012b: 11).

- Language hinders school achievement for immigrant students. In particular, PISA data show that, although there is no arrival age after which there is an immediate fall-off in performance, the most vulnerable immigrant students are those who arrived at a late age, unable to speak the host country language and from a country with weaker education standards (OECD, 2012b: 11–12).

- Lower performance is more strongly associated with a higher concentration of socio-economic disadvantage than with a higher concentration of immigrants or foreign-language speakers (OECD, 2012b: 12). PISA data highlight also that immigrant students are not evenly distributed across schools, as schools with a high concentration of immigrant students are generally more socio-economically deprived than other schools. In order to succeed in education, immigrant students often have to overcome multiple barriers related to immigrant status, language skills and socio-economic background (OECD, 2012a: 1). On average across OECD countries, some 15 per cent of immigrant students are in schools where more than 40 per cent of students mainly speak another language at home, and some 40 per cent are in schools where over 20 per cent of students mainly speak another language (OECD, 2012b: 12). In this sense, PISA data show that immigrant students face a major obstacle to success at school when they are concentrated in schools attended by students with similar socio-economic disadvantage (OECD, 2012a: 3). These findings suggest that it is not the mere proportion of immigrant students or of those who speak a different language that is associated with poor performance. In fact, there are many high-achieving schools with large proportions of immigrant students, which is often the result of specific education policies (OECD, 2012a: 4).

- Some education and social policies have different effects on immigrants and non-immigrants. PISA data show that in many countries the impact of higher parental attainment levels is weaker among immigrants in comparison with non-immigrant children, and therefore such a factor alone cannot explain immigrant students' outcomes. Indeed, an unexpected finding from the PISA survey concerns the presence of many immigrant children of highly educated mothers in disadvantaged schools, which seems to be correlated with the fact that they come from families with low-status occupations and lower incomes. In this perspective, the concentration of immigrant students in disadvantaged schools is a more powerful explanatory factor for their outcomes than either immigrant concentration in schools or the proportion of immigrant students who speak another language at home (OECD, 2012b: 13).

In particular, it must be observed that, in reading, immigrant students scored lower than non-immigrant students in 23 out of 28 OECD countries. Among

European countries the performance gap reaches a higher score in Italy (more than 72), Finland, Austria, Belgium, Sweden, Denmark and France (60 points or more) (OECD, 2012b: 34).

The Council of Europe recommends that integration of immigrant children into the education system should be taken in the following areas: adapting the system to their special educational needs; including lessons on the language and culture of the country of origin in mainstream school curricula; and promoting intercultural education for all (Eurydice, 2004: 15). The Eurydice network, which provides information on European education systems, has analysed the measures adopted in European countries to support immigrant children at school and specific approaches on two major issues related to their integration: communication between schools and the families of immigrant pupils; the teaching of the heritage language of the immigrant children (Eurydice, 2004, 2009).

In the European context, where measures to support immigrant children have been introduced, they correspond to two main models which are not mutually exclusive but can exist in combination within the same country:

- An 'integrated model' in which immigrant children are allocated to classes consisting of children of the same age in mainstream education, where they follow methods and the curricular content intended for native pupils. In this context, measures for support, fundamentally linguistic, are provided on an individual basis during normal school hours. If extracurricular tuition is provided, it happens outside normal school hours but always on school premises under the responsibility of the host country education authorities.
- A 'separate model' in which immigrant children are grouped separately from other children to respond to their special needs, and which may assume two forms: a mode of 'transitional arrangements', adopted for a limited period and with some lessons in the corresponding mainstream classes; and a mode of 'long-term measures' in which special classes for immigrant children are formed within the school for one or several school years, often in accordance with their linguistic competence (Eurydice, 2004: 41–2).

Regarding the orientation measures adopted to assist immigrant pupils and their parents, basically schools adopt the following types of measure:

- written information about the school system
- provision of interpreters
- special resource persons/councils
- additional meetings specifically for immigrant families; and
- information about pre-primary education (Eurydice, 2004: 37).

With regard to measures aimed at promoting parental involvement in the education of their children, half of the European countries use three main methods of promoting communication between schools and immigrant families: publication of written information on the school system in the language of origin of immigrant families; the use of interpreters; and the appointment of resource persons, such as mediators, to be specifically responsible for liaising between immigrant pupils, their families and the school. However, it must be observed that information on the school system, usually published centrally, is often provided only in a limited range of languages (usually the most widely represented) and addressing only general matters (like the structure of the education system, enrolment, assessment and orientation procedures, parental participation, and parental rights and obligations). Furthermore, although encouraged by the central authorities, the use of interpreters is rarely a statutory right, while the resource persons responsible for the reception and orientation of immigrant pupils often appear to be teachers, and rarely established figures (Eurydice, 2009: 7–17).

Another measure adopted is mother tongue instruction, carried out in various forms not often specifically designed for immigrant children. Usually such an opportunity is provided at the compulsory education level. If it is dependent on bilateral agreements it is often extracurricular, or if funded by the national education system it often appears to be dependent on availability of resources (Eurydice, 2009: 29).

A further level of intercultural commitment concerns the set of processes through which relations between different cultures are made explicit in school curricula. Several studies put in relation the state of the theoretical discussion and its correspondence in educational policies and in practice, at least in a number of European countries. In particular, Allemann-Ghionda highlights some issues that, with some differences among countries, are central in the conceptualisation of intercultural education in the European context:

- the intercultural potential of multilinguism and fostering bilingual education;
- the ways of including different religions or not in the curriculum, and the closely linked question of relativism versus universalism in the realm of value and the issue of laicism in public education;
- the integration and successful education of students with a migrant or ethnic minority background;
- and the intercultural dimension in the curricula of subject matters, beyond a narrow focus on migrants or minorities (Allemann-Ghionda, 2009: 138).

After 'multicultural' education became a topical issue in the USA, Canada and Australia in the early 1970s, the concept of 'intercultural' education also began to take root in some European countries with growing immigration flows (such as France, Germany, the UK, Belgium and the Netherlands). These first intercultural strategies focused mainly on measures addressed towards the sons and daughters of migrant workers in order to help them learn the host countries' languages and maintain their languages and cultures of origin. There was also some focus on making it possible for them to return to their countries of origin, taking the forms of an *Ausländerpädagogik* (pedagogy for foreigners) in Germany or of a *pédagogie d'accueil* (pedagogy of reception) in France (Grant and Portera, 2011).

From this perspective, while since the mid-1970s the priority in Western Europe has been to address immigrant students, from the 1990s onwards in Eastern Europe the concern has been mostly with ethnic minorities. Currently, however, the approach is generally shifting towards 'citizenship education', which involves a very wide range of forms of plurality and diversity – i.e. of culture, language, religion, gender and sexual orientation, ability/disability, socio-economic status etc. (Allemann-Ghionda, 2008: 1–6).

Comparative research carried out by Allemann-Ghionda on the approaches to intercultural education which have been developed in several European countries has highlighted that although in many contexts intercultural policies are enacted, the terminology and the approaches vary significantly (Allemann-Ghionda, 2008: v). In particular, with regard to the 'old' immigration countries, policies in France on cultural diversity are currently shifting away from intercultural education towards an approach aimed at linguistic and cultural assimilation, with solidarity, equal opportunities for all students and laity as the strategy's main concepts. In the UK, the shift has been from multicultural or 'anti-racist' education towards the academic achievement of ethnic minorities, with national cohesion, citizenship education and faith as the strategy's main priorities. Finally, in Germany, the school system seems characterised by early selection and tracking, making childhood education not fully accessible for all, and not always free of charge (Allemmann-Ghionda, 2008: v).

This study has also demonstrated that major problems in terms of intercultural engagement, which are widespread across European countries, are insufficient for quality assessment and control and for teacher education (especially in-service training), and involve little commitment to implementing European policies on intercultural education charges (Allemann-Ghionda, 2008: v). In fact, a general tendency in the education systems of the United Kingdom, France, Germany and Italy to encourage assimilation and exclusively teach the language of the host country has been noted (Allemann-Ghionda, 2008: 41).

Formulating recommendations for an integrated approach to newly arrived migrant children in an inclusive and comprehensive education system with a combination of discretionary and national monitoring of implemented policies and achievements of migrant children, a study promoted by the European Commission highlights that the main issue newly arrived migrant children face is segregation in lower-quality schools, often caused by the design of the education system itself such as early ability tracking or residence requirement as a prerequisite for enrolment (European Commission, 2013: 5–6). Furthermore the study identifies five types of educational support system adopting policies of linguistic support; academic support; outreach to and cooperation with migrant parents and communities; and intercultural education.

1. *Comprehensive support* model (adopted, for instance, in Denmark and Sweden), in which education systems are effectively inclusive and provide continuous support to development of linguistic skills, teaching support and assistance in transferring students to higher levels of education, with a strong focus on outreach to parents and local community and intercultural learning mainstreamed into education.
2. *Non-systematic support* model (adopted, for instance, in Italy, Cyprus and Greece), characterised by the randomness of the support provided, with no clearly articulated national-level policy to support the integration of newly arrived migrant children or – where it does exist – with no effectively resourced and implemented policy.
3. *Compensatory support model* (adopted, for instance, in Belgium and Austria), which includes all the types of support policies, with only academic support being a rather weak aspect, especially in a context characterised by early ability tracking and streaming systems. In this case, ongoing teaching of the host and mother tongues is provided. The support provided is essentially compensatory, aiming to 'correct' differences rather than tackling initial disadvantages.
4. *Integration model* (adopted, for instance, in Ireland), where linguistic support is not a central focus and the systems for welcoming newly arrived children, arrangements for assessing prior schooling and support programmes for underachieving students are well developed. Interchange between school, parents and local community is systematic, while intercultural learning is well integrated into the curricula.
5. *Centralised entry support model* (adopted, for instance, in France and Luxembourg), in which the focus is on the centralised reception of migrant children and the provision of academic support as the main drivers of educational inclusion. Centralised reception desks, assessment of prior schooling and welcoming arrangements for newly arrived migrant children are provided, and linguistic support and outreach to migrant parents and communities are also well developed (European Commission, 2013: 7–8).

Moreover, in Europe such an 'intercultural approach' – which in the great majority of its countries is incorporated in the general aims of the national curricula, or at least in other official documents – is embodied in three main aspects:

1. *learning about cultural diversity* in order to develop values of respect among pupils and, in some countries, also a fight against racism and xenophobia;
2. the *international dimension*, which provides an understanding of contemporary cultural diversity in its historical and social context (through the study of economic and social topics related to international relations and migration phenomenon); and

3. the *European dimension*, which focuses on the cultural characteristics of peoples and the history of European integration in order to develop a sense of common identity (Eurydice, 2004: 57).

Generally, in curricula of European education systems, this approach is related to specific skills, subjects or values that should be developed on a cross-curricular basis. Around half of the European countries have also identified certain subjects through which the intercultural approach should be developed, specifying contents, teaching recommendations, skills, values or objectives associated with the intercultural outlook. Never regarded as a subject in its own right, the intercultural approach is very often identified in terms of combining its integration into specific subjects (e.g., history, geography, foreign languages, religion, the language of instruction or citizenship education) and their cross-curricular aspects (Eurydice, 2004: 59).

This implies a global approach to the curriculum; or, as outlined by Lynch, a curriculum with a 'cultural breadth' – not aimed at covering everything about every culture, but in the sense that 'every teacher or every area of the curriculum or learning experience will be expected to deliver the full expanse of that cultural breadth' (Lynch, 1989: 44).

Analysing the forms of development of the curricula for plurilingual and intercultural education for the Council of Europe, several scholars highlight that the curriculum, which organises learning, is itself part of an 'experiential' and 'existential' curriculum which extends beyond the school. Its development and implementation cover numerous activities at various levels of the education system which interact among themselves: international (supra), national/regional (macro), school (meso), class, teaching group or teacher (micro) or even individual (nano). To ensure its overall coherence, curriculum planning must also cover several aspects of schooling: general aims, specific aims/competences, teaching content, approaches and activities, groupings, spatio-temporal dimensions, materials and resources, role of teachers, cooperation and assessment (Beacco et al., 2010: 7).

In this framework, there is a relevant role of individuals as 'intercultural innovators', involved in community development with the capacity to communicate across boundaries (Barn, 2011). The concept of 'intercultural competence', coined by Pedersen (1974), involves a wide range of components, such as:

- knowledge (cognitive skills), referring to the ability to analyse and understand a set of issues and think through the differences, ethical principles and values;
- life skills (emotional or soft skills), referring to cultural awareness, attitude of empathy, openness and flexibility and capacity to interact; and
- know-how (behavioural skills), referring to the field of action, to practical approaches and techniques and to the ability to experiment (Council of Europe, 2011).

This implies acquiring information (knowledge), adjusting behaviour (like skills) and developing abilities (know-how) (Council of Europe, 2011: 39).

Plurilingual and intercultural competence have been defined as the ability to use a plural repertoire of linguistic and cultural resources to meet communication needs or interact with people from other backgrounds, making it easier to understand otherness, to make cognitive and affective connections between past and new experiences of otherness, and to mediate between members of different social groups and their cultures (Beacco et al., 2010: 8).

The achievement of intercultural competences becomes essential in a life-long learning perspective, in an education system that fits the cultural discontinuity that characterises the present time. In this sense, the need for innovative educational planning aimed at building intercultural competences in the continuous education perspective has been highlighted: 'Such an educational project, that involves society as a whole, is also the pivot of a new pact between education and society, aimed at constructing a trans-national European education' (Onorati and Bednarz, 2010: 23). These pivotal elements, around which new advances in education should revolve, can be summed up as follows:

- *valuing experiential knowledge*, combining formal, non-formal and informal learning;
- *promoting reflexivity* as the meta-cognitive ability to reframe experience in a conceptual framework, making it transferable to other contexts;
- *fostering* an educational model that enhances individuals' ability to bridge social capitals by working itself as an occasion for a diversified sociality; and
- *tuning* between methodologies (online/presence, individual/cooperative), curricula (academic/vocational), educational approaches (deductive/inductive, theoretical/experiential) and cultural approaches (different ways of conceiving the role of education in society and the development of the person) (Onorati and Bednarz, 2010: 23).

Although in the European context the expression 'intercultural education' has an extremely broad meaning – for instance involving formal and informal education or pertaining to the concept of citizenship education – in education systems this dimension appears in the following explicit ways:

- Intercultural education or the inclusion of diversity in educational systems that are structurally inclusive (e.g., Italy).
- Intercultural education or the inclusion of diversity in educational systems that are structurally exclusive (e.g., Germany, Hungary).
- The focus is mainly on migrants or ethnic minorities and on the interaction with them as well as on their specific educational needs; although policies declare that all students are included (most countries).

- The focus is mainly on all students, and the curricula of most subject matter include an intercultural or diversity dimension. In other words, the intercultural or diversity dimension is claimed to be transversal (e.g., Sweden, Germany).
- Intercultural education is not part of the official policy, but an alternative concept like citizenship education is a specific statutory subject (e.g., the UK) (Allemann-Ghionda, 2009: 141).

Conclusion

Traditionally, school institutions have an 'integrative' function, as they are expected to develop a common core of knowledge, values and attitudes, building bonds between people of a certain society (Leeman, 2002: 40). Although there are several references in official papers on the contribution of immigrants' knowledge, skills and cultures to the 'enrichment' of the host society, often the focus of educational approaches still tends to be on the 'deficiencies' of incoming pupils (Le Métais, 2002: 19). In this sense, it has been observed that actually the European approach to interculturalism ends up being 'an economically driven series of tolerance', carried out only through top-down policies, while bottom-up approaches could allow a deeper possibility of redefining collective identities (Topolski, 2011: 86).

In particular, although the inclusion of diversity is celebrated as a value in most 'rhetoric' of educational policies, in fact in those highly selective and segregating educational systems inequality is still 'cultivated' (Allemann-Ghionda, 2009: 141). In reality, European states interpret the principles formulated by European institutions in a wide variety of ways, while theoretical debate as a national characterisation is less and less often noticeable, a comparison of the ways in which European educational policy is reflected in national policies emerges according to their particular political agenda and problems; each country chooses different priorities (Allemann-Ghionda, 2009: 140).

In this framework, a comparative analysis of European educational theories, policies and practice in schools shows several gaps between European pro-diversity policies and some national policies; between educational intercultural theories and educational policies in single countries; and between national educational policies aimed at developing intercultural education and their implementation in practice (Allemann-Ghionda, 2009: 141). Among the major reasons for this relevant divergence between the concept of 'intercultural education' and the normal routine of schools, which produce a shift toward neo-assimilationist policies and practice (sometimes even in flagrant contradiction of European pro-diversity policies), must be taken into account the following aspects: the question of monitoring and evaluating how planned curricula are applied is unresolved; in higher teacher education, intercultural education is not considered mandatory; in the analysis of results of the PISA survey, the OECD recommendation of support in learning the host language on behalf of students with a migration background does not envisage family or community languages; finally, the notion of intercultural education or of the inclusion of diversity in the curriculum is neutralised by structures of highly selective educational systems, organised according to a differentialist agenda, reproducing social selection (Allemann-Ghionda, 2009: 142).

In conclusion, a key current challenge remains for the whole European society: to assure equal opportunities to all its citizens, regardless of their cultural origin or social condition, through a consistent and enlightened approach to intercultural education.

References

Allemann-Ghionda, C. (2008). *Intercultural Education in Schools: A Comparative Study*. Brussels: European Parliament.

Allemann-Ghionda, C. (2009). From intercultural education to the inclusion of diversity: Theories and policies in Europe. In Banks, J. A. (ed.), *The Routledge International Companion to Multicultural Education* (pp. 134–45). London: Routledge.

Amin, S. (1989). *Eurocentrism*. London: Zed Books.

Armbruster, B. and Ahn, J. (2003). Multicultural education. In Collins III, J. W. and O'Brien, N. P. (eds), *The Greenwood Dictionary of Education* (p. 229). London: Greenwood.

Banks, J.A. (1993). Multicultural education: Characteristics and goals. In Banks, J. A. and McGee Banks, C.A. *Multicultural Education: Issues and Perspective* (2nd edn) (pp. 3–28). Boston: Allyn and Bacon.

Banks, J.A. (2001). *Cultural Diversity and Education: Foundations, Curriculum and Teaching* (4th edn). Boston: Allyn and Bacon.

Banks, J.A. (2008a). Citizenship education and diversity: Implication for teacher education. In Peters, M.A., Britton, A. and Blee, H. (eds), *Global Citizenship Education: Philosophy, Theory and Pedagogy* (pp. 317–31). Rotterdam: Sense.

Banks, J.A. (2008b). Multicultural education. In McCulloch, G. and Crook, D. (eds), *The Routledge Encyclopedia of Education* (pp. 393–6). London: Routledge.

Barn, G. (2011). *Making the Most of Diversity: Profile of Intercultural Innovators*. Strasbourg: Council of Europe.

Barn, R. (2012). Interculturalism in Europe: Fact, fad or fiction – the deconstruction of a theoretical idea. In *Unedited Workshop Proceedings: Debating Multiculturalism 1* (pp. 101–10). London: Dialogue Society.

Beacco, J.C. et al. (2010). *Guide for the Development and Implementation of Curricula for Plurilingual and Intercultural Education*. Council of Europe: Strasbourg.

Benhabib, S. (2004). *The Rights of Others: Aliens, Residents and Citizens*. Cambridge: Cambridge University Press.

Bernal, M. (1987). *Black Athena*. London: Free Association.

Chu, H. (1997). Multiculturalism. In Grant, C.A. and Ladson-Billings, G. (eds). *Dictionary of Multicultural Education* (pp. 182–3). Phoenix: Oryx.

Commission of the European Communities (2004). *Communication from the Commission to the Council, the European Parliament, the European Economic and Social Committee and the Committee of the Regions. First Annual Report on Migration and Integration.* COM(2004) 508 final. Brussels: Commission of the European Communities.

Commission of the European Communities (2008). *Green Paper. Migration and Mobility: Challenges and Opportunities for EU Education Systems.* COM(2008) 423 final. Brussels: Commission of the European Communities.

Council of Europe (1950). *The European Convention on Human Rights.* Rome: Council of Europe.

Council of Europe (2008). *White Paper on Intercultural Dialogue. Living Together As Equals in Dignity.* Strasbourg: Council of Europe Publishing.

Council of Europe (2011). *Constructing an Inclusive Culture. Intercultural Competences in Social Services.* Strasbourg: Council of Europe Publishing.

Cushner, K., McClelland, A. and Safford, P. (2012). *Human Diversity in Education. An Intercultural Approach* (7th edn). New York: McGraw-Hill.

Dancygier, R.M. (2010). *Immigration and Conflict in Europe.* New York: Cambridge University Press.

Dewey, J. (1997). *How We Think.* New York: Dover.

Dolton, P., Asplund, R. and Barth, E. (eds) (2009). *Education and Inequality across Europe.* Cheltenham: Edward Elgar.

European Commission (2013). *Study on Educational Support for Newly Arrived Migrant Children.* Brussels: European Commission.

European Union (2000). Charter of fundamental rights of the European Union (2000/C 364/01). *Official Journal of the European Communities.*

European Union – Council of the European Union (1999). *Presidency Conclusions, Tampere European Council, 15–16 October 1999.* 16 October 1999. http://www.refworld.org/docid/3ef2d2264.html.

Eurostat (2012). *Eurostat database.* http://epp.eurostat.ec.europa.eu/portal/page/portal/eurostat/home [retrieved December 2012].

Eurydice (2004). *Integrating Immigrant Children into Schools in Europe.* Brussels: European Commission Education, Audiovisual and Culture Executive Agency (EACEA).

Eurydice (2009). *Integrating Immigrant Children into Schools in Europe. Measures to Foster: Communication with Immigrant Families; Heritage Language Teaching for Immigrant Children.* Brussels: EACEA.

Figueroa, P. (1991). *Education and the Social Construction of 'Race'.* London: Routledge.

Freire, P. (1970). *Cultural Action for Freedom.* Cambridge, MA: Harvard Educational Review.

Geddes, A. (2003). *The Politics of Migration and Immigration in Europe.* London: Sage.

Gillborn, D. (2004), Anti-racism. From policy to praxis. In Ladson-Billings, G. and Gillborn, D. (eds), *Multicultural Education* (pp. 35–48). London: Routledge Falmer.

Giroux, H.A. and Shannon, P. (eds) (1997), *Education and Cultural Studies. Toward a Performative Practice*. London: Routledge.

Golz, R. (ed.) (2005). *Internationalization, Cultural Difference and Migration. Challenges and Perspectives of Intercultural Education*. Münster: LIT.

Grant, C.A. (1997). Multicultural education. In Grant, C.A. and Ladson-Billings, G. (eds). *Dictionary of Multicultural Education* (pp. 171–2). Phoenix: Oryx.

Grant, C.A. and Brueck, S. (2011). A global invitation. Toward the expansion of dialogue, reflection and creative engagement for intercultural and multicultural education. In Grant, C.A. and Portera, A. (eds), *Intercultural and Multicultural Education. Enhancing Global Interconnectedness*. London: Routledge.

Grant, C.A. and Portera, A. (2011). *Intercultural and Multicultural Education. Enhancing Global Interconnectedness*. London: Routledge.

Green, A. and J. Preston. (2006). Education and social cohesion: Re-centring the debate. In Green, A., Preston, J. and Germen Janmaat, J. (eds). *Education, Equality and Social Cohesion. A Comparative Analysis* (pp. 19–70). New York: Palgrave Macmillan.

Gudykusnt, W. and Kim, Y.Y. (2003). *Communicating with Strangers. An Approach to Intercultural Communication* (4th edn). Boston, MA: McGraw-Hill.

Gundara, J.S. (1986). Education for a multicultural society. In Gundara, J.S., Jones, C. and Kimberly, K. *Racism, Diversity and Education* (pp. 4–27). London: Hodder and Stoughton.

Gundara, J.S. (2000a). *Interculturalism, Education and Inclusion*. London: Paul Chapman.

Gundara, J.S. (2000b). Issues of discrimination in European education systems. *Comparative Education*, 36, 223–34.

Gundara, J.S. (2000c). The political context of intercultural policy. In Gundara, J.S. and Jacobs, S. (eds), *Intercultural Europe. Diversity and Social Policy* (pp. 45–61). Aldershot: Ashgate.

Gundara, J.S. (2002). The context of European unification and British devolution: Research issues for curriculum, knowledge and history. In Koppen, J.K., Lunt, I. and Wulf, C. (eds), *Education in Europe. Cultures, Values, Institutions in Transition* (pp. 75–88). New York: Waxmann.

Gundara, J.S. (2003). *Intercultural Education. World on the Brink?* London: Institute of Education, University of London.

Gundara, J.S. (2012). Intercultural education, vulnerable groups in vulnerable European nations. *Studi Emigrazione/Migration Studies*, 186, 302–24.

Heckmann, F. (2008). *Education and Migration. Strategies for Integrating Migrant Children in European Schools and Societies. A Synthesis of Research Findings for Policy-Makers*. Brussels: European Commission.

Holm, G. and Zilliacus, H. (2009). Multicultural education and intercultural education: Is there a difference. In Talib, M.-T., Loima, J. Paavola, H. and Patrikainen, S. (eds), *Dialogs on Diversity and Global Education*. Frankfurt am Main: Lang.

Houghton, S.A. (2012). *Intercultural Dialogue in Practice. Managing Value Judgment through Foreign Language Education*. Bristol: Language for Intercultural Communication and Education.

Jacobs, S. and Gundara, J.S. (2000). Introduction: Cultural diversity and social policy. In Gundara, J.S. and Jacobs, S. (eds), *Intercultural Europe. Diversity and Social Policy* (pp. 1–13). Aldershot: Ashgate.

Le Goffe, J. (2005). *The Birth of Europe. 400 to 1500*. Oxford: Blackwell.

Le Métais, J. (ed.) (2002). *A Europe of Differences. Educational Responses for Interculturalism*. Enschede: Consortium of Institutions for Development and Research in Education in Europe (CIDREE).

Leeman, Y. (2002). Multiculturalism, intercultural communication and education. In Koppen, J.K., Lunt, I. and Wulf, C. (eds), *Education in Europe. Cultures, Values, Institutions in Transition* (pp. 40–53). New York: Waxmann.

Leonardo, Z. (ed.) (2005). *Critical Pedagogy and Race*. Oxford: Blackwell.

Liebig, T. and Widmaier, S. (2010). Overview: Children of immigrants in the labour markets of OECD and EU Countries. In OECD, *Equal Opportunities? The Labour Market Integration of the Children of Immigrants* (pp. 15–52). Paris: OECD.

Lynch, J. (1983). *The Multicultural Curriculum*. London: Batsford.

Lynch, J. (1986), Multicultural education in Western Europe. In Banks, J.A. and Lynch, J. (eds), *Multicultural Education in Western Societies* (pp. 125–52). Eastbourne: Holt, Rinehart and Winston.

Lynch, J. (1989). *Multicultural Education in a Global Society*. London: Falmer.

Maalouf, A. (ed.) (2008). *A Rewarding Challenge. How the Multiplicity of Languages Could Strengthen Europe*. Brussels: European Commission.

McIntosh, P. (1998). White privilege and male privilege: A personal account of coming to see correspondences through work in women's studies. In Andersen, M. and Collins, P.H. (eds), *Race, Class, and Gender. An Anthology* (3rd edn) (pp. 94–105). Belmont, CA: Wadsworth.

Meer, N. and Modood, T. (2011). How does interculturalism contrast with multiculturalism? *Journal of Intercultural Studies*, 33, 2, 1–22.

Nusche, D. (2010). Policy for improving the educational outcomes of the children of immigrants. In OECD, *Equal Opportunities? The Labour Market Integration of the Children of Immigrants* (pp. 163–92). Paris: OECD.

OECD (2010). *Closing the Gap for Immigrant Students. Policies, Practice and Performance*. Paris: OECD.

OECD (2012a). How do immigrant students fare in disadvantaged schools? *Pisa in Focus*, 22, November.

OECD (2012b). *Untapped Skills: Realising the Potential of Immigrant Students*. Paris: OECD.

Onorati, M.G. and Bednarz, F. (eds) (2010). *Building Intercultural Competences. A Handbook for Professionals in Education, Social Work and Health Care.* Leuven: Acco.

Park, H. and Sandefur, G. (2010). *Educational Gaps between Immigrant and Native Students in Europe: The Role of Grade.* In Dronkers, J. (ed.), *Quality and Inequality of Education. Cross-National Perspectives* (pp. 113–36). New York: Springer.

Pedersen, P. (ed.) (1974). *Readings in Intercultural Communications: Cross-Cultural Counseling.* Chicago: Intercultural Network.

Peters, M.A. (2005). Critical race matters. In Leonardo, Z. (ed.), *Critical Pedagogy and Race* (pp. vii–ix). Malden, MA: Blackwell.

Philipson, R., Rannut, M. and Skutnabb-Kangas, T. (1995). Introduction. In Skutnabb-Kangas, T. and Philipson, R. (eds), *Linguistic Human Rights. Overcoming Linguistic Discrimination* (pp. 1–22). Berlin: Mouton de Gruyter.

Ross, A. (2008). *A European Education. Citizenship, Identities and Young People.* Stoke-on-Trent: Trentham.

Said, E.W. (1978). *Orientalism.* London: Routledge and Kegan Paul.

Silj, A. (ed.) (2010). *European Multiculturalism Revisited.* London: Zed Books.

Smith, G.P. (1997). Eurocentrism. In Grant, C.A. and Ladson-Billings, G. (eds), *Dictionary of Multicultural Education* (pp. 116–17). Phoenix: Oryx.

Smith, H.F. (2003). Intercultural. In Collins III, J.W. and O'Brien, N.P. (eds). *The Greenwood Dictionary of Education* (p. 185). London: Greenwood.

Spinelli, A., Rossi, E. and Colorni, E. (1941). *For a Free and United Europe. A Draft Manifesto.* http://www.altierospinelli.org/manifesto/manifesto_en.html [retrieved June 2013].

Steinberg, S.R. and Kincheloe, J. L. (2009). Smoke and mirrors. More than one way to be diverse and multicultural. In Steinberg, S.R. (ed.), *Diversity and Multiculturalism. A Reader* (pp. 3–22). New York: Lang.

Summer, W.G. (1906). *Folkways: A Study of Mores, Manners, Customs and Morals.* Boston: Ginn.

Thayer-Bacon, B., Frey, L.L. and McElrath, E.M. (2003). Multiculturalism. In Collins III, J.W. and O'Brien, N.P. (eds), *The Greenwood Dictionary of Education* (p. 229). London: Greenwood.

Titley, G. (2011). After the 'failed experiment': Intercultural learning in a multicultural crisis. In Ohana, Y. and Otten, H. (eds), *Where Do You Stand? Intercultural Learning and Political Education in Contemporary Europe* (pp. 161–80). Wiesbaden: VS Verlag für Sozialwissenschaften.

Topolski, A. (2011). Was European multiculturalism destined to fail? In *Unedited Workshop Proceedings: Debating Multiculturalism 2* (pp. 85–98). London: Dialogue Society.

UNESCO (2006). *Guidelines for Intercultural Education.* Paris: UNESCO.

UNESCO (2009). *Investing in Cultural Diversity and Intercultural Dialogue. UNESCO World Report.* Paris: UNESCO.

Wallace, C. (2008). Critical pedagogy. In McCulloch, G. and Crook, D. (eds), *The Routledge Encyclopedia of Education* (pp. 143–5). London: Routledge.

Woodward, A. and Kohli, M. (eds) (2001). *Inclusions and Exclusions in European Societies*. London: Routledge.

Woyshner, C. (2003). Intercultural education. In Collins III, J.W. and O'Brien, N.P. (eds), *The Greenwood Dictionary of Education* (p. 186). London: Greenwood.

Wulf, C. (2002). The other as reference point in European education. In Koppen, J.K., Lunt, I. and Wulf, C. (eds), *Education in Europe. Cultures, Values, Institutions in Transition* (pp. 19–39). New York: Waxmann.

Zmas, A. (2010). Immigration policies and educational inequality: A comparative perspective. In Govaris, C. and Kaldi, S. (eds), *The Educational Challenge of Cultural Diversity in the International Context* (pp. 135–51). Münster: Waxmann.

Chapter 2

Potential and Problems for Intercultural Education in the British Isles

Jagdish S. Gundara

Introduction

This chapter will examine the pressures on contemporary British society and polity during a period of contradictory changes. There is pressure for localisation, regionalisation on the one hand, as well as for centralisation at the national level. In contemporary terms the demands for devolution by Scotland and Wales and the rise of religiosity are perceived to present particular problems. The issue of multiculturalism as a policy issue is criticised by many as privileging issues of particular group identities and ignoring the larger question of a centralised British nation, and by others for ignoring the larger questions of inequality in Britain. The chapter deals with these complex issues by focussing on educational dimensions in relation to diversity, difference and inequality. Firstly, it addresses the question of multiculturalism and intercultural education and points the way forward in educational terms. Secondly, it addresses the challenges for developing 'communities of development and hope' through active citizenship at grassroots and local levels. Thirdly, it deals with the institutional challenges at the public level for developing features of transparency and good governance through joined-up intercultural agendas which can lead to greater levels of equality through social and public policy measures. This chapter argues that intercultural public and social policies are a step in the direction of actualising a cosmopolitan and social democratic polity in Britain. Education of citizens at formal and informal levels and greater levels of educational equality of outcomes within a state are important to enhance peace and stability in modern polities.

The following discussion on education and democracy in Britain takes as its premise that issues of multiculturalism pertain not only to the contemporary aspects of diversity based on linguistic, religious, nationality and social class but also to the historical diversities in society. There are, however, changing topographies of contemporary and historical aspects of differences and diversity, and they raise in their wake various complex issues for many societies across the world.

In the political domain the German Chancellor, Angela Merkel, has stated that multiculturalism in Germany had failed. As a person from East Germany, which did not come to terms with its fascist past, she probably has no understanding of the work done in the field of intercultural education by various *Länder* in the

Federal Republic of Germany before the merger of East and West Germany. The British Prime Minister, David Cameron, speaking in Munich, attacked Britain's multicultural policies and raised issues of national security as being endangered by these policies. His understanding of multiculturalism relates to the presence of immigrants who came to Britain in the post-World War II period. If he had a historical understanding of issues concerning the multinational and multicultural past of the lands that constitute England, Wales, Scotland and Northern Ireland he might have to revise his views about the failure of multiculturalism.

Multiculturalism

Social diversities which are evident in the British context are also evident in most other societies. In some ex-colonial European countries the experience of decline of imperial power and external colonialism, and the distance from it, allows the members of the polities to reflect on the dominant nature of historical 'internal colonialism'. This reflexive distance can provide an opportunity for nations to 'see themselves from the perspective of the defeated in the questionable role of victors who were called to account for the violence of an imposed and disruptive process of modernisation' (Habermas, 2007: 47).

In this chapter 'multiculturalism' is used as a descriptive term and refers to aspects of social and cultural differences in institutions, communities and societies. However, in many English-speaking countries 'multicultural' is used as a policy term and has led to interminable debates about 'political correctness'. In many European countries and other societies and international institutions multicultural policies are also perceived to have consequences for 'Western' and 'Enlightenment' values, which are perceived by critics as being undermined by 'the others', and especially Muslims in Europe. This tension between the religious and the secular has been highlighted by Ian Buruma (2010) and other contemporary writers. Another writer, Gilles Kepel (1997), argues that British and Dutch multiculturalism has echoes of the old colonial practices of indirect rule through organised religious and ethnic communities, and that this 'communal' approach prevents successful integration of Muslims and other immigrants in Europe. These issues of immigration, integration and the role of Islam are also raised by other authors, as are the dilemmas which have resulted from them for policymakers in most European societies (Caldwell, 2009; Anderson, 2009).

Another fairly strong critique of the use of multiculturalism as a policy term is that it tends to obfuscate the much bigger questions of inequalities in society. It tends to legitimise economic inequality and diverts attention away from the deeper issue of class politics in societies like the United States (Michaels, 2007). Worse still is the way in which conservatives in many societies try to underplay the importance of equality for all groups. Richard Wilkinson and Kate Pickett's research and book on 'evidence-based politics' initially received praise from British Conservatives, but soon after assuming power they used their right-wing think tanks to rubbish the authors' evidence (Wilkinson and Pickett, 2009; *The Guardian*, 14 August 2010: 3). However, they claim that where inequality exists in socially diverse communities: 'ethnic divisions may increase social exclusion and discrimination, but ill health and social problems become more common the greater the relative deprivation people experience – whatever their ethnicity' (Wilkinson and Pickett, 2009: 178). Where there are class differences, people nearer the bottom of society almost always face downward discrimination and prejudice. Where there is also racial discrimination there is greater social division and greater levels of discrimination which may impede the processes of intercultural understanding through educational and other social and public policy measures.

There is also another argument about the need to break from the national container of history and to develop a 'transnational memory'. This would enable societies to reflexively modernise by institutionalising a cosmopolitan civil society, having learnt lessons from the Holocaust, imperialism and colonial history. This normative cosmopolitanism would need to correct the democratic deficit of public institutions and create levels of institutional equality and interdependence. These measures would lead to cosmopolitan integration both internally and externally by reinterpreting the creative tension between unity and diversity. Beck and Grande state that this is 'a paradigm shift resting on the principle that diversity is not a problem but a solution' (Beck and Grande, 2007: 242). However, they recognise that living together can be explosive and therefore necessitates enhanced capacities for intercultural interaction (Beck and Grande, 2007: 249). The school curriculum and the learning process have an important role to play in giving substance to enhancing intercultural understanding.

This difficulty of living together is most pronounced for groups who are viewed as being very different by those who are settled and consider the norm as being the national sovereign territories which have boundaries. They view those groups which are nomadic as not having the same rights, and there is huge tension between settled and nomadic communities such as the Roma and Traveller communities in Britain and mainland Europe. The constitutional, human and social rights of these groups are ignored and their children's education is generally of a very low standard. This issue presents one of the greatest challenges for intercultural education in democratic societies and schools within them. In Britain the current government would like to withdraw from the European Convention on Human Rights and the European Court of Human Rights in Strasbourg. The historical memories of these politicians are very short because they do not realise that the human rights legislation draws on the English and Scottish Enlightenment and were drafted by British lawyers after World War II.

Within the British context, the devolution of Scotland, Wales and Northern Ireland is an indication of the political acknowledgement of the historical multinational nature of British society. This historical legacy presents ongoing challenges. Wales has a functioning Assembly but in Northern Ireland the Assembly has functioned sporadically, while Scotland has a Parliament which has greater powers than an Assembly.

The complex processes of devolution, centralisation and integration are simultaneously taking place within many socially diverse societies. It is important to reflect on the features of democracy, citizenship and public and social policy issues within most societies generally. There is also a need to educate young people about the multicultural nature of societies and the importance of democratic features and cosmopolitan citizenship issues within such complex societies and regions. The multicultural contexts in historical and contemporary terms are dynamic and not static. There are also transcultural crossings, shifts and leaps which can result in dissensus since the dominant group may attempt to undermine consensus to remain dominant. There is an ethical imperative to engage in dialogue on issues of difference in society. While the need for grounding by many groups can be understood, it can be temporary and changing, and based on critical reflection. Grounding and uncertainty can go together and open up possibilities which are not necessarily relativist in nature. They can emerge in pedagogical terms where dissensus and consensus can be seen to be contingent on changing circumstances. In Raymond Williams's terms this would require the unlearning of the 'inherent dominative mode' (Williams, 1958: 376). This sort of perspective can form the basis for intercultural dialogue and intercultural education.

The liberal market economies have deepened the divide between winners and losers, but the elite continue to use political rhetoric and conventions of compromise. They try not to allow the basis of discontent and opposition to 'respond energetically or imaginatively to new challenges' (Judt, 2010: 157). While democratic societies provide constitutional protection for dissent, there is a general swing towards conformity and the minority dissenters may find themselves as outcasts. Neither at the level of citizen nor of contemporary intellectual are there informed discussions about public policy issues, which are undertaken by policy specialists and think tanks.

In the US the mantra of holding taxes to a minimum and 'keeping the government out of our affairs' is further strengthened by the demagogy of keeping 'socialism' out of government. In Switzerland a referendum banned the building of minarets by Muslims; in Britain citizens have accepted high levels of closed-circuit television usage and intrusive policing; and in most European countries citizens find it difficult to challenge economic policies. The education systems bear part of the responsibility for not teaching young people to be well-informed critical citizens and allowing them to remain apolitical. Young people are more likely to join single-issue interest groups but do not engage in 'the management of public affairs' and the development of strategies to dissent within the law. This can happen if young people develop a new language of politics which recasts public conversation (Judt, 2010: 156–73). This is partly the result of young people not being taught history properly and the absence of an understanding of who 'we' are and who the 'others' are. A critical reading and understanding of the past can help young people refine their analytical skills in order to understand the complexity of contemporary societies. At the underlying level the absence of the study of history may add to the failure of citizenship education to deal with issues of dissensus.

Consideration of such a pedagogic practice is necessary because most states face similar issues which have led to pressure on political, economic and social systems. At this level contrasting valuations can be placed on politics and the market and reinforce 'confidence in the civilising power of a state that they expect to compensate for *market failures*' (Habermas, 2007: 47). There are pathological consequences of capitalist modernisation which require ongoing political evaluation to promote citizens' 'awareness of the paradoxes of progress' (Habermas, 2007: 47). This could form the basis for bringing together differentiated regions in most continents in order to develop cosmopolitan strategies beyond national boundaries.

Education has a powerful role to play in strengthening democracies and making them more inclusive. It can also enable young people to understand their rights, obligations and responsibilities as active citizens within most complex democratic societies. This presents educational institutions with the challenge of bridging divides by providing diverse groups with access to social goods in society. They can also assist in nurturing conversations which can lead to the creation of shared values within the public domain and public institutions. However, educational processes should not only be considered to be taking place in the formal school system; they should also include the use of visual media and a critical reading of media messages.

There are also some elements of diversity which can be counterproductive if they conflict with citizenship and liberal democratic principles. Given that there are deep divisions caused by historically derived 'hidden hatreds' and uneven development, what can be done to develop new friendships and creative imaginations? There is already a legacy of exclusive and negative imaginations of racism, xenophobia, chauvinism and sexism. These issues pose complex challenges to teachers of citizenship trying to bridge these divides which cannot be dealt with easily through rational discussions. While at the classroom level these issues present pedagogical challenges, they also present institutional challenges. In democratic educational institutions, intercultural and anti-racist policies disallow negative behaviours. These policies can also be used to provide greater levels of access to knowledge, skills and shared values through institutional initiatives. Hence, while there has been the Holocaust and genocide of particular groups and peoples, the role that educators along with other public and social policymakers have to undertake is how to build solidarity and commonality between and within these different groups at the transnational level. The issue at this level is: without losing sight of the particularities of a loss of different groups, what can be done to bridge the divides between different groups?

To ensure that young people do not accept binary divides but adhere to their rights, obligations and responsibilities, the political culture has to have a broad basis. It cannot be based on a narrow, national, dominant group or on the acceptance of simplistic ethnic divides. Young people need to develop notions of inclusivity which symbolically and substantively are based on inclusive good values from all groups, and which capture the imagination and engage the disenchanted young people, especially those from subordinated and marginalised communities.

Cosmopolitan constitutional and human rights principles and other progressive and democratic struggles can also form part of this teaching and learning process.

Amongst many young people the notion of being part of and belonging to complex localities is important. Hence, the acceptance of territorial belongingness which is not exclusive but shared is worth exploring within schools and youth clubs. There is a need to develop non-exclusivist neighbourhoods which, rather than being no-go areas for some, are what Bookchin (1992) has called 'confederal communities'. This entails turning biological affinities into social affinities. Such communities would be based on shared resemblances which are neither racist nor patriarchal. This necessitates the revamping of the old Greek concept of *paidea* or the German notion of *Bildung* to develop their interactive and intercultural aspects within complex and socially diverse schools and communities. These purposes of education ought to ensure that they are enablers of citizens in contributing to the life of communities and societal institutions. These confederal values ought perhaps to give a new meaning to an intercultural *paidea* or an intercultural *Bildung*. Chinese and Indian civilisations also embody similar notions which can lend strength to developing intercultural shared value systems that strengthen the social affinities within multicultural polities in Europe. These types of measure should in fact provide greater credibility to issues of teaching and learning about citizenship.

Communities of Development and Hope

Processes of devolution, national or regional integration and mass migration place great pressure on national educational systems to engage in teaching democratically at local levels while recognising the centralisation of power at national or supranational levels (Baumann, 2007). Democratic schools and socially diverse classrooms can organise teaching and learning which enables young people to understand the complexity of societies and develop shared understanding. Provision for lifelong learning and informal education can also form the basis of inclusive learning communities which have collective voices and cut across communal divides. Education systems need to create public spaces so that whole democratic communities at the local level can influence educational and public policies in general. This type of learning within both modern cities and rural areas has to be connective since both these contexts are at the intersection of the local, national, regional and global – and also since there are intersections of perceived, conceived and actual lived space. As David Harvey (1989) states, the compression of learning is needed because of space/time compression, and learning is not restricted to formal or informal but also occurs in the contexts of family, community and workplace. Hence, both rural and urban communities become 'learning communities' through active learning strategies which are sustainable.

These types of development can contribute to the rebuilding of communities and the establishment of a connection with what Judith Green calls 'communities of development and hope' (Green, 1998: 431). Individuals and groups need a sense of agency as the citizens of a democratic society which moves beyond the merely institutional basis and engages with issues of exclusion within diverse communities. It allows for what Green refers to as deeper democratic features of diverse and complex modern societies. These features include a critical understanding of intercultural issues highlighted by indigenous or immigrant minorities. In some contexts such groups are defined as 'others' and demonised. However, these diverse communities also present the possibilities of complex interactions at individual and community levels to form the basis of resemblances and fraternities across group divides.

Hence, deep democracy has dynamic and imaginative features which draw upon and connect one's own stories and those of the community. One's personal knowledge confers the confidence to deal with issues and to contribute to public life and public institutions with greater competence. It also has the potential to initiate and help shape public and social policy from a local context. Such a development of a collective critical consciousness would contribute to rebuilding the 'public square', as discussed by Cornel West (1994). The public square includes public institutions and the need to engage with issues of deep divisions, democratic and intercultural relations and to turn exclusions into inclusions. Schools and other civic institutions which have greater levels of autonomy need to be supported, as Green writes:

> For their effectiveness in facilitating public discussions, coalition development and multinational community building [...] fostering deeply democratic attitudes and by offering opportunities to develop skills and capacities that active democratic citizenship requires. (Green, 1998: 437)

Small beginnings at grassroot and community level are one way of initiating involvement with deep democracies. They use experience as a basis of active citizenship, which can form the beginning of developing broader analysis and conceptualisation of citizenship engagement, not necessarily based on established political parties or machines. An impressive recent British pioneer in this field, the Novas Scarman Trust, till recently sponsored small self-help projects in run-down communities. An enormous amount of work in this field was pioneered by the Trust's former director, Matthew Pike, and the Trust has functioned in all nine regions of the British Isles. The projects set up in local areas were not just temples of democratic talk, but were of the 'can-do' mentality which leads to practical action at local community level, using the community's own capacities and initiatives. They included the turning of a derelict rubbish dump into a small park; reopening and running a closed-down village shop on which the community depended; and enabling a group of jobless youngsters to acquire the house they were squatting in – renovating it as a hostel, and then going on to renovate other derelict properties. Initiatives also included the provision of practical skills, training for jobs and generating local economies through micro-economic projects (Scarman Trust, 1999). The way into these instrumentalist initiatives has included the generation of interest in the creative faculties of those who are marginalised in society and to engage them by using their imaginations and imaginative faculties. In short, they have been a way of using community assets to reduce inequalities and bridge group divides.

Transparency and Good Governance

There are numerous hurdles in developing community involvement and transformative institutions in the present context because:

> Persistent fundamentalism and differentiation in religious, ethnic and national identities are juxtaposed with increasingly interpenetrated cultures. It is a context of global economic competition along with global consciousness of disparities of wealth and well being. (March and Olsen, 1995: 7)

What makes divisions based on the above issues particularly threatening to the prospects of deep democracy is the success of appeals to ethnic, gender, religious, racial and ethnic identities which undermine confidence in reason and the Enlightenment and, coupled with the pessimism engendered by uncertainties and introspection during the early years of the new millennium, which may have led to a decline in confidence not only in democracy but also in good governance. At this level it is particularly important that governments in democratic polities are transparent. The pressures of an economic urban and rural underclass, rising populations and depleting resources are a major challenge which most states at the international level need to confront. These pressures can lead to greater divides through pressure of economic globalisation.

Institutions in society have an educative role so that they can foster sacrifices not selfishness, and self-discipline through cooperation (March and Olsen, 1995: 49). Invoking the civic and the collective consciousness develops notions of the common good and requires the shaping of a sense of inclusive solidarity based on a sense of security and belonging. Specific personal identities need to be shaped to that of being a citizen, so that the private self is confirmed in the public domain through critical conversations and evaluations. This requires the state to provide a framework within which the social and cultural pluralism of multiethnic and multicultural societies can establish a sense of inclusive and collective solidarity. March and Olsen write:

> Part of the craft of democratic governance is developing institutions that simultaneously accommodate the ideals of pluralism and diversity, institutions that are capable of maintaining trust and mutual affection within a polity while simultaneously accommodating enduringly in constituent subgroups demands based on family ties, religion, ethnicity, language or personal affinity. That craft involves strengthening identities based on broad and long term conceptions of

a community of citizens and a concern for others in that community, including future citizens and unborn generations, and developing institutions that encourage both solidarity and civility. (March and Olsen, 1995: 55)

The statecraft entailed in cultivating this community of citizens who are defined by a bundle of rights, duties and responsibilities should be an essential aspect of diverse polities where the ethos of civic virtue is absent. Nevertheless, introducing a civic education which critically informs young and adult learners in diverse polities of their roles in society is a complex task. It entails an involvement in critical public debate based on insights which acknowledge the legitimacy of multiculturalism and which can accept both conflict and opposition as aspects of the knowledge required to deal with the complexities of life not only in a national society but also within the larger and developing cosmopolitan polity.

Such a political life assumes that the young citizens have a set of identities rather than one dominant or singular identity. It also assumes that good governance will empower the positive experiences of the key political identities. It entails the management of conflicts as well as inconsistencies. Deep democracies, however, also need to deal with seeds of deep conflict, and also the simpler ones of self-interest and public interest which are under continual tension. Education for democratic citizenship entails the learning of rules needed to negotiate reasonably in situations of such complex conflicts and to become active citizens in complex communities.

Establishing processes which are acceptable to learners requires teachers and learners alike to understand the difficulties of teaching and learning in diverse polities, and of the resolution of conflicts through deep conversations and mediation of differences. In many cases there can also be an agreement about what constitutes 'the common good'. In a democratic context, teaching and learning demands accepting a commitment to the democratic processes, even when differences and contradictions remain unresolved. The powerful rules governing democratic negotiation and civility are not only difficult to teach but also to learn. Nevertheless, knowledge, skills and competencies can be acquired and sharpened through education and democratic learning experiences in democratically organised schools and institutions.

Democratic engagement is more complex in societies which have higher levels of inequality and social differentiation. Hence, greater levels of equity between rights, resources, competencies, knowledge and organisational capacities would help the chances of democratic accommodations and solutions being worked out.

The objective may include not only education in the obligations and rights of a policy's key identities but also the establishment of widespread agreement on the main substantive purposes and ends of the policy, a sense of common good and common destiny. A key objective is to produce a political community within which citizens can discuss political issues in an atmosphere of mutual trust, tolerance and sympathy (March and Olsen, 1995: 244). The absence of these measures and the inability to strengthen cohesive democratic cultures may lead to the fragmentation of such polities or to alternative models of authoritarian government (Dahl, 1998: 145–65).

Most contemporary societies embody complexities, paradoxes, contradictions and a deepening of differences as a result of high levels of socio-economic inequality. These contradictions need to be addressed in forthright ways in all areas of public, social and private lives to enable aspects of deep democracy to be forged. At a community level there needs to be more interaction between enablers and can-doers who are active citizens in many countries around the world. Some community activists in England had managed to develop micro-economies using assets within the community. These have, however, been reversed in the last few years because it is perceived as an unimportant issue of public policy, despite the inner-city riots by young people in 2011.

In the absence of these engagements the linguistic, cultural, religious and nationality divides have become deeper and are creating exclusive imaginations of differences and divides. There is no substantive thinking or public policy development to enhance intercultural understanding to create empowered communities which are stable or peaceable. Hence, it is critical that educational measures are instituted to ensure that separatised groups do not 'bowl alone' but 'bowl together' (Putnam, 2000; Putnam and Feldstein, 2003). However, in Britain – where the government has used the rhetoric of 'Big Society' – very little has been done to achieve grassroot public engagement: serious thinking about how to connect communities which have suffered fragmentation, deep divides and impoverishment because of the corrosion of community solidarities as a result of the changes brought about by neo-liberal economies. The government's thinking about this field has a feel of *noblesse oblige* which harks back to the thinking of Edmund Burke (Norman, 2013). Current coalition government policies are not based on a critical analysis in qualitative and quantitative terms which take account of the gravity of the increasing gaps in social class and racial terms. The harking back to religious identities in disadvantaged communities and also at the level of schools in a secular societal context requires public policy measures to reverse increasing insularity and cultural and social divides.

Education Policies, Practices and Civil Society

Schools, universities and institutions of lifelong learning have an important role to uncover the hidden and ignored pasts of most European societies in order to build a more inclusive notion of their polities. Such a critical understanding of the complexity of societies can be acquired through work within individual academic disciplines as well as interdisciplinary studies by teachers and learners.

Schools and universities can also assist education systems in devising the intellectual basis of inclusive policies which can assist in making contemporary societies more socially just. These include the asymmetries resulting from social-economic inequalities. In the absence of integrative or inclusive policies which governments need to develop and implement, progressive forces can become galvanised and reinforce singular identity politics and strengthen singular identity-based organisations and activities. In the new millennium schools and higher education systems also face the more complex task of having to use the highly specific concerns expressed by identity-based organisations, as well as the intensification of issues of racial, ethnic and gender-specific politics, that challenge the possibilities of reconstructing a more inclusive and shared basis of knowledge which is part of the mainstream educational curriculum. Yet, as Peter Kwong, discussing issues in the US, writes:

> The objective of defining identity should not be an abstract theoretical exercise.
> In fact, the original mission of ethnic studies and Asian American studies was
> to end racism in the spirit of the larger struggle for equality and social justice.
> (South End Press Collective, 1998: 65–6)

In the case of Britain, Prime Minister Cameron might be right about the failure of policies of either multiculturalism or interculturalism – but this is because they have never been tried. The focus on education has been on disadvantages and deficit construction of the immigrant 'others'. Educational debates and policies have centred on defining children of immigrant origin as ethnic minorities, and have by and large portrayed them as a problem. In cases where they have not achieved well in the educational system they are defined as 'ethnic minorities'. In 1965 the policy of assimilation was followed by a policy of bussing children of immigrant families from local schools if their numbers exceeded 30 per cent, and this policy was only abandoned when it was declared discriminatory by the courts 10 years later (Tomlinson, 2008). Government and local authority policies during the 1960s and 1970s focussed on the teaching of English as a second language. This focus continued despite the fact that the 1975 Bullock Report, 'A Language for Life', stated that children should not forget their first language.

With the enactment of the Race Relations Act in 1976 came the recognition that there were issues of racial disadvantage in a range of areas of social policy. In the 1980s there was recognition that Britain was a 'multi-ethnic' society and there was a long debate on the implications of this for schools and the education system generally. This culminated in the enactment of the Education Reform Act (ERA) in 1988, whose purpose was to strengthen the singular English identity in the context of a historically and contemporaneously socially diverse Britain.

The categorisation of 'ethnicity' was used in monitoring students' performance in schools (Tomlinson, 1983) and ran the risk of stereotyping groups and communities. In the case of children of immigrants from the West Indies, many were diagnosed as educationally sub-normal and were placed in schools for sub-normal children, where they could not achieve as well as children in mainstream schools (Coard, 1971). In many cases this diagnosis was incorrect because the children used the Creole language while the teachers assumed that they were 'misusing' the English language. The issue of English as a second language has not been resolved for those who are English, as second-language learners and children of Bangladeshi origin still continue to do poorly in school, but teachers continue to misdiagnose this as an issue for these learners.

After various House of Commons Select Committee Inquiries, the Department of Education and Science set up the Rampton Committee (1981) and the Swann Committee (1985) to focus on the needs not just of children of West Indian origin but of all minority ethnic children. The uneven statistical evidence was not able to chart achievement differentials even within a particular group. Hence, the higher achievement by black girls as opposed to boys was not recorded. Amongst the Asian communities the higher levels of achievement by East African Asians was different from the lower levels by sections of the Bangladeshi and Pakistani communities (Archer and Francis, 2007). However, there was no clarity on whether it was the children who were underachieving or if it was the education system that was failing them (Gillborn, 2008).

These issues are further complicated because of the impact of racism and socio-economic differences on pupils' educational outcomes. There have only been patchy measures undertaken by schools and some local education authorities as a corrective to these negative features, which basically necessitate educating the majority and dominant English population. The studies on educational achievement in schools did not reveal the nature of children's school experience or of the learning and teaching processes. Many studies in the 1980s were more qualitative in nature; they examined the issue of school processes and mapped the complexities and multiple and changing nature of students' lives in complex institutions (Tomlinson, 2008).

The issue of student subcultures, and especially of resistance to racism, was one of the main features, and this related to the way in which teachers played a significant role in the difficulties children experienced (Mac an Ghaill, 1988). Young children in inner-city areas drew on discourses about 'race', and these influenced their relationships both inside and outside school and the classroom (Connolly, 1998). There are differentials in the experiences of Asian students who, despite being assessed as 'good', were not seen to be doing well (Troyna, 1991). However, children of Afro-Caribbean background from a different aspect were seen to be doing worse because they were based in 'low achieving schools [...] and were caught in a loop of disadvantage' (Foster, 1990). Afro-Caribbean boys were seen by many teachers as having behaviour problems; they were over-represented in numbers excluded from school; and students and teachers alike were influenced by discourses about black males (Sewell, 1997).

Intercultural education in the context of a multicultural Britain has not received the type of serious attention it merits, and issues of racism which need to be challenged through institutional anti-racist policies have been very sporadic. Multicultural and anti-racist school policies caused enormous controversy and were seen as simplistic (Donald and Rattansi, 1992; Gilroy, 1990).

Gillborn (2008) argues that government policies, instead of eradicating racial disadvantage in education, focus on social control and assimilation and use the argument of social cohesion to do this. The change in policies is reflected by an increased focus on issues of social class, poverty and disadvantage and a decreased focus on issues of racial disadvantage and inequality.

The educational establishments have articulated policies and practices by focussing on 'ethnic' definitions and identities as stated earlier, and these too have negative connotations and ignore the intergenerational changes which have taken place within communities that migrated to Britain after World War II. Notions of 'ethnicity' may be misplaced, partly because some of these identities may result from racism and the social exclusions which have led to the development of 'siege mentalities' which have jelled into 'siege communities'. These mentalities might include a focus on religious identity to safeguard a community.

The Macpherson Report (1999) into the death of Stephen Lawrence pointed out that 'institutional racism' existed not only in the British police force but also in the education system. Following this report there was the enactment of the Race Relations Amendment Act (2000), but this has not helped resolve issues of social justice; and issues have instead been articulated around a very limited notion of citizenship and national cohesion.

In educational terms market forces have been allowed to operate schools: education is seen as a matter of consumer choice, and the setting up of free schools over which local education authorities have no control.

The educational initiatives outlined above do not demonstrate any consistency or clarity of understanding about educational issues for multicultural schools and communities. Therefore, there has been very little effective action at a formal educational level. There was also a need to deepen democracy to strengthen the institutions of civil society, especially in the so-called non-governmental sector. A weaker civil society can increase the 'narcissism of small differences', as Freud states, and can fragment communities and societies; identity-based movements or single issue politics need not necessarily lead to balkanisation. Conversely, forging overlapping interests can allow the development of a movement with a broader base of popular support and political power which can help to establish frameworks and influence the state institutions to become more just, inclusive and democratic. Here the issue of human rights is particularly important in the demands for greater justice for socially excluded groups. Those who have worked around these issues are also able to see the connections between them and develop agendas on a broader front, based on these interconnections. However, this joined-up globalisation is not yet a reality, partly because of the democratic deficit in national, regional and international institutions. However, unfortunately neither the Council of Europe, the African Union nor the UN system has developed coherent policies and action-oriented approaches to deal with this complex set of issues. It is possible that national education systems can develop effective strategies to deal with some of these broader issues and can act as enabling agencies in this process. Organisations like UNESCO have developed agendas such as Education for All (EFA), the International Covenant on Economic, Social and Cultural

Rights and Universal Primary Education, yet issues of equalities do not feature very prominently within them or their schools.

Over the years the Council of Europe, which started as a political institution based on levels of mutualities, has developed increasingly as a norm-based organisation which has involved itself not only in conflict resolution but also in asserting issues of human rights within democratic contexts to develop values of democracy, diversity and human rights among young people. Yet, as its membership increased after the fall of communism these progressive initiatives have been undermined by the new member states on very narrow nationalistic grounds.

Many of the European and post-colonial ideals of democratic states which were formulated in the post-World War II period to avoid the catastrophes of interstate violence have been negated. There is also growing evidence of these becoming more institutionalised in an effective manner not between but within many countries. The devastation and ethnic cleansing in southeast Europe has occurred 50 years after these abominable ideas were defeated in World War II. Moreover, a multicultural and multilingual Europe is a powerful counterweight to other regional organisations which do not embody the vast elements of social diversity. The same is the case for countries in other continents where ethnic cleansing has taken place. On the other hand, these differences, when channelled through appropriate educational initiatives, can lend strength to developing greater levels of fraternity and unity.

Citizenship and Difference

The challenge for citizenship is to mould the one out of the many, and to construct appropriate educational responses to difference and diversity within the numerous modern societies. Education policy initiatives of anti-racism or multiculturalism which are directed solely at immigrants or indigenous minorities and do not include the dominant groups or majority populations may not be useful. The essentialist rhetoric of some of these policies in some contexts has led to the 'othering' of groups and created binary oppositions (e.g. majority/minority, belonger/non-belonger, black/white). Given these divides and the varying levels of inequality, Marshall (1977) asserts that the state also tries, through citizenship, to initiate a 'tendency towards equality' by creating basic conditions leading towards social equality. It is also a dynamic and an active not a passive concept. Hence, social equality can be achieved by removing hindrances like 'institutional racism' and exclusionary practices such as 'glass ceilings', whereby women or minorities never reach the top tiers of institutions or organisations.

Education systems also face the challenge of helping to build inclusive polities along with other social and public institutions by accommodating notions of difference and also by creating conditions of belongingness of diverse groups. In educational institutions such initiatives can be 'creative moments' since notions of citizenship can be used to develop integrative mentalities by reducing inequality and differences between groups.

Equality and Democratic Engagement

How can there be a framework for universal norms which can encompass particularistic demands and establish solidarity? Citizenship as a modern concept is realisable only in the context of a democratic and constitutional state. Modern citizens have rights which have been acquired after long struggles and which cannot be easily ignored or denied. One of these rights is the access to institutions within a society – and is particularly relevant for girls, women or vulnerable groups. In some cases it is not the state but a patriarchal or otherwise particular community that may deny women their right to education or employment.

The conferring of citizenship rights entails opposing such particularistic practice which would deny girls or women equality in education or employment. At this level public institutions need to distinguish which values of different communities are acceptable and do not violate the universality of the rights of girls, women or vulnerable groups. At this level there are fairly serious issues about public and private domains amongst groups with few shared political identities, and fears that their legitimate religious, traditional and familial rights would be infringed and lead to the homogenisation of minority communities and their cultures. There can be three important ways of ensuring that this does not happen, by making sure that:

1. the modern constitutional principles used by the state are universalistic and cosmopolitan, and not purely those of the dominant nation of shared descent and culture;
2. secular notions are reviewed to ensure that they are not oppositional to faiths and religions, but have an interpretation which protects the rights of all groups to believe or not believe and which protects legitimate private rights;
3. the asymmetries in socio-economic terms are reduced between majorities and minorities; and issues of fairness, equality, mutuality, reciprocity and social justice are dealt with seriously.

Hence, there are institutional and structural bases of exclusivity to be removed. If citizens are excluded or marginalised within the education system, does the state stay neutral or does it intervene? In other words, is the state fair or is it impartial? Rawls, using the difference principles, would argue that the 'better off' should not do better than the 'worst off' (Rawls, 1971: 60, 124, 132, 199). So, to accord equity the state is 'fair' but not impartial. In a democratic context a citizen is entitled to education and knowledge to equalise their life chances. Hence, the state has a role in creating a level playing field, and in educational terms it can do this by intervening. This is especially true where marginalised or excluded minorities are subordinated by dominant or majority groups.

Contemporary societies also currently face a dilemma because old solidarities and mutualities have been destroyed, especially as the younger generation are divided into winners and losers. The notion of a citizenship education during the period of economic globalisation that the losers owe nothing to the winners, is a difficult but critical issue. Habermas writes:

> Today, as the nation-state finds itself challenged from within by the explosive potential of multiculturalism and from without by the pressure of globalisation, the question arises of whether there exists a functional equivalent for the fusion of the nation of citizens with the ethnic nation. (Habermas, 1998: 117)

Constitutional principles, human rights declarations, and progressive and democratic struggles can also form part of this teaching and learning process.

Deep Citizenship

Within most contexts internationally the narrow nationalistic and destructive power a government can unleash needs to be restrained. As Habermas writes about Europe:

> A culture that has over the centuries been torn apart more than any other by conflicts between city and country, ecclesiastical and secular power, the competition between religion and science, and the struggles between political authorities and antagonistic classes, had to learn the painful lessons of how differences can be communicated, oppositions institutionalised, and tensions stabilised. The recognition of differences, the mutual recognition of others in their otherness, can become a distinguishing mark of a shared identity. (Habermas, 2007: 44–5)

Notions of how to develop deep democracy based on deep social participation and citizenship require urgent attention because the private market has no public obligations and the role of mixed economies becomes more important. The role of social capital amongst citizens is now also recognised by the World Bank.

Deep democracy demands deep citizenship. The activation of civic values in public and private domains puts into place a new non-traditional understanding of citizenship. Here deep democracy can be assisted by eliminating the previous private/public divide:

> The fundamental change in the way in which the particular and the universal are related to the public and the private is to admit the civic virtues to wide areas of

life: most generally wherever one can act towards the universal, therein lie the civic virtues and therein lies deep citizenship. (Clarke, 1996: 118)

Some Future Directions in Education

British and European education systems need to seriously re-examine the earlier history of the Mediterranean which involved interactions between Greeks, Egyptians and Phoenicians (amongst others) in that complex region. These interactions have left a legacy of complex knowledge which has been largely ignored by the North European historiography of the eighteenth and nineteenth centuries. Greece has been viewed as the 'pure childhood' of Europe and thus set a basis for Eurocentrism in the construction of knowledge about this continent. This issue needs to be revisited to form a much more inclusive basis of knowledge within European education systems. For instance, during the eleventh and twelfth centuries Muslim, Jewish and Catholic scholars formed an intercultural basis of constructing knowledge inherited from ancient Greece which laid the foundation for knowledge leading to the Renaissance.

These earlier historical aspects of intercultural intellectual collaboration in European history can form the basis for a non-Eurocentric, transnational curriculum for schools in the twenty-first century. For instance, a transnational history curriculum could lead to friendships across national boundaries by delimiting triumphalism and militarism.

Measures to reduce educational inequalities are needed to engage disenchanted young people by reinstating the power of education and not to merely 'school' young people, which replicates the existing socio-economic roles and divides. The exciting task of educating young people to improve their life chances requires interculturally educated teachers who are not merely 'trained' but also 'educated'. These teachers need to understand the theory and practice of learning and teaching as well as the rich, diverse and complex underpinnings of society and communities reflected within a school's curriculum and functioning.

The divides within many city communities can be bridged through common state school systems provided by accountable and democratically elected local authorities: good comprehensive educational measures to ensure a common and shared curriculum which draws on the broader intercultural pool of knowledge as a basis for the official school curriculum. This ought to build on the subjectivities of knowledge which young people bring to the school. This would form the basis of developing common and shared public democratic values.

In Britain and many other European countries concepts of the 'secular' and the 'religious' are perceived as being oppositional. The reality in most polities is that secular constitutional democracies protect the private rights of groups to believe or not to believe; to attend or not attend church, mosque or temple. The patriarchal dimensions of faith may restrict citizenship and the human rights of girls and women; and in the public domain and institutions rights should remain inviolable. Private institutions may 'instruct' believers about a particular faith. The role of educational institutions is not to instruct but to inculcate the critical faculties amongst the learners and to educate young people across particularistic group divides based on singularised identities. School also cannot afford to ignore the multiple, hybrid and 'mestizo' identitities of many young people. In this respect the educational institutions may choose to educate learners about secular societal values and inter- and multifaith issues.

The neo-liberal economic model is used in Britain in judging school performance by publishing league tables and setting narrow performance targets. This process entails an inspection system with no space for intercultural and anti-discriminatory policies and practices which regulate behaviours. Perhaps European schools could follow the system in Finland which allows schools to self-evaluate. This ought to contain an important dimension of the absence of racist and xenophobic behaviours and measure the state of intercultural understanding within schools.

Democratic school practices which provide a lived reality on the basis of democratic engagement can contribute to the learning of citizenship and human rights values which are then translated by young learners into active citizenship values and engagement within their communities and society generally. This in turn can form the basis to create safe and stable inclusive communities of 'development and hope'. It also provides a basis for protecting the rights of new as well as old minority groups like the Roma people in Europe.

Conclusion

This chapter aimed to initiate a more informed and rational political and policy dialogue which can lead to evidence-based research on intercultural public and social policies in Britain and Europe generally. It is anticipated that these can help to tackle meaningfully some of the underlying challenges which are laced with social and class divides. The current tokenistic and rhetorically oriented multicultural policies only help to strengthen superficial, simplistic identity-based politics and sustain siege communities and mentalities. The secular state has the duty to protect the autonomous and private religious and traditional identities of its groups. However, state support and funding of schools and other institutions is an intrusion into the private domain. It also helps to entrench particularistic group identities and diminishes the broader integrative powers of the state. The state, therefore, has an even greater obligation to strengthen inclusive public institutions and protect the constitutional and human rights of all citizens. This necessitates the enhancement of public spaces for cross-group conversations. These are necessary to build reciprocity and trust across divides in multicultural communities also divided on a class basis.

Narrowly based state policies also obviate the development of politically creative and imaginative capacities of citizens to help in the process of revitalising statutory and civic institutions and cultures. These citizen initiatives can genuinely help the state in resolving some of the underlying causes that feed narrow nationalism, xenophobia and racism.

Conversely, the political cultures and many institutions on the European continent have the capacities to remove democratic inequalities and deficits. These capacities draw on both the past and on contemporary struggles of the underclasses, subordinated and oppressed groups, to acquire democratic and citizenship rights. The seeds of these experiences are reflected in many communities, localities, regions and national states. To enhance cosmopolitan citizenship the European Union and the Council of Europe provide the constitutional and institutional basis to help build a stable, peaceable and diverse European continent.

References

Anderson, P. (2009). *The New Old World*. London: Verso.

Beck, U. and Grande, E. (2007). *Cosmopolitan Europe*. Cambridge: Polity.

Bauman, Z. (2007). *Liquid Times: Living in an Age of Uncertainty*. Cambridge: Polity.

Bookchin, M. (1992). *Urbanization without Cities: The Rise and Decline of Citizenship*. Montreal: Black Rose.

Buruma, I. (2010). *Taming the Gods: Religion and God in Three Continents*. Princeton: Princeton University Press.

Caldwell, C. (2009). *Reflections on the Revolution in Europe*. London: Allen Lane.

Clarke, P.B. (1996). *Deep Citizenship*. London: Pluto.

Coard, B. (1971). *How the West Indian Child is Made Educationally Subnormal in the British School System: The Scandal of the Black Child in Schools in Britain*. London: New Beacon.

Connolly, P. (1998). *Racism, Gender Identities and Young Children: Social Relations in a Multi-Ethnic, Inner-City Primary School*. London: Routledge.

Dahl, R.A. (1998). *On Democracy*. New Haven: Yale University Press.

Donald, J. and Rattansi, A. (1992). *Race, Culture and Difference*. London: Sage.

Foster, P. (1990). *Policy and Practice in Multicultural and Anti-Racist Education*. London: Routledge.

Gillborn, D. (2008). *Racism and Education: Coincidence or Conspiracy?* Abingdon: Routledge.

Gilroy, P. (1990). The end of anti-racism, *New Community*, 17 (1), 71–83.

Green, J. (1998). Educational Multiculturalism: Critical Pluralism and Deep Democracy. In Willett, C. (ed.), *Theorizing Multiculturalism: A Guide Current to Debate*. Oxford: Blackwell.

Habermas, J. (1998). *The Inclusion of the Other: Studies in Political Theory*. Cambridge, MA: MIT Press.

Habermas, J. (2007). *The Divided West*. Cambridge: Polity.

Harvey, D (1989). *The Condition of Postmodernity: An Enquiry into the Origins of Cultural Change*. Oxford: Blackwell.

Judt, T. (2010). *Ill Fares the Land*. London: Allen Lane.

Kepel, G. (1997). *Allah in the West: Islamic Movements in America and Europe*. Stanford: Stanford University Press.

Mac an Ghaill, M. (1988). *Young Gifted and Black: Student–Teacher Relations in the Schooling of Black Youth*. Buckingham: Open University Press.

March, J.G. and Olsen, J.P. (1995). *Democratic Governance*. New York: Free Press.

Marshall, T.H. (1977). *Class, Citizenship and Social Development*. Chicago: University of Chicago Press.

Michaels, W.B. (2007). *The Trouble With Diversity: How We Learned To Love Identity And Ignore Inequality*. New York: Henry Holt.

Norman, J. (2013). *Edmund Burke: Philosopher, Politician, Prophet*. London: HarperCollins.

Putnam, R.D. (2000). *Bowling Alone: The Collapse and Revival of American Community*. New York: Simon and Schuster.

Putnam, R. and Feldstain, L.M. (2003). *Better Together: Restoring the American Community*. New York: Simon and Schuster.

Rawls, J. (1971). *Theory of Justice*. Cambridge, MA: Belknap Press of Harvard University Press.

The Scarman Trust (1999). *Getting Self-Propelled: The Can Do Challenge*. London: The Scarman Trust.

Sewell T. (1997). *Black Masculinities: How Black Boys Survive Modern Schooling*. Stoke-on-Trent: Trentham.

South End Press Collective (1998). *Talking about a Revolution: Interviews with Michael Albert, Noam Chomsky, Barbara Ehrenreich, Bell Hooks, Peter Kwong, Winona LaDuke, Manning Marable, Urvashi Vaid, and Howard Zinn*. Cambridge, MA: South End Press.

Tomlinson, S. (1983). *Ethnic Minorities in British Schools: A Review of the Literature 1960–1982*. London: Heinemann.

Tomlinson, S. (2008). *Race and Education: Policy and Politics in Britain*. Maidenhead: Open University Press/McGraw-Hill Education.

Troyna, B. (1991). Underachievers or underrated? The experience of pupils of South Asian origin in secondary schools. *British Education Research Journal*, 17 (4), 361–76.

Wallerstein, I. (1991). *Unthinking Social Science: The Limits of Nineteenth Century Paradigms*. Cambridge: Polity.

West, C. (1994). *Race Matters*. New York: Vintage.

Wilkinson, R. and Pickett, K (2009). *The Spirit Level: Why Equality is Better for Everyone*. London: Penguin.

Williams, R. (1958). *Culture and Society, 1780–1950*. London: Chatto and Windus.

Chapter 3

Interculturalism, Diversity Policy and Integration in France: A Succession of Paradoxical Instructions

Martine A. Pretceille

In France, intercultural education has always been linked to the immigration and schooling of 'foreign' pupils despite numerous attempts to move away from this specificity via extension of the term to other sectors such as language learning, French as a foreign language in particular, intercultural communication, intercultural management and training for expatriates. It is in the context of this migration problem that we present an analysis of the policies and evolution of interculturalism in France.

Today, immigration sees its plural recognised. A process linked for many years to economic immigration from former French colonies, immigration is now accepted not only as a way of structuring society but also as a permanent movement with increasingly complex and diversified methods. This is not a marginal phenomenon but rather a phenomenon that affects all sectors of society. Immigration is also new in the sense that it is becoming increasingly similar to countries historically and traditionally considered as immigration countries such as the USA, Canada and Australia.

Immigration today is not the same as it was before, and we still do not know what it will look like in the future. We should also consider the European area and the Schengen area, both of which give populations greater mobility. Thus Gypsies, Roma, migrants and travellers are all mixed together despite differences in their history, status and social and economic situations. We cannot discuss the evolution of intercultural education without mentioning the successive contexts and the different developments and decisions made in a more general context than that covered by education. In fact, the intercultural issue stretches beyond the educational domain to become a social and political challenge, a challenge recognised by local authorities through neighbourhood and town policies.

However, social and educational policies are caught in a vice between paradoxical orders: an increasingly complex law and subject to random incidents, crises, emergencies; and a social world that is deeply but confusingly marked by an ethnicisation of situations. In addition, it should be noted that, in its recommendations, Europe is increasingly insisting on the issue of integration rather than that of immigration.

From Intercultural to Equal Opportunities

Driven by the European Council, it is through the expression 'intercultural activities' that the intercultural problem has been introduced into primary schools in France. Introduced in the context of learning the language and culture (Ministère de l'Éducation nationale, 1975, 1978), interculturalism was designed to better integrate foreign pupils into the French school system while respecting their cultural identity and facilitating their readaptation to their country of origin should they wish to return. The context was marked by the economic crisis, suspension of the immigration policy (1974) and the Stoléru laws that introduced a policy of encouraging the return of migrant workers. In 1978, the expansion of intercultural activities to all schoolchildren corresponded to a consistent failure of the Stoléru laws, the stabilisation of migrant populations and the recognition of immigration as something structural and not just temporary. We will not refer here to the many analyses carried out on the paradoxes and ambiguities as well as on some advances in intercultural education (see Abdallah-Pretceille, 2011).

The 1980s were a real turning point for policy. In fact, thanks to the 1981 memorandum on Priority Education Zones (ZEP), the schooling of migrant children is no longer the subject of specific measures but is considered one of the ways of fighting social and cultural inequality. It was also in this period that town policies and positive discrimination policies developed at the territorial level, such as *développement social des quartiers* (1983) and *opération 'banlieue 89'* (1989).

The French suburban crisis of September 2005, the causes of which were, according to some, ideologies or challenges attributed to either economic and social inequalities or to a failure in the French integration model, was the chance to present a notion well known in educational fields, that of equal opportunities, and to extend this to society as a whole.

The notion of equal opportunities comes from the school register to embrace all social initiatives and to pave the way for differential treatment, which will neither be affirmed nor denied. Thus we are witnessing a paradox to better deal with the question of cultural heterogeneity; it is dissolved in a series of measures and initiatives that circumvent legal obstacles (notably the issue of the recognition of minorities). In fact:

> positive territorial discrimination that forms the basis of urban policies is never politically displayed or claimed; on the other hand, it is systematically watered down by themes related to emergencies and priorities, which have become, over the years, a window to the perception of neighbourhoods and public action strategies. (Doytcheva, 2007: 77)

At the same time, silence surrounds intercultural activities. The latter have not gone away; they are simply minimised or ignored.

The logic of differentiation of the public is necessary for the preponderance of emergency, local and fairness for all. In terms of social and educational action, equal rights logic leads to the abandonment of differentialist positions so only one issue is dealt with, that of all publics without distinction. Institutional initiatives continue and multiply. We can mention:

- a ministry of employment, social cohesion and housing and the promulgation in June 2004 of a law providing for a social cohesion plan based on three levers: employment, housing and equal opportunities;
- a ministry dedicated to the promotion of equal opportunities and aided by six 'equal opportunities' prefects, including three in the Parisian region (2005);
- the creation in 2006 of a national agency for social cohesion and equal opportunities responsible for working in the suburbs;
- a High Authority dedicated to combating discrimination in favour of equality (HALDE). In terms of the recommendations contained in Bernard Stasi's report, the law implemented on 30 December 2004 replaces the European directive dating from 29 June 2000 relating to the implementation of the policy on equal treatment for all, regardless of race or ethnic origin. The High Authority's powers are gradually increasing so as to permit this agency to issue administrative sanctions. For example, the measures proposed include legislation relative to the practice of testing for recruitment, the French Audiovisual Board's (CSA) obligation to promote diversity within the French audiovisual sector. HALDE will be scrapped in 2011 in favour of a Rights Advocate.
- a name change from Social Action Fund (FAS) to (Action Fund for Integration and the Fight against Discrimination (FASILD). This change is linked to the adoption of the 16 November 2001 law pertaining to the fight against discrimination. FASILD's role is evolving such that its mission is based on three key priorities:
  - the welcoming of new arrivals with the implementation of devices being gradually extended to the whole territory, including a veritable welcome and integration contract;
  - integration, extended to access to rights and knowledge of duties, social promotion and professional conditions;
  - the fight against racism and discrimination.
- The replacement in 2002 of the Training and Information Centres for the Schooling of Migrant Children (CEFISEMs), created in 1975, with Academic Centres for the Schooling of Newcomers and Travellers (CASNAVs). Since 1990, the CEFISEMs saw their mission redefined according to needs at the time, namely the importance of ZEPs and violence prevention. Changes in the migratory population led to further adjustment of its missions. In addition to refocusing on strictly linguistic

and pedagogical actions, CASNAVs are defined as expertise centres for managers (cohort monitoring and assessment of welcome devices, etc.). Their link with local educational authorities rather than with training centres (often former teacher-training colleges) translates to a change in direction, level of intervention and working methods.

Let us also remember that the National Pedagogical Education Centre (CNDP)-Migrants became part of the CNDP in 1998 and was called Town-School-Envrironment (VEI). Similarly, the semantic field of reference is also changing and reflects the desire to consider the diversity of situations. As an indication, we will mention the following changes:

- the terms 'discrimination' and 'inequality' are used synonymously and almost systematically;
- 'newcomers' are now called immigrants, children of immigration, and second-generation immigrants;
- 'first language' has replaced 'mother tongue';
- 'populations with specific characteristics' refers to newcomers and travellers who move in the same circles;
- the terms 'foreigners' and 'immigrants' are no longer significant when taken out of context. Any use of absolute terms is more a sign of stigma than consideration. An expression like 'x% of foreign pupils' is recognised, in texts, as no longer being significant.

Such euphemisms reflect the sensitivity of the issue and the caution with which issues and target audiences are identified. This is encouraging, as it reflects the complexity of the problem; but it is also indicative of the fact that the weight of representations, like the weight of groups and circumstances, increasingly leads social actors closer to a 'politically correct' form whose logic may be the final dissolution or denial of the problem.

Between Differentiation and Lack of Differentiation, Paradoxes, Ambiguities and Procrastinations

Whatever the formulation (political diversity, fight against discrimination, positive discrimination, intercultural education and multicultural education etc.), all decisions, initiatives and recommendations range from the recognition of a specificity, differentiation between individuals, but also from a fierce determination not to mark, not to differentiate – a desire fuelled by fear of destroying a form of social cohesion.

Positive discrimination is no longer reserved for foreigners and migrants. It now concerns many social categories (economically weak populations, marginalised populations, issues of sexual orientation, etc.) and geographic areas (suburbs in particular). Thus, 'the need to carry out an action to facilitate the integration of immigrants is combined with the idea, somewhat contradictorily, that this action needs to blend in with existing social programmes' (Doytcheva, 2007: 85).

However, any complacency by neutralising and sanitising formulations contradicts attempts to solve a problem that is not named and to display, at the same time, a political desire to find solutions. We fall into this blind alley in which France has been for many years.

Social and educational action remains mired in the dilemma between affirmation and caution. The absence of a ministry with an interministerial dimension responsible for the development and implementation of an immigration policy is significant. Immigration remains the prerogative of the Ministry of the Interior and Religious Affairs, which reduces the issue to a question of flow of input, output and safety. The 2007 creation of the Ministry of Immigration, Integration, National Identity and Solidarity Development was not able to resist (scrapped in 2009) the confusion between issues, not to mention two ideologies perceived as contradictory in the context of the period. The increase in words to describe this ministry translates, again, the blurring and uncertainties that surround any discussion or action on this issue. For many years other countries, such as Great Britain and other nation states opted to officially claim to want to deal with civil and ethnic issues related to immigration.

The French tendency to water down this issue altogether only delays things and aggravates the passionate and ideological climate that systematically surrounds this issue:

> Subsuming integration into social action has two significant consequences: on the one hand, the constant concern to translate the individual into universalist socio-economic categories, removing the cultural dimension in favour of large national regulatory instruments such as work, education and health; secondly, inclusiveness actions are addressed at *immigrant populations* to the extent that they are a component that is excluded. But generally speaking, that is to say in non-specific and non-discriminatory terms, integration affects inconsistency. (Doytcheva, 2007: 101)

This logic of equal rights between foreigners and nationals leads to the abandonment of former particularistic and differentialist approaches and to the desire to incorporate the issue of foreigners into common law.

The idea of integration – previously reserved for 'foreigners', 'immigrants' and 'children and adolescents of immigrants' – now addresses any individual who participates in the civic space and who shares the same values (see Haut Conseil à l'Intégration/High Council for Integration, 2011). Integration becomes synonymous with avoiding stigmatising origins. Differentialism and the right to be different are no longer appropriate. However, this concept is in direct contradiction with another social phenomenon, namely the recruitment of actors from diverse backgrounds to manage fairly actions related to diversity. We find the same contradiction when the political parties refer to the number of members and candidates at elections 'from diverse backgrounds'.

In various texts from 2002, we have tried to use a single expression, welcome and integration. The welcome and integration contracts, in place since July 2003, consist in providing the newcomer with a civic and linguistic education, and social and personalised professional support. This contract, which is signed voluntarily by the foreigner, commits the newcomer to 'respecting the Republic's values, laws and rules of law as well as taking training offered to them'. The welcome and integration contract is designed for immigrants arriving in France with documentation. The question remains for those who are undocumented. The interference of principles and intentions means (although this is still under debate), indirectly, that the integration contract has become a means of immigration control at the expense of integration.

Discourses and contradictory practices relative to differences, whether recognised or not, lead to another paradox – that of the encystment of individual and/or group identities into 'prison-identities', which causes anger or rage in people who can no longer define themselves and who are instead assigned an identity (a label) by an authority, such as 'immigrant', 'second generation' and now 'from diversity'. This obligation to belong, which is often aimed at devalued and marginalised groups, causes a return to exacerbation reactions.

In fact, regardless of the formulation and actions undertaken, we always come back to the same dilemma: how can we combine ethnicity and integration? How to initiate a political, social and educational process that goes far beyond this series of injunctions that are even more paradoxical than ethnicity and integration maintaining strained relationships subject to the vagaries of economic, political and international conditions, which are also subject to ideological fluctuations. Hesitation in successive policies shows interference between integrative tradition in the French Republic and the emergence of new, poorly stabilised models, misunderstood and attempting to register the specific individual and group into a coherent whole.

Intercultural Education and Citizenship

In the same vein, the call to citizenship – including participatory life at neighbourhood level – again leads to misuse of the ethnic issue. We recognise the presence of foreigners while continuing to deny the specific characteristics of distinction.

The intercultural issue has often been used as a cure for social and educational problems. Currently, the intercultural issue is involved in the fight against social violence, incivility and citizenship education. The sense of 'cure' is always the same. There has been an inflation of discourse on citizenship, which is also often confused with civility. Reference to citizens is almost non-existent, and this needs to be investigated. In fact, in France, 'citizens' are people of French nationality. So how can we integrate people who live in the territory but do not have, do not want or cannot have French nationality? The shift from the term citizen to that of citizenship avoids answering this question by looking to unify practices, duties and requirements. Similarly, we can see a shift in meaning between citizenship and morality. This systematic recourse to discourse on values to retrain social ills presents moralistic excesses of which history has, unfortunately, already given some painful examples. This type of call to citizenship works as a leitmotif and in fact serves as an outlet and good conscience to those who, precisely, no longer engage.

This inflation of references to citizenship via schools, companies, media, suburbs etc. is associated with a hard-hitting discourse on 'the loss of values', a loss mainly attributed to young people – and more specifically 'to young people from the suburbs' – as if adults and seniors have always shown an increased sense of values (fascism, totalitarianism and the wars in the twentieth century suggest the opposite). The word 'suburb' is now a stigma that contributes to this general confusion and adds to this semantic and axiological jumble. The geographic definition of suburbs has given way to a sociological definition that works as a marker, a categorisation, a differentiation – with one of the direct consequences being distancing and thus a form of rejection. This stigmatisation is a cause of violence in itself. Therefore, attempts to combat violence with analysis procedures, which are themselves symbolically violent, are contradictory and paradoxical.

This incantatory call to morality, to citizenship whose content is never really explained and remains unclear, may cause the return of a moral order. This is all the more dangerous because this call comes with a security discourse, also doubled by references to 'zero tolerance' built in dogma, an even more pernicious slogan that invalidates the notion of tolerance. While in the past (especially the more recent past) politicians sought to resolve problems through improving structures and institutions, this is currently through improved social and moral behaviour. Certainly, if the axiological dimension is important and necessary, it should not be reduced to forms of moralising injunctions against one type of audience to evade the question of the absence of a collective project at the level of society as a whole. Morality would only, in this context, be a way of regulating problems and crises.

In France, the Republican tradition of schooling combined society and school. This complementarity cannot be questioned outside of a national democratic debate or through decay, even less by cyclical initiatives taken in an emergency and without reference to a widely discussed and shared collective perspective. Which type of citizen should the school create? This is a classic question today formulated from the 'what is citizenship' question, a shift that is not merely semantic but raises questions too.

This absence of a comprehensive plan is concealed by the multiplication of timely initiatives through the development of an instrumental policy. Everyone – in their neighbourhood, at their school, in their establishment, in their 'zone' – tries to find a local and contextual solution. Thus there are numerous emerging projects of varying quality and length which, in the absence of overall coherence (coherence should not be confused with cohesion here), reduce initiatives aimed at consolidation, remediation and correction initiatives, through reinforcement of the law and security measures. We are now seeing a development of the legal to the detriment of the social; regulation of problems by way of functionality, technical expertise (including social expertise), that corresponds, finally, to avoid in terms of confirmation, not just of values, but also of references and norms.

This instrumentalisation of the social facilitates, in the best cases, improvement of social cohesion, which lies at the level of 'techniques' introduced to reduce fractures, but which make the economy a reflection and work relative to axiological coherence – that is to say relative to values. This explains the inflation of measures; these are always timely and uncertain because they are selected in an emergency. However, the search for efficiency does not just include measures, even good ones. Is it necessary to move away from this sociality without standards, which bears violence through anomie as well as all the security excesses? Without a collective project, without lines of force, the ethical risk is of only being the extra soul of consensus, to use an expression coined by French philosopher Alain Badiou. This explains the development of expert arguments, pragmatic arguments, which tend, ultimately, to compensate for failures in meaning.

Thus the question is namely how to establish or re-establish agreement between shared values and norms, and how to make them more visible. In fact, we cannot talk about integration in schools and society without specifying the frame of reference in which foreigners will mix and then integrate. This is important because the different places for socialisation (school, neighbourhood, family, leisure centres, associations etc.) no longer work in harmony in terms of values and norms. This explains the development of conflicts between structures and the development of alternative and synchretic behaviours among individuals.

Therefore, problem-solving through talking and discussion, which was, in the past, the subject of general agreement, is no longer the subject of consensus at present. Some individuals and certain groups tend to systematically apply the principle of violence when it comes to settling conflicts. The less clearly schools show their references, the more they encourage conflicts relative to norms, and the development of sectarian folds and communities. Lacking agreement on this, the educational system runs the risk of being reduced to a mere transmitter of knowledge and of losing its identity and one of its missions: creating citizens. If this dimension is abandoned, we need to deal with the idea that the school only manages and regulates knowledge, a function that preceded the development of educational consumerism and the commodification of knowledge. The fact that the financial cost is small or reduced (through a public service) will have no effect on a school's new consumerist direction.

Axiological cropping of the educational sector is a prerequisite for educational and pedagogical efficiency; reframing should be in terms of the heterogeneity and complexity of the social and academic fibre. In this perspective, integration is defined more as an affiliation, from objectified and common bases or from 'a desire to live together', than as a mere filiation. The logic of the contract cannot grow out of any ethical agreement.

In a group or a homogenous society there is more evidence and shared implicits. It is not necessary to systematically repeat the codes. At present, this axiological coherence can only be communicated by intergenerational tradition and transmission given the extreme diversity of populations. Currently, we are suffering less from an absence of values than we are from their affirmation and collective objectivation. We now need to guarantee this process through objectivation, discussion and debates, which is another way of running with the idea of a deliberative, and not statistical, democracy (through the addition of ballots for example). It is clear that this agreement on norms and shared values cannot be achieved through coercion or imposition of one group or another. Any contract idea not linked to an ethical approach is just a social pragmatic with no sustainable efficiency.

The School System: Stuck between National Directives and Local Adaptations

In practical terms, despite official directives on intercultural education, key players in the school system constantly swing between the desire to preserve the principle of equality and resistance to the facts: differences present themselves in a lawless and often sudden manner. Introduced by some and retracted by others, differentialist or communitarian trends are constantly evolving. The dilemma is always the same: should we consider the origins, visible or not, of pupils? Official texts clearly state that the school is 'a place for social, cultural and, ultimately, professional integration'. A present mastery of the French language is seen as a key factor in this integration.

We can see this desire to break down the borders between natives and foreigners in several national education memoranda. For example, a 2002 memorandum on the enrolment and schooling of first- and second-degree foreign pupils clearly stipulates in its introduction that 'under current legislation, no distinction can be made between pupils of French nationality and those of foreign nationality in terms of access to education' (Ministère de l'Éducation nationale, 2002c). Now the priority is granted to the territory, that is to say the presence of child migrants in a territory makes education compulsory. Reference is also made to the United Nation Convention on the Rights of the Child (November 1989), which 'guarantees the child the right to education outside of any distinction relative to their nationality or personal circumstances'.

In order to remove any ambiguity, it is specified that 'it is not the responsibility of the Ministry of National Education to check the documents held by foreign pupils and their parents relative to rules governing their entry and stay in France'. In the same vein, the law is waived for 16–18 year-olds, the age at which possession of a temporary residency card or residency card is compulsory. In addition, 'the refusal to educate a young person who is not subject to the schooling obligation must be justified' (Ministère de l'Éducation nationale, 2002c). This refusal may be justified by pedagogical reasons.

Considering that this is a sensitive subject, very clear instructions concerning discrimination/equal treatment between French children and foreign children are given regarding the continuation of studies, exam registration, academic status and the learning contract. All this data is indicative of the gap that exists between the goals of education – which cannot be subject to the vagaries of the economy, voting, anxieties or fears – and negative representations disseminated by or rooted in the population. Note that, as a result, official texts are more accurate and therefore much longer. The spirit of legalisation gradually permeates all sectors. The intercultural dimension is absent from all official texts.

The Welcome Obligation

The welcome duty and obligation is subject to specific instructions, thereby revealing the difficulties encountered in practice. The references used are those of republican principles, proof that they were often forgotten, or simply ignored.

> The welcome applies to both pupils who are newcomers to France and other pupils.
> The welcome obligation refers to common law and the schooling obligation.
> Parents of foreign nationality benefit from the same rights as French parents (right to vote and eligibility to be elected as representatives on school boards).
> (Ministère de l'Éducation nationale, 2002c)

The welcome function for pupils involves an action aimed at families in order to make them aware of 'how the educational establishment works'. This simple notification furthers the idea that French society is now structurally heterogeneous, and thus implicits and evidence on school are no longer necessarily shared. This simple reminder, which may seem silly to outsiders, is significant so that French schooling – public and consistent in its methods and objectives – is seen as 'granted' by the locals. French teachers often do not see the need for presentation and explanation.

In the same vein, there is a suggestion that schools are moving closer to local authorities to enable 'better knowledge of French culture, values and institutions by pupils and their parents' (Ministère de l'Éducation nationale, 2002a). Similarly, there is a suggestion that this presentation is in the first language. This is a big win, at least in terms of official instruction, because in practice recourse to the first language already takes place despite circumstances and best efforts.

If directions are more focused and texts longer, they are also accompanied by recommendations for flexibility and adaptation. The general trend is to operationalise and evaluate procedures by opting for a form of contractualisation; this may be social or educational.

Back to Linguistics

To widen our perspective beyond a strict focus on immigration, population mobility has become a characteristic of the school system and has encouraged the modification of measures taken in the 1980s to include new parameters. The adjective 'non-francophone' is no longer taboo, and we find this used in various memoranda.[1]

The main challenge when it comes to schooling new arrivals is mastery of the French language because it is considered that, with minimal linguistic knowledge, integration of migrant students is not possible and social exclusion is certain. In addition, texts establishing CASNAVs encourage a refocusing of activities based on a linguistic approach to social integration.

The High Council for Integration recommended in 2011 that it should 'be written in establishments' guidelines that French must be spoken'. Despite these guidelines, mastery of French is holding back many children and pupils. Although we cannot carry out a detailed analysis here, one hypothesis is that if language is a factor in social integration, some groups and individuals ignore this principle as they are concerned about communitisation, and also because the social lift is broken and mastery of the French language is no longer a guarantee of employment.

Reception and monitoring arrangements are now the subject of specific focus, and many initiatives are taken. By way of example, let us use the welcome centre in Toulouse, which has prepared a skills record detailing information concerning the migration project and schooling: 'The schooling of newcomers concerns all educational teams.' This emphasis on the concept of teams and collaborative projects reveals the resistance and tendency of some teachers to discharge their responsibilities onto specialised teachers. In addition, it is specified that language teaching is the responsibility of the whole teaching team and not just specialised teachers. Co-responsibility is invoked directly and not just suggested like it was in the past.

Teaching Language and Culture of Origin (ELCO)

The 1960s set a benchmark for the Enseignement des Langues et Cultures d'Origine (ELCO) programme. Its main objective was to provide children with an education allowing them to easily return to the school system in their country of origin. It was during this period that so-called intercultural practices were developed. With encouragement and recommendations from the European Council, ELCO saw its missions and working methods evolve. In schools, ELCO was also subject to contradictory pressures:

---

1   We can refer to the work published by Martine Abdallah-Pretceille in 1982 entitled *Des enfants non-francophones à l'école. Quel apprentissage? Quel français?* Paris: A. Colin- Bourrelier (out of print). At the time, talking to non-francophone pupils was deemed incorrect and unacceptable.

If the number of enrolments in ELCO fell by 25% between 1994 and 2003, today, while enrolment shows a steady increase (an increase of nearly 16% over the previous six years, especially in primary schools), both the control and the effects of this device are grey areas. In fact, teachers are not very closely monitored by academic bodies. Thus it leads to the following paradox: rising enrolment and a disavowal expressed by the actors at the school. The latter question, the relevance of the device, constitutes a brake to integration by reinforcing community references. This evolution is revealed in the geographic origin of pupils (a significant increase in pupils from Algeria, stabilisation for students from Tunisia and the gradual disappearance of European languages with the exception of Portuguese). (Haut Conseil à l'Intégration, 2011)

For the High Council of Integration, the integration process, and thus the creation of social cohesion, goes beyond the question of immigration. Therefore, it recommends that ELCO be scrapped given that it contradicts the objective of integration. This echoes the ideas voiced in the Ministry of National Education's general report of 2006, which recommended the integration of ELCO into modern language classes.

Starting in 2001, when it was decided to promote the acquisition of a modern foreign language as part of compulsory education, it was suggested that teaching the language and culture of origin should be gradually integrated into this generalised language learning in order to encourage diversification of the languages studied at school. Partner countries were invited to match the French programme to integrate courses into lower-school curricula to encourage the extension of the teaching and learning of language to college.

The Religious Aspect

At the start of the twenty-first century, the intercultural question expanded into the religious domain. In 2003, the European Council raised the issue of the 'new intercultural challenge relative to education: religious diversity and dialogue in Europe'; then, in 2004, a conference was held in Oslo on the 'religious dimension of intercultural education'.

The expansion of culture into religion – or, more specifically, the recognition of religion in culture – does not change either the nature of the problem or the paradigm of the analysis. Any discourse on culture (and *a fortiori* on religion) is simply the expression of a point of view likely to be confirmed or contradicted by other points of view. In this sense, it is not the reflection of an objective reality but the result of a social, political and linguistic activity. Like language, culture and religion are ways to present oneself and others. Anchored in history, politics, economy, psychology etc., conditioned by relationships with others, enrolled in a context, in a time and place, cultures and religions are subject to confinements and should avoid dogmatic and fundamentalist discourse. Similarly, according to Bourdieu, there is no language autonomy relative to production conditions; there is no culture or religion outside the confines of communication and enunciation. Culture and religion are at the crossroads of two determinations: relational logic and belonging or reference logic. Religions do not exist outside of individuals who follow them and modify them. 'Religious forgery' is constantly present. Current conflicts in testimony are cruel.

Recourse to the religious dimension of intercultural education covers a series of ambiguities and responds to multiple complementary but paradoxical objectives and challenges. The desire to respond to all registers at once has the potential to cover a consensus panel likely to shatter at the first sign of difficulties. Religious dimension? religious teaching? religious event? intercultural education? education? tolerance education? interreligious education? etc. based on formulations subject to controversy.

The French tradition of secularism has reduced the possible options. Therefore, there is no possibility of including religious teaching in public (i.e. state) schools. The limitation of the religious dimension only partially solves the problem – on the one hand, because an event is not religious in principle. Like all other events (psychological, sociological, anthropological, historical and economic) its qualification is the result of analysis. Overinvestment in any one of the variables relative to the others runs the risk of artefact. The religious dimension is one of many and is part of a network of meanings and interpretations. It may not be isolated. Granting the religious aspect a specific status, out of context, constitutes adopting a non-scientific and ideological approach.

In France, the question becomes one of teaching religion in secular schools (Debray, 2002). It is disconnected from any intercultural issue and remains at the level of lesson content and teacher training. However, from some initiatives, silence fell again, but the question is especially prompted by the emergence of so-called 'religious' codes in everyday classrooms and schools – the Islamic veil, 'halal', Ramadan, diversity, teaching content, catering etc. – in a climate of tension, mutual distrust, misunderstanding and power relations, disguised or not.

In a report, Rossinot (2006) pointed out that, since 2006 – in conformance with the law passed on 15 March 2004 concerning secularism in schools – the wearing of insignia or dress manifesting religious affiliation had not been for the difficulties related to the management of religion in public schools but had resulted in a diversification of claims from pupils.

On these different points, we find the same blurred logic, words of caution or free interpretation of ministerial directives and memoranda that are not always in agreement with each other.

The Need for Networking and Partnership with All Local Actors

This is clearly about an end to the isolation of schools and educational facilities. Dedicated measures from the relevant interministerial committee aimed at integration fall under town policy when it comes to integrating newcomers, with the introduction of Local School Support Contracts (CLAS) aimed at young residents of priority urban education zones[2] or Local Education Contracts (CELs).[3] These measures provide the partnership with an institutional framework.

The Fund for Action and Support of Integration and the Fight against Discrimination (FASILD) is a privileged partner for schools. Similarly, CASNAVs are defined as bodies for cooperation and mediation with institutional partners and school associations: 'Interfaces between national education and other services or local resource networks; the aim is to inform our partners, govern relations and cooperate with competent representatives relative to solving problems collectively' (Ministère de L'Éducation nationale, 2002b).

Partnership and networking induce the division of responsibilities and further evoke the expression of co-responsibility. The focus on school is reduced compared to a more global vision that tries to simultaneously consider education, socialisation, integration and inclusion. The reference site becomes larger: the territory rather than the school.

National guidelines are based, or should be based, on decentralised services in regions and departments. At departmental level, a steering committee is established to welcome migrants in which national education should participate as much as possible. We tend to establish a welcome platform, or even a counter, to welcome all pupils of migrants.

In 2001, a framework agreement was signed between the Ministry of National Education, the Ministry of Employment and Solidarity and the Social Action Fund. For those who do not know much about France, it is not easy to get interministerial agreements signed. National education authorities have been invited to share action and support for integration with relevant associations and other state-run organisations. However, between national and local projects, the challenge is tricky and action options are always likely to be at fault; this blurs, even anaesthetises, the readability of initiatives.

Agency for the Development of Intercultural Relations for Citizenship (ADRIC)

Created in 2003, ADRIC's work is based on the confluence of ideas as well as on networking and multi-partnerships. Its innovation is based on the intercultural paradigm for practices, and not to create an objective in itself. ADRIC aims

---

2   This device includes the local education contract. The objectives of the CLAS are to: contribute to school success and social integration; improve the quality of the school support offer; increase parents' involvement in their educational role; create conditions to enable real consideration of parents' roles by associations when it comes to school support; and guarantee equal opportunities.

3   CELs aim to implement an educational plan designed by different partners invested in education for children and young people (teachers, parents, associations and elects etc.) and to bring all funds together consistently: those of local authorities, youth ministries, National Education and Research, Sports, Culture, City, *Caisse d'Allocation Familiale*, and action and support fund for integration and the fight against discrimination.

to raise awareness of, develop and promote democratic citizenship, equality, freedom and secularism by focusing on an intercultural approach. This approach avoids a double pitfall:

- Overvaluation of cultural variables leads to explaining away everything with cultural differences without distinguishing socio-historical, economic and political dimensions in situations encountered, and reduces people to an immutable cultural identity;
- Negation of cultural diversity, which ignores the significance of interactions between individuals and groups and obstructs constructive communication based on the identification of divergences and convergences of contacts to build bridges and promote understanding.

For ADRIC, it is not about denying cultural factors or making them the only variables in the actions of individuals or groups. The French intercultural approach allows not only for the identification of cultural references operating within interactions between individuals or groups, but also for awareness of the socio-historical, economic, psychological and political impact in the formation and references and their evolution.

With this action and reflection method, ADRIC helps with the fight against violence and discrimination (related to gender, sexual orientation, origin, social class and beliefs) while providing better support for the public (including descendants of immigrants). Therefore, the agency works in partnership with the social actors involved in different structures (e.g. education and territorial social action).

In addition, since 2008, ADRIC has developed a knowledge and experience capitalisation activity through the establishment of methodology guides. This has resulted in both theoretical and practical works providing key analytical approaches and operational elements of understanding and means of conflict resolution. Four guides have already been published:

- 'Coping with violence and discrimination: Supporting immigrant women' (2008)
- 'Acting on secularism in the context of cultural diversity: Received ideas relative to citizen behaviour' (2009)
- 'Newly immigrated women: From welcome to integration' (2011)
- 'Parenthood in all its forms: For an intercultural approach with families and professionals' (2012).

These tools are disseminated throughout the territory in the context of awareness and support days for professionals based on these topics. In 2011, ADRIC also led awareness and training initiatives. The following are some of the most common topics requested by social actors:

- welcome and support for immigrant women
- gender equality
- the fight against sexual violence
- cultural diversity management
- the fight against discrimination
- interculturality
- support, integration and inclusion for young immigrants
- support for parenting in an intercultural environment
- welcome for infants and interculturality
- secularism, citizenship and diversity of religious expression.

The partners that require these types of intervention are schools and vocational training institutions (38 per cent); local authorities and state agencies such as prefectures, DRJSCS (27 per cent);[4] and social sector organisations – social centres, social landlords, host organisations and support families and people in difficulty (16 per cent).

The professionals involved in this training are from various sectors: local authority employees (20 per cent); teaching and educational staff (17 per cent); social workers and community health workers – including animators, educators, interpreters, counsellors in social economy (15 per cent); state officers (2 per cent); trainers and lawyers (1 per cent), local politicians (1 per cent) and staff working in welcome and support for tenants, including building custodians (1 per cent). There is also a non-professional group participating in this training: students (high schools, colleges) and their parents (36 per cent) as well as volunteers and inhabitants (7 per cent).

A Training Example: Interculturality and Equality[5]

In a Parisian college where the majority of pupils belong to privileged families and interact with pupils from lower social classes, there is an acute divide between students in some classes. One class has considerable differences in reading abilities, general culture and behaviour; in another class, 22 of the pupils have grades that are good or even excellent, whereas the opposite is true for six underprivileged students in a different situation (due to lack of equipment, disruptive behaviour and absenteeism).

The teachers – very invested in their pedagogical and educational missions, very committed to the principle of public schools, particularly the principle of equality – struggle to deal with such heterogeneity in the classroom, especially when under pressure from upper-class families anxious to guide their children towards prestigious schools. This situation poses the following questions:

---

4   Directions régionales de la jeunesse des sports et de la cohésion sociale (Regional Directorates of Youth, Sports and Social Cohesion).

5   Académie de Paris, February–April 2012/February–April 2013.

How can we overcome socio-cultural divides?

How can we help all pupils progress and succeed?

How can we 'live together' in the classroom and beyond by establishing shared values?

How can we honour the equality objective?

Initial training conducted in 2012 by ADRIC allowed educational staff to approach the issue of heterogeneity in all its dimensions, especially when heterogeneity or diversity leads to inequalities: in terms of culture, family support for education, access to information and social capital, self-development and social compartmentalisation and ethnicisation differences etc. Reflection has focused on several areas: diversity and equality between boys and girls, shared values, citizenship and the relationship between school and family. In 2013, ADRIC's expertise was once again required to support educational teams with the co-construction of specific action in order to:

- identify, from reflection performed in 2012 and existing practices, teaching and educational approaches constructed from the 'common' (between pupils, pupils and teachers, and professionals and families);
- reflect on actions likely to resolve existing conflicts, to reaffirm the heterogeneity of pupils as being an asset and to make diversity a lever for learning and 'living together';
- work on a common approach to the citizen and democratic values that need to be shared and defended in educational practice and in the school environment.

In conclusion, we can only comment on the difference between the inflation of devices and directives whose follow-up and coherence are not always guaranteed and some form of political blindness resulting in hesitation, without denying paradoxical injunctions, but not clearly reaffirming the fundamental republican values.

References

Abdallah-Pretceille, M. (1992). *Quelle école pour quelle intégration?* Paris: CNDP/Hachette.

Abdallah-Pretceille, M. and Porcher, L. (1996). *Education et communication interculturelle*. Paris, PUF (2nd edn 1999).

Abdallah-Pretceille, M. (2003). *Eduquer et former en contexte hétérogène: Pour un humanisme du divers*. Paris: Anthropos.

Abdallah-Pretceille, M. (2011), *L'éducation interculturelle*, Que sais-je?, no. 3487, Paris: PUF.

Debray, R. (2002). *L'enseignement du fait religieux dans l'école laïque. Rapport au Ministère de l'Éducation nationale*. Paris.

Doytcheva, M. (2007). *Une discrimination positive à la française? Ethnicité et territoire dans les politiques de la ville*. Paris: La Découverte.

Haut Conseil à l'Intégration (2011), *Rapport. 28 janvier 2011*, Paris: La Documenttion française.

Lazaridis, M. (2001). La scolarisation des enfants de migrants: entre intégration républicaine et mesures spécifiques. *VEI Enjeu*, 125, 198–208.

Ministère de l'Éducation nationale (1975). *Bulletin officiel de l'Éducation nationale (BOEN) no. 15* (April).

Ministère de l'Éducation nationale (1978). *Bulletin officiel de l'Éducation nationale (BOEN) no. 36* (September).

Ministère de l'Éducation nationale (1997). *Contrats d'accompagnement scolaire: Circulaire du 1 juillet 1997*. Paris.

Ministère de l'Éducation nationale (2000). *Contrats educatifs locaux: Circulaire interministérielle du 9 juillet 1998, complétée par la circulaire interministérielle du 25 Octobre 2000*. Paris.

Ministère de l'Éducation nationale (2002a). *Convention-cadre entre le ministère de l'Education nationale, le ministère de l'Emploi et de la Solidarité et le Fonds d'action sociale pour les travailleurs immigrés et leur famille (FAS). Bulletin Officiel no. 10* (25 April). Paris.

Ministère de l'Éducation nationale (2002b). *Missions et organisation des centres académiques pour la scolarisation des nouveaux arrivants et des enfants du voyage (CASNAV). Circulaire no. 2002–102* (25 April). Paris.

Ministère de l'Éducation nationale (2002c). *Modalités d'inscription et de scolarisation des élèves de nationalité étrangère des premier et second degrés. Circulaire no. 2002–63* (20 March) *– BO no.* 13 (28 March). Paris.

Ministère de l'Éducation nationale (2002d). *Organisation de la scolarité des élèves nouvellement arrivés en France sans maîtrise suffisante de la langue ou des apprentissages. Circulaire no. 2002–100* (25 April) *– BO special no. 10* (25 April). Paris.

Ministère de l'Éducation nationale (2006). *L'enseignement de la langue et de la culture d'origine. Rapport à monsieur le ministre de l'Éducation nationale, de l'Enseignement supérieur et de la Recherche. Rapport – no. 2005–090*. Paris.

Rossinot, M.A. (2006). *La laïcité dans les services publics. Rapport du groupe de travail Présidé par M. André Rossinot*. Paris.

Chapter 4

Intercultural Education in the German Context

Otto Filtzinger and Giovanni Cicero Catanese[1]

Migration and Cultural Diversity in Germany: Development and Characteristics

The Federal Republic of Germany (FRG) has developed into a multicultural society through periods of immigration from European and non-European countries. At the end of World War II, approximately 11 million ethnic German war refugees came to western Germany from the former eastern territories of Germany and Eastern European countries with German minorities. Later, there was a return of ethnic Germans from the former Soviet Union, especially from the republics of Kazakhstan and Siberia – to where ethnic German immigrants had been deported from Russia – as well as return migrants from Poland and Romania. In total nearly 4 million ethnic Germans have returned to Germany in various waves of migration, constituting its largest group of immigrants by far (Berlin-Institut für Bevölkerung und Entwicklung, 2009: 7).

Starting in the 1950s and 1960s as Germany underwent post-war reconstruction, the German Labour Agency recruited what it called 'guest workers' (*Gastarbeiter*) from Mediterranean countries to compensate for war-related losses of working-age men. The first agreement was signed with Italy in 1955. There followed treaties with Spain and Greece (1960), Turkey (1961), Portugal (1964), Tunisia and Morocco (1965) and Yugoslavia (1968). This recruitment of workers led to an expansion of foreign workers after 1969. Restrictions were put into place in 1973 with a ban on further recruitment. This halt to further immigration was valid until 1975. But the number of immigrants living in Germany dropped only marginally in 1976–78. In the early 1980s there began a long-term phase of family reunification, with a concomitant increase in the birth of children of immigrants.

In response to the high level of youth unemployment, in 1977 a federal-state commission (*Bund-Länderkommission*) issued 'Proposals for continued development of a comprehensive policy plan for the employment of foreign workers' (*Vorschläge zur Fortentwicklung einer umfassenden Konzeption der Ausländerbeschäftigungspolitik*), something which had previously been driven

---

1   Otto Filtzinger is the author of the first six sections, while Giovanni Cicero Catanese is the author of the final sections.

purely by the needs of the labour market. A 1979 memorandum between the federal government's commissioner for migrant issues and the Foreign Workers' Coordination Committee (*Koordinierungskreis Ausländische Arbeitnehmer*) proposed measures for the social integration of the children of migrants and their descendants (Kühn, 1979).

The economic crisis of 1980–82 and its aftermath were met with contradictory policies towards immigration and immigrants. The increase in unemployment led to measures against illegal employment that largely affected immigrants. Offers of return bonuses of 10,000 German marks were largely ignored. On the other hand, requirements for legal residency status and naturalisation provisions were eased, and special rules were also introduced for immigrants' spouses and children born in Germany and abroad (Filtzinger, 2001).

The German Democratic Republic (GDR) also engaged in an active recruitment of foreign workers after the borders were closed with the building of the Berlin Wall (1961). However, intergovernmental agreements with socialist countries Cuba (1978), Mozambique (1979) and North Vietnam (1980) made immigration to East Germany possible. These incomers were primarily unmarried workers who lived in segregated housing completely isolated from the German population and, like other minorities, were the targets of discrimination and received little respect. In 1979, 190,000 foreign workers were in the GDR. Almost all were fired after the fall of the Berlin Wall. After reunification, there were gradual waves of immigration from other countries to the former East Germany, but much less than the numbers flowing into the former West Germany (Krüger-Potratz, 1991: 151–89).

Armed conflicts, political and religious persecution, economic and social emergencies and natural catastrophes were other reasons for the increasing immigration into the reunified Federal Republic of Germany. In recent decades, many immigrants have come from further and further afield, and from non-European cultures that in the public consciousness were even further distant.

Despite the increase in immigration, German politicians clung to the political fiction that Germany was not an 'immigration country'. This reflected the dominant wishful thinking that immigration could be restricted to bringing in required labour which would then rotate out of the country. In this view, immigration and return migration would balance each other out and would be driven by the needs of the labour market. There were indeed some who did see themselves as 'guest workers', who would come to Germany for a short time, earn a lot of money and then return home. Economic and family realities, however, often let the dreams of a return go unfulfilled, even for those from the EU who had gained the freedom of movement around the continent. Those who did go home soon came back to Germany, but this time often with spouse and children in tow. Many children were affected by such back-and-forth migration, often negatively – affecting academic success both in their country of origin and their new home.

German policies on immigrants tried to curb further migration for a long while. The conscious use of the German term *Zuwanderung* and avoidance of the more permanent-sounding *Einwanderung* reveals a migration policy that openly contradicted the facts on the ground while avoiding finding a strategy to integrate Germany's new residents. It was not until the beginning of the twenty-first century that German migration policy came under pressure from demographic developments. These changes were reflected in the reform of residence and citizenship laws in 2000, which, among other things, granted German citizenship to children born in Germany to immigrant parents, regardless of their parents' nationality. This reform resulted in more than half of the 15.7 million 'immigrants' in Germany holding German citizenship by 2010.

Another step forward was taken with the first National Integration Plan (2007). The German government's National Action Plan for Integration (*Nationaler Aktionsplan zur Integration*, 2011) was designed to 'strengthen cohesion and achieve participation'. This new political line of integration and participation is also evident in the 2012 report by the Federal Commissioner for Migration, Refugees and Integration (*Beauftragte der Bundesregierung für Migration, Flüchtlinge und Integration*) on the situation of foreigners, which reported on the measures being taken to promote political, social and cultural integration.

According to the Federal Statistical Office (*Statistisches Bundesamt*), nearly 1.08 million people immigrated to Germany in 2012: 765,000 from European countries, especially southern and eastern Europe. Most came from Poland (176,000), followed by Romania (116,000) and Bulgaria (59,000). The number of immigrants from countries most affected by the financial and economic crisis – such as Greece, Spain, Portugal and Italy – is also increasing. This is the highest rate of immigration since 1995. The educational level of immigrants has been rising in recent years. The percentage of immigrants who were university graduates rose from 30 per cent in 2005 to 44 per cent in 2009.

In May 2013, the federal government organised the 2nd Demographic Summit, where academics, social organisations and citizens discussed the negative growth and rapid ageing of the German population. Representatives of the business community asked to make it easier for skilled workers to immigrate. The president of the German Association of Chambers of Commerce and Industry estimated that 1.5 million foreign workers would have to be added to the German workforce by 2025. Germany should therefore be made more attractive to skilled migrants by developing a better 'culture of welcoming' (*Willkommenskultur*).

The increasing number of immigrants was accompanied by a growth in xenophobic and prejudiced sentiments among the broader population, exacerbated by unprofessional handling of the 'asylum seeker problem' since 1980–81. In recent years, fears about Islamist alienation and religious fanatics prone to violence have spread. The lack of nuance in media reporting has not helped. Hate speech in Facebook posts and music videos and songs full of calls for violence against foreigners, Jews, people with physical and mental disabilities and homosexuals are helping to fuel right-wing sentiments that have often resulted in physical violence. The recently revealed murders by the far-right terrorist cell National Socialist Underground (NSU) have shaken up politicians and the population alike. However, these numerically small right-wing groups have no supporters in the Bundestag and are largely rejected by the general population. Nevertheless, these provocations are making efforts to have objective discussions more difficult. These efforts include the federal government's establishment of a forum on Islam, initiatives for Christian–Jewish–Muslim dialogue and the establishment of umbrella organisations for various Muslim communities that abhor acts of violence.

The new multicultural Germany – which can be described as multinational, multiethnic, multilingual and multireligious – was created not only by migration but also by two other social, political and economic transformation processes: Europeanisation and globalisation. All three influence each other and have led to cross-cultural and transcultural transformations. The cultural diversity is also seen in a variety of forms of cohabitation among different social groups of men, women, bisexual and homosexual people; of young, adult and old people; of disabled and non-disabled people; and by members of religious, political and free-living groups. The result is a multifaceted society resulting in rapidly changing, vividly coloured variations like those in a kaleidoscope.

Multiculturalism in Educational Institutions

In the first phase of foreign-worker immigration, there was a wide variety of ideas for the inclusion of these 'foreigners' children' (*Ausländerkinder*) across the different German states (*Länder*), which, according to the German constitution, are responsible for education policy.[2] As family reunification increased and the number of children born in Germany to migrants rose, compulsory school attendance meant that their numbers also rose in the country's elementary and secondary schools. Day-care centres, where attendance is voluntary, initially saw less impact from the rise in numbers of immigrant children.

Different states established ethnically based day-care centres and elementary classes, partly due to the wishes of the immigrant parents and partly to cope with what the schools felt were insufficient skills in German, the usual language of instruction. This helped to meet the wishes of migrant parents who wanted to preserve their language and cultural identity, and also maintained the political

---

2   In addition to 'foreigners' children' or 'children of foreigners' (*Ausländerkinder*), other terms have come into common usage, including: 'children/youth without German passports', 'immigrant children/youth' (*Migrantenkinder, Migrantenjugendliche*) or 'children of immigrants' (*Zuwandererkinder*). In the meantime, these children have come to be designated in official German statistics as 'children with a migrant background' (*Kinder mit Migrationshintergrund*). In the literature and research, we now speak mostly of 'people with a migrant background' (*Menschen mit Migrationshintergund*). This term aligns with that issued by the Federal Statistical Office in 2004, defined as 'all migrants after 1949 to the present territory of the Federal Republic of Germany, as well as all persons born in Germany with at least one parent who migrated after 1949 or who was born in Germany as a foreigner', regardless of what passport they currently own (Die Beauftragte der Bundesregierung für Migration, Flüchtlinge und Integration, 2012: 102–3).

fiction of a rotating migrant workforce by ensuring that these 'foreign' children and families would be ready to return 'home' when the time came.

Since the 1980s, but not all at once, the states began to integrate the children of immigrants more fully into the German education system. These children were either taught in their parents' native language, as suggested by the European Council, or received instruction in that language from native speakers. While this additional instruction has been abolished in some states, Rhineland-Palatinate still offers instruction in 15 'languages of origin' (*Herkunftssprachen*).

The number of children and young people with a migrant background in the German education system has risen steadily since the first phase of the family reunion plan in the 1980s. This applies to all levels, from nurseries (0–3 years) to upper secondary schools: 30 per cent of children not from a migrant background attend nurseries (school before age 3), while only 16 per cent of children from a migrant background do. Since 2013, a new national law guarantees all children 12 months and older a place in these nurseries as well as equal access to early childhood care facilities. An average of 85.7 per cent of children with a migrant background attended childcare centres in 2010. Currently, virtually all have preschools, and schools have a considerable number of pupils with a migrant background.

In recent decades, larger and medium-sized cities in Germany have become so diverse with respect to nationality, ethnicity, language and religion that schools with children of more than 10 different nationalities and languages are not uncommon. The proportion of pupils who leave school with admission to university has increased by 36 per cent from 2005 to 2010. However, the proportion is much lower than their German counterparts, 36 per cent of whom graduate from high school with admission to university. Only 15 per cent of students with a migrant background do the same. The school drop-out rate among young people with a migrant background is, however, on the decline. The proportion of apprentices with a migrant background rose from 31.4 per cent in 2009 to 33.5 per cent in 2010, while 65.4 per cent of apprentices were from a German background (Die Beauftragte der Bundesregierung für Migration, Flüchtlinge und Integration, 2012). The national Pact for Apprenticeships and Young Skilled Workers (*Pakt für Ausbildung und Fachkräftennachwuchs*) has set a goal of increasing the number of youths with a migrant background who participate in Germany's famous apprenticeship and vocational training programmes.

The length of stay and the many social contacts in the destination country over time change the cultural socialisation of the family and lead to the formation of multiple, overlapping identities for children and adolescents. With the steady increase in multicultural partnerships and families, the German/foreigner dichotomy is beginning to blur in everyday educational practice. Cultural diversity is part of the daily life of children and adolescents. In their daily relationships, they register physical and linguistic differences; different modes of expression in gestures, facial expressions and body language; different behaviours and emotional reactions; the use of different cultural and religious rituals; ways of dressing and different table manners. In this multicultural context, new forms of transnational and transcultural cohabitation are developing in educational institutions that involve children and parents of German background. Even if this is experienced by many as invigorating, it also leads to intercultural tension, misunderstanding and conflict not only between people with and without a migrant background, but also among different migrant groups themselves.

However, cultural diversity is not only manifested in the presence of children and families with the cultural differences described above; it is also present in children with various impairments and special needs, even if most of these children attend special schools designed for their needs. The group of children and young people with different cultural backgrounds because they have exceptional physical and/or gender needs is numerically much smaller than that of children and adolescents with a migrant background. All in all, children today reflect a broad diversity of family backgrounds and values as well as history of socialisation.

Many schools no longer consider multiculturalism primarily as a problem but as an educational resource. They use the children's everyday experiences of multicultural living to encourage intercultural learning. The German Youth Institute (*Deutsches Jugend Institut*, DJI) conducted interviews with children in 2000 which revealed just how many children see and experience multicultural living as the norm. Many adults, however, view multiculturalism as a phenomenon that is changing the norm. While children are more open and less removed from diversity, adults connote diversity with difference and otherness.

The public debate and published opinion regarding the differences of migrants and with regard to other human differences is often still concerned with prejudices, stereotypes and fears that make it difficult to prepare children at home and in school for life in a constantly changing political, social and cultural environment.

The educational policies of the German states still struggle to establish a consistent, inclusive system, even if the special schools for different groups of foreigners no longer exist. However, there are still special preschools and schools for disabled children. Last but not least, the highly tracked German education system, with its selective ways of gaining access to higher education, means that equitable educational opportunities are still not guaranteed for all children. There are many others factors that cause educational disadvantage, such as the social and financial situation of the family or family-related educational success. Also, the fact that many states have recently introduced mandatory standardised screenings for German-language skills before school enrolment has made it more likely that so-called linguistic defects will be discovered and 'children at risk' identified. These assessments designed to sort children affect children with a migrant background as well as many children of German background. The language skills of the children in their non-German mother tongues have received little attention from the schools.

Scientific Research into the Problems Associated with the Inclusion of Children and Adolescents with a Migrant or Different Cultural Background in the Education System

This section will present a selected overview of research into intercultural education.[3] Research into changes in education brought about by the experience of migration only began in the 1970s, initially from primarily pedagogical and praxis-oriented perspectives. This evolved into the initial theories for the academic discipline of 'education of foreigners' (*Ausländerpädagogik*) and target group-focused 'research about foreigners' (*Ausländerforschung*). In the 1970s and 1980s, this focus led to intercultural and international comparative studies to evaluate instruction at reception level, instruction in the native tongue and intercultural education (Gogolin and Krüger-Potratz, 2006: 145–7). The first methods for researching integration were proposed in 1982 but only began to take hold at the beginning of the twenty-first century.

More intensive work on developing educational theory and a change of perspective on issues of migration and cultural pluralisation that went beyond pedagogical praxis to include broader, more empirically based research in education began in the late 1980s and early 1990s. Education research began to deal more and more with the integration of 'foreign children' (*Ausländerkinder*) in schools. Preschool and extracurricular areas received separate treatment as they were considered part of social work's task of providing intercultural education. In addition, other educational approaches emerged: encountering the other (*Pädagogik der Begegnung*), diversity education, peace education, conflict education, developmental intercultural education, Europeanisation education. Meanwhile, intercultural education became open to questioning prejudicial and gender-biased education and opening up prospects for integrative, socially inclusive pedagogies.

Since the late 1990s, studies conducted by migrant welfare agencies have shown the levels to which children of migrants are affected by poverty and disadvantage in the education system, which can be attributed in part to a lack of an intercultural praxis in education. The problem of participation in the education process was taken up in various reports (see *Bund-Länderkommission*, 2003 and the OECD's annual education report, for example). In 2012, an expert commission report expressed a desire that all future studies of the impact of non-parental childcare in early childhood take into account the needs of children with a migrant

---

3   Gogolin and Krüger-Potratz (2006: 135–94) give a good overview of comparative research into intercultural and international education from 1960 to 2006. Also important is the overview of migration and integration as a research subject prepared by the German Youth Institute (Bednarz-Braun, 2013: 73–4). The report of the Beauftragte der Bundesregierung für Migration, Flüchtlinge und Integration (2012: 642–4) provides an overview of recent migration and integration research. Theories and research about racism are presented in Auerheimer (2012: 93–105).

background and other disadvantaged children, in particular how this relates to a child's future performance in school (Die Beauftragte, 2012). A 2005 government report also addressed the need for special support services for children and young people with a migrant background (Bundesministerium für Familie, Senioren, Frauen und Jugend, 2005: 175).

Another focus of migration and integration research seeks to standardise the terminology used to describe this population and to clarify the term 'migrant background' (*Migrationshintergrund*), which has been in official use since 2004 to label statistics on 'foreigners' (Bundesministerium für Bildung und Forschung, 2005). Terms such as 'foreigners' (*Ausländer*) or 'Germans with foreign roots' (*Deutsche mit ausländischen Wurzeln*) are deemed problematic because they are oriented exclusively at a person's legal status, obscuring more complex features of the immigrant experience. The term 'migrant background' is likely to open up new fields of research and intergenerational issues. However, this term is criticised in some scientific fields because it aggregates two distinct units and thus assigns the persons concerned a label and separates them from the general population.

From 2006 to 2011, the German Youth Institute commissioned a research project on themes of 'migration, interaction and inter-ethnic coexistence', which dealt primarily with the intercultural relations of children and adolescents. The findings showed that their success and their intensification depended crucially on an enabling environment. A report on the experience of children and youth with a migrant background collated research data in the educational context.

The Max-Planck-Institut fur Bildungsforschung Berlin has made the issue of social inequality an important research field. Its education and pedagogy department had a particular focus on issues of migration and integration until 2010. Special consideration was paid to family background in the transitions from one educational institution to the next (Die Beauftragte, 2012: 642).

Currently, education and educational processes in the immigrant community are a main topic of research. The Nationales Bildungspanel (NEPS), an interdisciplinary network devoted to educational excellence, collects longitudinal data over the entire life of children to improve the medium- and long-term data available for empirical research. Included is data on educational attainment of people with a migrant background. It is assumed that a migrant background has some impact on the acquisition of skills and on educational decisions (Die Beauftragte, 2012: 650–53).

The OECD'S Programme for International Student Assessment (PISA) study of the educational disadvantages experienced by children of a migrant background identified one of the causes as reduced levels of language development in the preschool years (Roux and Stuck, 2005). Since 2009 the Ministry of Education has been promoting a research initiative into language diagnostics and development (*Bundesministerium für Bildung, Sprachdiagnostik und Sprachförderung, FISS*). This helps to explain the explosion of speech therapy and materials to develop monolingual language skills that have hit the early education market in recent years. The educational establishment has been quite critical of the funding given to the many, mostly politically motivated language support programmes added in the various states for failing to take into consideration the actual needs and motivation of children. These programmes especially ignore the way children learn language through early socialisation. Many of the states' programmes continue to emphasise the acquisition of skills in the language of instruction prior to entering primary school rather than a child-centred pedagogy of language development.

However, when the state of Baden-Württemberg's EVAS project (*Evaluationsstudie zur Sprachförderung von Vorschulkindern*) evaluated the effectiveness of these targeted additional language-support measures in preschool children, it noted that 'targeted early language training with specific programmes and concepts does not lead to better language skills than nonspecific promotion of language in the preschool everyday' (Hofmann et al., 2008: 297). The evaluation of the language support programme in Rhineland-Palatinate came to a similar conclusion when it ascertained that the success of such language-support courses depended on 'the process quality in the language support group, the kindergarten group and the school as a whole' (Kammermeyer et al., 2011: 457). In this context, it is interesting to note that the state of Thuringia has not set up a language support programme, but has still done very well compared to the other states in the PISA study. It is welcome news that the Ministry of Education's FISS initiative was extended in 2012 to include an emphasis on 'language education'.

In addition to linguistic studies on early language acquisition, there is also a large amount of research in Germany and abroad on the early bilingual and multilingual language acquisition of children and adolescents (see Reich et al., 2002; Buttaroni, 2011). The research still remains more focused on the diagnosis and treatment of language delays and language disorders, as well as the methods for acquiring and promoting German as a second language (Bundesministerium für Bildung und Forschung, 2005: 169). What sets research into multilingualism apart is the inclusion of children's first language(s); forms of expression commonly used by multilingual children; and information about the child's linguistic background, as well as assessment of the parents' language skills in the first and second languages (Lengyel, 2012: 21).

The 'Early Chances' (*Frühe Chancen*) programme put in place in 2010 at 4,000 day-care centres in Germany recommends early language development. However, it neither does justice to the multilingual situation in childcare facilities nor considers the European mandate to promote multilingualism for all EU citizens with early multilingual education (Ministerium für Bildung, Familie, Frauen und Kultur des Saarlandes, 2008).[4]

---

4 The Institut für Interkulturelle Pädagogik im Elementarbereich e.V. has developed a research-based and tested European language portfolio for children aged 3–7 as part of a project to promote early multilingualism to take advantage of the potential available in early childhood and to make use of the interest of children growing up in a monolingual context (Filtzinger et al., 2011).

Critical Reflection on the Current State of Research and Desiderata for the Future

For the continued development of concepts and strategies for intercultural education, more attention needs to be paid to all of the facets of how a multicultural society is continuing to develop. There needs to be a critical assessment of current theories, the selection of research topics, with research grants and commissioning processes and the research methods and results. The potential of interdisciplinary research remains less exploited: 'The heterogeneous structural connectivity makes it difficult, however, to see an overview of key issues and makes a substantive debate about concepts, the development of methods and theories, and the production of cross-disciplinary contexts all the more difficult' (Die Beauftragte, 2012: 654). The focus of research should not only be on the integration of people with a migrant background, but also on the conditions, the needs and abilities of children and adolescents with a different cultural background – as well as on developing strategies to implement structural and participatory education in schools and other places of education. There is also a lack of academic support and evaluation of innovative intercultural projects.

There remain far too few investigations into how children and adolescents themselves view their intercultural environment, although the 10th report on children and adolescents in 1998 expressed their desirability (Bundesministerium für Familie, Senioren und Jugend, 1998: 95–107). The German Youth Institute project 'How children experience multicultural life' (*Wie Kinder multikulturellen Alltag erleben*, 2000) should be mentioned here for its interesting methodology, which included surveying the children themselves.

Unfortunately, there have been almost no action research projects that foresee the active participation of those affected and take into account their experiential knowledge in developing questionnaires and research designs as well as managing and evaluation research processes.

Intercultural Education Strategies and their Implementation in Schools

Pedagogical Concepts of Intercultural Education

There have been three main streams in the changed pedagogical landscape as it responds to the experience of immigration which can only partially be considered sequential developments and are not strictly separable from one another (Filtzinger, 2013: 221–30). Inclusive pedagogy goes beyond the initial situation rooted in the experience of migration and looks at cultural diversity within society with regard to a variety of human differences.

Ausländerpädagogik
'Teaching foreigners' sees integration as a process of assimilation and compensation. Its interventions were targeted primarily at integrating the second

generation of guest-worker families. Children of migrants were largely described as 'problem children' (*Problemkinder*), with difficulties attributed primarily to family or individual causes related to their foreign origin and their cultural otherness. As a result, the pedagogical efforts focused above all on adaptation to the educational and behavioural standards and values of the receiving society. Special programmes tried to compensate for the 'deficits' of the 'children of foreigners/foreign children' (*Ausländerkinder*). This focus on the children's difference promoted their stigmatisation and pushed ethnicity and nationality to the foreground while ignoring training for everyday life and education itself. These methods also neglected to pay attention to the shared situations and needs of all children. Unreflective pedagogical attempts to force assimilation prevented addressing the real everyday conditions of life for the migrant families.

Interkulturelle Pädagogik

'Intercultural pedagogy' developed from the critique levied against *Ausländerpädagogik*. By the late 1970s, one began to speak of intercultural education, especially in early childhood education circles.[5] By the early 1980s, intercultural pedagogy had become programmatic. It focused more on the skills and strengths of migrant children, with integration understood as an interactive process. Foreign and native children were now treated in common as the target group for instruction. Through 'encounter' (*Begegnung*), otherness (*Fremdheit*) would be broken down, mutual understanding awakened and differences bridged through tolerance. Cultural exchange was viewed as mutual enrichment. Intercultural education has the goal of shaping the multicultural experience of all children and adolescents in such a way that they feel comfortable and can use their experience creatively and productively to develop the ability to act and make their way through life in an open society marked with migration.

Anti-racist pedagogy

In the aftermath of xenophobic statements and attacks on migrants by extreme right-wing activists, the Anglo-American concept of anti-racism training came into vogue. This training sees itself as more political than purely educational. It accuses intercultural pedagogy of assimilating migrants into the receiving society and criticises it for reducing institutional and political problems to cultural differences. Above all, it makes the native population into the problem as they refuse to grant immigrants equal rights and discriminate against and segregate them. With increased cultural diversity, racist behaviours were also on the rise between different immigrant groups. The anti-racist training favoured

---

5   The German language makes a distinction between *multikulturell* and *interkulturell*. While multicultural describes the social situation created by people of different cultural backgrounds living together, intercultural designates a programmatic, pedagogical reaction to this situation. Multicultural means coexistence of different cultures; intercultural refers to interactive integration of different cultures.

emancipatory training in self-esteem, self-initiative and conflict skills and promoted uncovering and removing discrimination, segregation and bias. Many topics of anti-racist pedagogy came to be included in many school curricula. The Berlin project *Kinderwelten* (children's worlds) worked against the formation of prejudice within childcare facilities (Wagner, 2010). Didactic models were developed for the schools which linked to key elements of intercultural and anti-racist pedagogy (Auernheimer, 2012: 147–53).

Intercultural pedagogy of inclusion
In recent years, the UK concept of inclusion has come under discussion in Germany. This referred initially to the integration of persons with disabilities. The UK National Curriculum put students at the centre of pedagogical action in the 1990s. It postulates the creation of appropriate learning challenges, adapting to different learning needs, helping students overcome learning disabilities and valuing the skills of individuals and particular groups of students. In Germany, the term inclusion first came to be used in the social sciences and social work, but it then entered discussions about teaching children with a migrant background. In the educational realm, it concerned primarily the inclusion of children with special needs and disabilities in the general classroom. There are already some inclusive nurseries and day-care centres. The first social work courses of study in early childhood inclusive education have already been developed. Intercultural pedagogy of inclusion celebrates cultural diversity and all human differences, and lets all children and adolescents participate in an emancipatory developmental and education process.

Multicultural and Intercultural Models of Educational Institutions

The German education system is marked by a variety of institutional models because the states are free to design their own educational policy and schools. Below, some of the institutional models for both public and private schools as they have been introduced in different states at different times are described typologically. Attention will be paid above all to how these models affect children from migrant or different cultural backgrounds.

Nationality-based schools
These are institutions where migrant children of a single nationality are normally taught by teachers sharing the same nationality or native language. This model corresponds to the concept of rotating immigrant populations promoted by German politicians and the desires of the migrant parents, and also fits the concept of separating the 'foreign children' for compensatory education. But, as immigration for the long term became almost the rule, the number of schools attended solely by German children and those attended exclusively by non-German children dropped steadily. Only a few parallel or preparatory classes remain of this last group; otherwise, they have mostly disappeared. This development was helped

by the increase in the number of nationalities who had come to Germany. One advantage of the nationality-based schools was that the migrant children learned their parents' language particularly well, thus creating a good basis for later bilingualism. The homogeneity of the education in the family and school and the associated integration into that immigrant nationality group mostly did not result in segregation or self-separation, but instead promoted a stronger sense of 'internal integration' (*Binnenintegration*) – a kind of psychological adjustment and acceptance of integration into the receiving society.

Multinational/multicultural/multilingual schools

This type of institution has become de facto the norm nowadays, having spread since the demise of the nationality-based schools and the mass migration of many different nations and cultures first to the larger cities and then to the smaller towns and villages. These schools accept all children living in Germany. A higher or lower proportion of the children have various non-German nationalities, countries of origin and native languages. They reflect the German population mix as a whole. These schools, however, expect a high level of adjustment to the national educational objectives. They make little reference to cultures of origin and provide little or no support for the native or parental languages of children with a migrant background. They also rarely use the multilingual reality on campus to promote the plurilingualism which has been named as one of the general goals of European education.[6] Thus good opportunities to develop core skills in intercultural, multilingual education for all children are being wasted.

Bilingual/bicultural schools

These are mostly found in German border regions with neighbouring countries. For example, German-French schools were established to promote cultural understanding after the end of World War II. German-Danish schools respect a linguistic minority in the north of Germany, and German-Polish and German-Czech schools promote reconciliation after the fall of the Berlin Wall. In the 1970s, the Staatsinstitut für Frühpädagogik in Munich developed a concept for bilingual and bicultural education especially for day-care centres which was implemented both in Munich and in some other German states. This bilingual/bicultural model was limited to certain larger cities with large migrant populations in day-care centres and schools from primary through to upper secondary level. There were also, albeit just a few, German-Turkish and German-Italian schools. This model offered children of non-German-speaking parents the chance to develop their

---

6   The terms multilingual and plurilingual are mostly used synonymously, but the European Council has suggested that they should be distinguished. Multilingualism refers to the proximity of languages in bi- or trilingual countries (such as Belgium, Canada, Switzerland and Luxembourg) and what has become the everyday life of many European immigrant groups. Plurilingualism is the ability of individuals or groups to understand and speak more than one language. Both concepts are used in this latter sense.

parents' language in parallel with German as a second language. Children with German-speaking parents had the chance to learn another language from use in the classroom and playground. The teachers were usually native speakers of German paired with native speakers of the second language who would bring the cultural skills from their culture of origin. The bilingual German-English schools, often called 'international', also practised a de facto bilingual model with German offered as a foreign language. The few European schools (*Europaschulen*) are a kind of multilingual institution with bilingual classes or groups. These bilingual/bicultural schools have come under criticism for not addressing the much wider linguistic and cultural diversity in today's society.

The inclusive school

In recent years there has been a growing interest in the introduction of inclusive schools. But the widespread and well-established parallel system of special schools for children with various disabilities is already under pressure from the requirements of the UN Convention on the Rights of Persons with Disabilities (2006), binding on Germany since 2009.[7] Special schools are being partially transformed into so-called integrative schools catering for children with and without disabilities. However, to date full integration of children with disabilities has only been ordered in the state of Bremen. The development of an inclusive education system as demanded by the UN Convention with full inclusion of children with special needs and disabilities is moving very slowly and is being counteracted by the introduction of upper secondary schools for the highly gifted.

Church schools

It is mostly the Catholic and Protestant churches in Germany that take advantage of the constitutionally guaranteed freedom of non-governmental bodies to establish private schools with state recognition. These church schools are most commonly preschools (ages 2–6); in some regions, they make up to 50 per cent of the early childhood education system. These schools are also attended by children of other faiths. The two state Christian churches as a rule, however, do not allow non-Christian teachers to be hired. Interns, intercultural aides, language aides and other assistants might be exempt from this rule. Recently, even a few Muslim childcare centres have opened. Among secondary schools, the number of church schools is considerably lower.

Gemeinschaftsschule

'Community schools' are gaining ground as an alternative model to the three-track secondary school system prevalent in Germany (i.e. *Hauptschule, Realschule, Gymnasium*). The *Gemeinschaftsschule* keeps all students within the same school and uses flexible transitions between the different secondary diplomas

---

7   Klemm (2010) gives a good overview of the status quo and the challenges facing inclusive education.

on offer in Germany. It has become an option, in theory, in all 16 states. The *Gemeinschaftsschule* is often attended by children with a migrant background and by children from socio-economically disadvantaged families who hope to have a better chance of gaining a higher-level secondary diploma in these schools.

All-day schools

Many of the schools described above have recently become institutions where children receive care and instruction for the entire day while their parents work. This is considered a politically desirable development. After some initial hesitation, even the church schools are increasingly beginning to offer this form of care/ school blend. And, while migrant parents/families may have a stated preference for childcare to be provided by family members, more and more are sending their children to all-day schools.

A Real-World Example

A relevant example of intercultural learning through early multilingual education is the *IPE-Institut für Interkulturelle Pädagogik im Elementarbereich e.V.* in Mainz. The institute has developed a European language portfolio for children aged 3–7 in Germany which has been recognised by the European Council. In paragraph 4.7 of the portfolio, teaching consultant Giovanni Cicero Catanese describes his work with the project and the practical testing conducted in three Mainz childcare centres.

Measures and Challenges for the Design of Intercultural Education

Intercultural education intends to shape the multicultural experience of children and adolescents in such a way that they feel at home in their country of residence and can use their experience creatively and productively to develop the skills and orientation necessary for life in a society marked by cultural diversity within a democratic Europe, and in a world that is experiencing a global information and communication revolution. This is the standard against which the quality of intercultural education and pedagogical orientations needs to be measured.

Opening up to Other Cultures

At the end of the 1990s, there was a discussion about opening up communal social services in Germany to the needs of an ever-growing migrant clientele by breaking down the barriers to access and integrating migrants into the structures. In this context, the need to open up schools to other cultures also came to be expressed (Filtzinger, 1995: 115–17). The discourse on this issue can be understood as a critical complement to the concepts of immigrant education and intercultural social work. Elements of diversity education from the US and human rights instruction from England, Canada and France came to be included (Diehm, 2009: 61–2), with their emphasis on other disadvantaged groups such as women, people with physical and mental disabilities, members of religious minorities, ethnic groups, and homosexual, bisexual and transgender people. Prengel (1995) tried to collate the shared elements of intercultural pedagogy, feminist pedagogy and integration pedagogy into one of diversity. The Berlin *Kinderwelten* project described above (Wagner, 2010), building on the anti-bias approach by Louise Derman-Sparks, brought other aspects of diversity less often considered into the discussion around intercultural pedagogy. A pedagogical orientation which is sensitive to difference and bias can strengthen the individual development of one's identity to be able to encounter other people with empathy and respect (Diehm, 2009: 62).

Opening up to Other Cultures in Educational Policy

Some states, many towns, and non-profit children's and adolescent groups, clubs, foundations, projects and initiatives as well as numerous childcare facilities and primary schools have developed concepts and ideas for opening up to other cultures. The German federal government developed a national plan of action in 2011 with the motto 'Strengthen Cooperation – Make Participation Real' (*Zusammenarbeit stärken – Teilhabe verwirklichen*). This plan abandons the older forms of intervention based on deficits and opens up new perspectives for education. This was also seen in the 2012 report of the Federal Commissioner for Migration, Refugees and Integration, which reported on the concrete implementation of integration goals in 2010–12.

Improved participation should be achieved by transforming foreigners' advisory councils (*Ausländerbeiräte*) into councils for migration and integration which would also deal with educational questions. Another part of this is automatic German citizenship for migrants' children who are born in Germany, which brings identity conflicts which they then have to resolve as they reach adulthood. A general formal recognition of double citizenship could thus make multiple identification easier.

Opening up to Other Cultures in Schools

Opening up to other cultures in schools poses a great challenge for children, parents and teachers. It assumes a mutual and trusting acceptance of those involved and openness to cultural, national, ethnic, religious, physical, sexual and linguistic diversity. Figure 4.1 describes some elements of the concrete process of opening up to other cultures in schools.

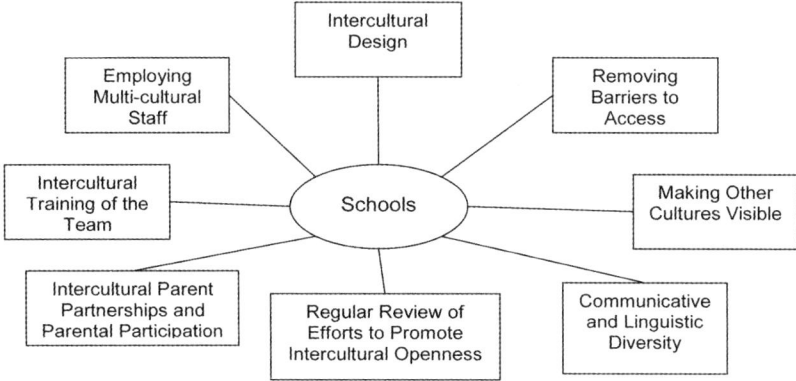

Figure 4.1   Elements of opening up to other cultures

Intercultural dimensions in school design
Schools reflect the cultural diversity of society, but few have taken intercultural openness as part of their core curriculum. A school team should develop ideas for intercultural education from the multicultural experiences of the school. Parents and children should also be included in this process. Creating a written plan allows these concepts to be reviewed on a regular basis and give parents and other partners the chance to take the school at its word. The European dimension should also be clearly recognisable in the concept because it opens up a double national and European sense of belonging as part of children's process of developing their identity (Filtzinger, 2010: 15–17).

Intercultural training of staff
Intercultural education is still not satisfactorily addressed in the training of professional staff in schools, which is why this is an important topic to be addressed at continuing education events. Because processes for opening up to other cultures are most effective when they are designed within their target environment and when those who will be involved in their implementation participate, team meetings, collegial consultation and training (with external consultants as required) are suited for promoting the dynamic process of opening up to other cultures.

Hiring multicultural staff
An important building block in opening up to other cultures is the presence of multicultural staff on the team. They can represent different cultural facets: as men or women, as people with a migrant background or a person with a disability or other cultural characteristics. With children of migrant background sometimes making up more than 30 per cent of the student body, it is ridiculous that this group is not reflected more in school teams. Staff from other cultural backgrounds are much more commonly found in day-care centres than in schools. Multicultural staff

can also be important sources of insight within the team, and offer children and parents from other cultural background an opportunity to identify with someone similar. Multicultural teams manifest the multicultural diversity of the school to the outside world. It is still very rare to see head teachers from non-German cultural backgrounds. That there is a lack of teachers with a migrant background is clearly related to adolescents failing to obtain the necessary academic qualifications due to disadvantage in school. There are also other reasons why leaders might have problems with staff from other backgrounds. For example, there are very few male staff members in preschool and primary school settings, even if most seem to agree that they would be advantageous. Also, the employment of men and women with disabilities in schools is rather rare.

Intercultural parent partnerships and participation
The recent official recommendations in favour of stronger parental involvement in education are not being fulfilled in many schools. Some of the most often mentioned reasons why parents with a migrant background do not participate in the activities of day-care centres and schools include: 'The parents aren't interested'; 'the parents don't appreciate school'; 'the fathers don't have time or don't want to'; 'the migrants withdraw into their own culture'. Even if such statements were true, one ought to ask whether what is on offer sufficiently takes into account the interests and needs of parents. One should invite them to activities which are not so dependent on language-based communication. Intercultural parent partnerships means including parents – with their heterogeneous situations, opportunities and expectations – as partners in the planning and execution of pedagogical activities. Sponsorships can serve as a transition to this. The goal remains: to turn this educational partnership with parents into a collaborative constructive process. An exchange of professional expertise with parents' experience of raising their own children offers teaching staff the opportunity to become more familiar with different families and their lives, and gives parents the opportunity to become familiar with the culture of public education. Parent participation is above all else an institutional participation of the parents. Parent associations should include the full spectrum of parents: fathers and mothers, Germans and migrants, different professions, as well as parents with disabilities or who have children with disabilities, those who are in same-sex partnerships and those who are single parents. Unfortunately, most of these associations do not envision participation where parents might have a say in what gets decided.

Removing barriers to access
Making buildings barrier-free is required for all children, parents and staff with disabilities. But there are also barriers that are less visible, such as quotas or when schools discreetly or openly advertise that they have no foreign students. For the same reason, some schools view hiring staff from migrant backgrounds with scepticism; if they were interested in opening up to other cultures, they would have already hired them to make the school more attractive to migrant parents. There

are also some schools that make a point of stating that they speak only German on school grounds, or that they do not observe religious dietary restrictions, or that their Muslim staff do not wear headscarves. At entry into primary school, the required skills in the instructional language of German are often a very difficult hurdle for children of non-German origin to cross. Also, parents of children with disabilities may find it hard to find a regular school that will take their child.

Making interculturality publicly visible
Interculturality is visible when it can be seen on posters, books, recordings, invitations, parent newsletters in different languages; when other languages can be heard in the halls and when consumables, games and clothing from other cultures are on hand – that is, when schools make their intercultural activities publicly available through the media and events.

Communication and linguistic diversity
Communication is the fundamental pillar of human interaction. It is not reducible to linguistic communication. Linguistic communication is not reducible to a single language. Language education is not reducible to learning German. Becoming open to other cultures means becoming open to a diversity of languages, creating a climate that is friendly to communication and language that allows the children to become familiar with a broad spectrum of communicative options – what Loris Malaguzzi calls the '100 languages of children'. For language development, it is significant that all children, multilingual and monolingual, can expand their communication skills in everyday situations. In all schools, there is linguistic diversity: from dialects to standard language, from minority languages to global languages, from sign language to Braille, from 'perfect' to 'broken' German. In this area, the close ties between language development and intercultural education become clear. When insular groups of majority-language speakers are given advantages instead of recognising the linguistic diversity at both the individual and collective level, this results in processes of exclusion between those children who speak German well and those children 'who are at risk' instead of an expansion of communicative and multilingual competence of all children.

Regular assessment of interculturality
To ensure the quality of interculturality and its continued development, schools will need to review their practices from time to time. With reflection orientated towards identifiable standards, the status of openness to other cultures can be checked on an annual basis and adjusted accordingly.

Opening up to Other Cultures as a Challenge

Childcare facilities have become more open to other cultures sooner, more often and better than primary school facilities. But the biggest catch-up is with secondary schools. There has already been some progress in opening these up to other cultures, but there must be further efforts to spread the idea of inclusion and its consequential implementation at different policy, administrative, skill and decision-making levels as well as in the schools themselves. These levels need to become better connected. There are major differences between the German states in the implementation of integration and inclusion. The challenge is of not making children and youth adapt to the schools, but rather to have the schools adapt to the needs and skills of the children and adolescents. Cultural diversity is a task for intercultural educational policy as well as a challenge for independent and relevant research into intercultural education in order to develop suitable guidelines for citizens with cultural and other differences to live together in communities and to design processes for opening up to other cultures that are based on real-world experience. The intercultural challenge is the cooperative construction of an open intercultural society that includes all groups with different cultural backgrounds in an interactive, inclusive development process and that makes use of the human resources of all citizens to:

- guarantee the communicability of different cultural codes;
- handle political, social and cultural conflicts with fairness;
- work together in solidarity and democratically to build an open, multicultural society;
- achieve the highest levels of equality among citizens;
- make the country's schools European, intercultural, multilingual, inclusive and participatory places where children and adolescents can help forge paths to a democratic and pluralistic European Union of freedom, peace and rule of law.

The European Language Portfolio at Preschool: Analysis of an Experiment in Germany and Prospects

Numerous Council of Europe documents emphasise that all languages, not only national European languages, must be upheld and protected. These include official, regional and minority languages, migrant languages and the languages of major trading partners (European Commission, 2007: 23).

Indeed, in a move towards fostering and expanding multilingual education, at the end of the 1990s the Council of Europe laid down the criteria for the development of a new instrument, the European Language Portfolio (ELP), with the intention of making a significant contribution, within a common framework, to the recognition of language skills acquired both during school years and through personal life experiences.

All models of the European Language Portfolio (ELP) have three parts: The Language Passport, The Language Biography and The Dossier. Learners are able to use each of these parts according to their individual needs in different learning contexts. It may be that the parts have different names if deemed to be more practical by those using them. This is the case of the 'Junior' Portfolio model developed by the Centre for Information on Language Teaching (CILT), where the Passport, Biography and Dossier are called 'The Languages I Know', 'What I Know and Can Do in Languages' and 'My Dossier' respectively. In this case, giving the three parts different names makes their function and use easier for young learners to understand.

- *The Language Passport* provides an overview of the learner's skills in various languages, defined in terms of ability according to the various levels of the Common European Framework. The Language Passport records the formal language certificates obtained (exams, qualifications etc.) and outlines learners' language learning and intercultural experiences. It also includes information relating to partial language skills as well as learning assessments by the educational institution of both the teacher and the learner. In order to promote recognition of the ELP in Europe and facilitate the mobility of individuals, the Council of Europe has designed a standard version of the Language Passport for young and adult learners (15/16+ years). It contains some pages that cannot be changed, while allowing users to add others according to individual needs.
- *The Language Biography* illustrates the processes involved, rather than results or outcomes. This section of the ELP is based on the idea that reflecting on their own learning process encourages learners to be motivated to learn languages, thus affecting the results achieved. This pedagogical function is associated with the Biography documentation's function, which is more extensive and detailed than the information provided in the Passport. In fact, the Biography gathers all information regarding learners' language experiences, from first contact with the languages studied to opportunities for exposure to the language(s), including environments outside school (on holiday, at home, watching television, films etc.). The Language Biography encourages learners to become involved in planning their own learning process, helping them to assess at what point they are on their learning path and what they can do to achieve their objectives and/or bridge any gaps. It also fosters multilingualism. On this note, this section of the ELP contributes to achieving the objective of promoting all of a learner's language skills, including their knowledge of languages or dialects spoken within families.
- *The Dossier* provides the learner with the opportunity to select and present the materials that record and illustrate the experiences and skills outlined in the Language Passport. This section of the Portfolio takes on an important educational function, especially for young learners, who are able to demonstrate their learning achievements, thereby highlighting the language and intercultural experiences obtained both inside and outside of the school environment (Ministero della Pubblica Istruzione, 2006).

Analysis of the ELP's aims, principles and functions gives rise to new and exciting areas of research in the field of education and intercultural dialogue, starting with a number of basic considerations about the use and possible future developments of this tool. It is this framework that provides the basis for the linguistic and educational project which will be described in the following pages, a project that has focused on assessing the feasibility of the above tool in a specific field of education: preschool. To allow a better understanding of the subject matter and context, from now on the German preschool will be referred to by the German word 'kindergarten'.

Dissemination of the European Language Portfolio in Germany and Current Trends

Before describing the project carried out in Mainz, it is necessary to clarify several aspects in order to understand the current historical framework within which this initiative is placed.

Since the early 1990s, an idea which had already found fertile ground in the United States for nearly a decade slowly but surely spread across Germany: for teaching to be centred on the principles of pragmatically oriented self-learning, detached from evaluations and marks but linked to the needs of the individual; enhancing their skills rather than focusing on shortfalls. These elements, together with a focus on the biography of each learner to set out individual learning plans, underpin the educational concept of the ELP (Kolb, 2007; Fthenakis et al., 2009; Brauer et al., 2012). From this point, several books were published on the subject and several recommendations were drawn up at ministerial level to encourage teachers to use the Portfolio tool in its various forms.

It is worth remembering that, in Germany, the organisation of schooling falls within the institutional responsibility of the *Länder* (federal states) rather than a centralised ministry, which means that in each region there may be a varying use of the Portfolio. Despite the widely varied results, however, it is not difficult to see how the subject of children's active participation in the construction of knowledge and in the biographical reconstruction of their own learning path is gaining strength to compete with the exclusively evaluation-based approach towards knowledge, which is extraneous to the individual. Nonetheless, parallel to the openness towards this qualitative and biographical approach, one can observe an enormous amount of effort made by a large number of psycholinguists and educators to develop tests that are able to classify language skills in German by way of points systems, scores and levels of competence (Jampert et. al., 2005; Reich, 2007; Kany and Schöler, 2010). Many of these tests, however, currently remain subject to criticism, due both to the inflexibility of the standards and because they are often designed on the basis of monolingual children, without taking into account aspects of bilingual or multilingual development.

Therefore, on one hand, there is an increasingly urgent need to guide students through the learning process to foster an independent and self-aware learning experience that enhances individual skills and knowledge acquired both in formal contexts (school) and non-institutional settings (family, associations, etc.). On the other hand, there is a tendency to resort to standardised tools that can serve as a screening mechanism from the early age of 4–5 years in order to identify language shortfalls that could hinder a child's academic career. This trend is the result both of objective needs – that is to say, with a large group of children who learn German as a second language (L2) who could benefit from observation tools that shed light on any language difficulties and offer relevant solutions – and of an educational policy trend, which is tied to the monocultural and monolinguistic tradition of schooling in Germany (Gogolin, 2008).

Although the idea that children of foreign origin using their mother tongue could have a negative influence on the development of the L2 has practically disappeared from the scientific literature in the field, it is still a belief commonly held by teachers and educators. In order to bridge this divide, a large number of scholars have recently focused their efforts on promoting pedagogical tools.[8] These were of a qualitative nature with biographical records of the learning process, above all to foster an attitude aimed at motivating students by highlighting their individual skills and experiences rather than focusing exclusively on areas of weakness.

Moreover, it is proving increasingly necessary to develop not only 'preventative' actions concerning the German language, which focus primarily on children of foreign origin, but also, first and foremost, programmes that are able to promote multilingualism as early as kindergarten among all children, especially – to use an unkind assignation – for the 'monolingual natives' who, in a few years, will be able to see the disadvantage of monolingualism in a predominantly multilingual Europe. This framework underpins the project described in the next chapter.

Experimental European Language Portfolio Model in the Kindergarten Goetheplatz: Process and Results

The pedagogical project that we intend to illustrate, in light of the introduction of the European Language Portfolio in several kindergartens in Mainz, was divided into several phases to take advantage, especially in launching the experimental phase, of the useful 'platform' provided by the decade-long collaboration between the IPE-Institute and the Goetheplatz Municipal Kindergarten in Mainz.[9] The phases of the project can be summarised as follows:

---

8   See, for example, Tracy, 2007; Reich, 2008; Fthenakis et al., 2009; Protestantischer Kindergarten Regenbogen and Institut für Bildung im Kindes- und Jugendalter, 2010.

9   The project documentation – developed and carried out in collaboration between the IPE-Institut für Interkulturelle Pädagogik im Elementarbereich e.V and the Goetheplatz Kindergarten and other general activities of the IPE-Institute – is held in the institute's library and is available to the public. The most recent documentation is also available online (http://www.ipe-mainz.de).

1. feasibility study of an ELP model for children aged 3–6, which is already in place in Spain, and its adaptation to the situation of the school in which the first experiment took place from September 2007 to June 2008;
2. development of a new ELP model (September 2008–June 2010);
3. support in disseminating the pedagogical work of the ELP in various kindergartens (from 2011).

The first phase of the research was dedicated to identifying the ELP models which already exist and are approved by the Council of Europe for the 3–7 age group. In September 2007, the following were found to be accredited:

- the Polish model for children aged 3–6 (Centralny Ośrodek Doskonalenia Nauczycieli, 2007)
- the Spanish model for children aged 3–7 (Ministerio de Educación, Cultura y Deporte España, 2003)
- the Turkish model for children aged 5–9 (Bilfen Schools, 2007).

After requesting an original copy of each of these three models from the relevant national ministries, we proceeded to examine their features and adaptability to the context of the experiment.

The two which were considered to be the most suitable were the models from Spain and Poland, since the Turkish model – due to the very structure of Turkey's educational system – is aimed at children who have just begun the primary education and literacy stage. The Polish model is presented in an interesting way for the child, in the 'shape of an accordion'; it contains a progression of sections dedicated to each year of age from 3 to 7 years. This helps to clearly visualise the evolution of the learning process and makes it possible to highlight the events that characterise the various stages of the child's life. The final choice, however, was made in favour of the Spanish ELP model, since it has both material which is directly available to the child – the Portfolio in the strict sense – and a teacher's guide for its use. The guide outlines several activities that can be organised into small groups to fulfil the various sections of the ELP.

Some of these activities were later selected, translated into German and carried out over the period of one school year. Subsequently, an assessment of this experience was carried out (Cicero Catanese, 2010). These assessments gave rise to the next phase of the project, which was the development of a new ELP model effectively adapted to the German context, while retaining the inspiration of the above-mentioned models.

The New European Language Portfolio Model for Children Aged 3–7

The new model – released in the autumn of 2011 (Filtzinger et al., 2011) and recorded by the Council of Europe as issue '2011.R002' – is made up of two elements:

1. a teacher's guide (in German), which introduces the theme of multilingualism and multilingual education in Europe and gives useful indications regarding how to use the second element;
2. the pages that constitute the ELP itself, aimed at children aged 3–7 (in German, Turkish, Italian and English).

Yet what are the activities performed at the kindergarten through the use of the European Language Portfolio? In the following section, we will attempt to summarise some of these activities and to understand the pedagogical impact that they can have, as seen during the experimental phase and in the ongoing process of disseminating the materials in several other schools, which, in different ways, enables us to receive their comments, criticism and ideas.

The pedagogical ELP project is open to all children who, regardless of their mother tongue(s), are able to come together and exchange information about their experiences with different languages in a primarily playful manner. It should be emphasised, once again, that the European Language Portfolio is not an instrument for children of foreign origin, but rather a documentation tool available to *all* children.

The main topics suggested by the model developed in Mainz include: my name and its meaning; my family and the languages that we speak at home; the languages I 'encounter' every day; the languages I 'encounter' at school; places I've visited; colours, numbers and body parts in different languages; recipes from around the world; my contact with other cultures.

Through interviews with children, it is possible to trace the languages spoken within the family or at school; and, together, we can provide the chance to become 'detectives or reporters in the search for languages'. Indeed, for children, actively seeking this information is very exciting, as they can ask their parents or other adults, as well as their buddies, what languages they speak. Given that preschoolers are unable to read, once this information has been collected, every language found can be represented by, for example, a coloured or a smiley face) that will be used from then on in the ELP to refer to that language whenever necessary (for instance to be drawn alongside photos of the children's parents or buddies to illustrate what languages they speak). It is not important, especially in an early stage, to establish the criterion of 'identifying' a language, or that it is spoken correctly by children who claim to know it. What is important is the identification process itself: a language can, in fact, be identified if the children listen to music in that language, or if their grandfather speaks it, or if they hear it during a trip and find it strange or incomprehensible. Even the dialectal forms play an important role and may be 'collected' in the Portfolio.

The Portfolio itself can be a topic of discussion and practical experience, in presenting children with both the ELP and the various book formats. The teacher can show and verbalise their form, content, structure (number of pages, designs) in order to demonstrate the different formats and topics that distinguish the various books.

During the subsequent activities, the children are then offered topical inputs (e.g. travelling) that can be elaborated upon by referring – as in the case of the experimental phase – to the child's real experiences (e.g. the 'big' places they have visited, in foreign countries, as well as the 'small' ones, such as visiting relatives in another city, or even the 'journey' from home to school) through which inspiration can be drawn for language activities, such as describing landscapes, people they have met and, potentially, the languages they speak.

A flexible pedagogical approach geared towards the everyday proved to be a 'winning' formula – both in the experimental phase of the project and in its subsequent stages – with regard to the motivation of the children as well as their families. Indeed, families greatly appreciated the school's interest in their biography, language and culture, being no longer seen and considered as problematic issues but rather as something that enriches. (Some parents told of how, on some occasions, school or medical staff had advised them not to speak their mother tongue, saying that it would run the risk of their children not being able to learn the German language.) Here, parents were able to share their own background with the children – with stories about their childhood, country of origin – and perhaps in another language, depending on their ability. This is a pedagogical and mental approach that may face initial challenges and be met with scepticism among both teachers and families. Efforts to overcome these difficulties, however, have proved effective.

Not only did parents feel a sense of enrichment of their cultural background (e.g. when they were supported with the idea of speaking their native language at home), but teachers (through the ELP's biographical approach) also shared something about themselves with the children, who showed a clear interest in sharing in these experiences. It was interesting to see, for instance, how children as early as in the experimental stage suggested to teachers to fill in their own Portfolios, an idea that was immediately met with enthusiasm. This meant that both children and their families felt that teachers were closer to their daily lives, with positive effects on parent–teacher meetings, where teachers reported a greater level of openness and trust.

The activities of the European Language Portfolio can be implemented in a flexible manner, both in terms of content and the number of participants. As most of the activities are suitable for small groups (five–seven children), some of them may be appropriate for group sessions (such as in circle activities). In the experimental phase, several activities were carried out regularly, at least once a week, yet the nature of the ELP is that many of the daily topics offer the opportunity to reflect upon the language. It follows that every daily event can provide inspiration to capture the child's attention towards the subject. For instance, during an excursion to a park, the children of one school 'explained' to the teacher how some plants, or parts of them (leaves, colours etc.) have different names in the language spoken at home compared to German. Through simple ideas involving the children's skills in their own languages it is therefore possible to achieve a form of language education which is motivating, and with a pragmatic approach. To provide yet another example, the topic of one's own name – its meaning, the letters from which it is made up and how they are written differently in other cultures – opens up a world of interest for children towards languages; it strengthens their personal identity and promotes an attitude of curiosity towards other cultures. This was shown by the suggestion by the same children to visit the municipal library, where there are many books written in different languages and with different characters. Indeed, today there are many books and materials on the market, including multimedia in multiple languages, which undoubtedly makes it easier to introduce children to the world of languages.

In its experimental phase, the programme also provided evening meeting with parents, who were informed of the project's aims and methods. During these meetings, families had the chance to discuss, reflect and exchange information on the various aspects related to the language development of their children (mostly bilingual or trilingual) and to understand the importance of multilingual education for their children.

The project was made possible thanks to the contributions of the Robert-Bosch Foundation, the Training Fund of the city of Mainz, the Ministry of Education, Science and Culture of the Federal Region of Rhineland-Palatinate, and the head of migration policies of the same federal region.

Reflections and Further Developments

The feedback that followed the publication of the new model of the European Language Portfolio; the outcomes on the courses offered to teachers from more than 30 kindergartens; and the interest of several public and private organisations operating in various parts of Germany (and also in other countries such as Austria, Belgium and Serbia) in introducing the ELP project into the structures they manage brought into sharp focus ideas and educational materials which support early multilingualism for all children which demonstrate the skills of multilingual children of foreign origin, and which raise awareness of monolingual children in terms of openness to new languages and cultures.

On a strictly educational level, the experimentation of the ELP has, above all, given rise to clear indications about the feasibility of this tool in a preschool establishment. The work related to the language Biography, as well as the collection of materials for the Dossier, was met with great interest by children, with clear positive effects on their general level of motivation towards learning and the development of metalinguistic awareness. This last aspect was most clearly seen in the older children (5 years and over); yet not to be underestimated are the long-term results that can be achieved by exposing younger children to activities on the topic 'language' in a conscious and direct way.

In this regard, there is the undeniable advantage for monolingual children in participating in activities such as those proposed by the ELP. These broaden their cultural and language knowledge through contact with other languages and their sounds, laying solid foundations for the development of a sense of awareness and understanding for fellow learners who come to school – with different language backgrounds – to learn the official language of the place. Full success cannot be achieved in this process, however, without the involvement of both migrant and non-migrant families. The Portfolio may be an opportunity for families to gain better mutual knowledge (through activities to which all parents are invited) as well as an opportunity for the school to provide, with the biographical work carried out through the Portfolio, more accurate advice to families regarding their children's language development. Moreover, parents can participate in the 'creation' of the Portfolio along with their children by helping them to collect important materials or by filling in with them the parts that relate to the family's language history.

Mention should also be made here of the Language Passport. In the experimental phase, this was certainly the most complex part to carry out, in as much as the question is raised as to whether it is indeed necessary or whether the self-assessment skills it requires can be observed as early as in this age group. The issues and questions that arise from the Language Passport deserve a thorough reflection that would go beyond the scope of this chapter. Here, it may only be reported that many children who have worked with the ELP for more than one year have shown (albeit in the under-6 age group) attitudes that give a clear indication of the development of the earliest forms of metalinguistic skills and the ability to reflect on their own skills. It is for this reason that, in any case, we have developed a simplified form of the Language Passport.

Concluding Remarks: Ideas for the Implementation of the ELP – The 'Three Pillars'

In this last phase, a few years on from the launch of the project, there are three of what might be considered to be the 'pillars' that underpin our work to develop further the European Language Portfolio in early childhood:

1. The first is to reinforce the use of this instrument and its underlying concept in preschools, to make fostering multilingualism in preschools 'part of the curriculum'.
2. The second pillar is to extend the language biographical initiative to the age group below 3 years. Germans kindergartens are, in fact, slowly becoming structures that accept children not only from 3 years of age, but also younger. This change can, therefore, offer the possibility to carry out biographical work primarily with families.
3. third pillar is represented by the transition from kindergarten to *Grundschule* (primary school), which in Germany is still struggling to ramp up structural reforms in terms of intercultural aspects. The ELP activities can certainly pave the way for the development of greater continuity and consistency in the implementation of programmes aimed at fostering multilingualism.

References

Auernheimer, G. (2012). *Einführung in der Interkulturelle Pädagogik*. Darmstadt: Wissenschaftliche Buchgesellschaft.

Bednarz-Braun, I. (2013). Migration und Integration als wissenschaftliches Thema. *DJI Impulse. Das Bulletin des Deutschen Jugendinstituts*, 2.

Berlin-Institut für Bevölkerung und Entwicklung (2009). *Ungenutzte Potentiale. Zur Lage der Integration in Deutschland*. Berlin.

Bilfen Schools (2007). *Avrupa Dil Portfolyosu; Onay Model no. 85.2007 / European Language Portfolio: Accredited Model no. 85.2007.*

Brauer, G., Keller, M. and Winter, F. (2012). *Portfolio macht Schule. Unterrichts- und Schulentwicklung mit Portfolio*. Seelze-Velber: Kallmeyer and Klett.

Bundesministerium für Bildung und Forschung (2005). *Migrationshintergrund von Kindern und Jugendlichen. Wege zur Weiterentwicklung der amtlichen Statistik*. Bonn.

Bundesministerium für Familie, Senioren und Jugend (1998). *Zehnter Kinder- und Jugendbericht. Bericht überdie Lebenssituation von Kindern und die Leistungen für Kinderhilfen in Deutschland*. Bonn.

Bundesministerium für Familie, Senioren, Frauen und Jugend (2005). *Zwölfter Kinder- und Jugendbericht*, Bonn.

Bund-Länderkommission (1977). *'Vorschläge zur' Fortentwicklung einer imfassenden Konzeption der Ausländerbeschäftigungspolitik*. Bonn.

Bund-Länderkommission (2003). *Förderung von Kindern und Jugendlichen mit Migrationshintergrund. Gutachten von Gogolin, I., Neumann, U. und Roth, H.-J.*, Bonn: BLK Geschäftsstelle.

Buttaroni, S. (ed.) (2011). *Wie Sprache funktioniert. Einführung in die Linguistik Pädagoginnen und Pädagogenm*. Hohengehren: Schneider Verlag.

Centralny Ośrodek Doskonalenia Nauczycieli (2007). *Moje pierwsze europejskie portfolio językowe Nr. akredytacji 87.2007*. Warsaw.

Cicero Catanese, G. (2010). *Das Europäische Sprachenportfolio. Anwendungs- und Entwicklungsmoglichkeiten zur Unterstützung einer interkulturellen und mehrsprachigen Bildung in vorschulischen Einrichtungen*. Münster: Waxmann.

Commissione delle Comunità Europee (2007). *Relazione sull'attuazione del piano d'azione 'Promuovere l'apprendimento delle lingue e la diversità linguistica'*. Brussels: European Commission.

Die Beauftragte der Bundesregierung für Migration, Flüchtlinge und Integration (2012), *9. Bericht über die Lage der Ausländerinnen und Ausläner in Deutschland*. Berlin.

Die Bundesregierung (ed.) (2011), *Nationaler Aktionsplan Integration. Zusammenhalt stärken – Teilhabe verwirklichen*. Berlin.

Diehm, I. (2009). I*nterkulturelle Pädagogik im Elementar- und Primarbereich in europäischer Perspektive von programmatischen Verengungen zu neuen Problemsichten*. In Röhner, C., Henrichwark, C. and Hopf, M. (eds),

Europäisierung der Bildung. Konsequenzen und Herausforderungen für die Grundschulpädagogik. Wiesbaden: VS Verlag für Sozialwissenschaften.

DJI (Deutsches Jugendinstitut) – Projekt 'Multikulturelles Kinderleben' (ed.) (2000). *Wie Kinder multikulturellen Alltag erleben.* Munich: Ergebnisse einer Kinderbefragung.

Filtzinger, O. (1995). Gesellschaftliche Entwicklungstendenz und Interkulturelle Öffnung. In Barwig, K. and Hinz-Rommel, W. (eds) (1995), *Interkulturelle Öffnung sozialer Dienste.* Freiburg im Breisgau: Lambertus.

Filtzinger, O. (2001). Politica migratoria in Germania e integrazione degli immigrati. *Studi Emigrazione/Migration Studies*, 144, 877–93.

Filtzinger, O. (2010). Die interkulturelle Dimension im Konzept von Kindertagesstätten. Ein entscheidender Schritt auf dem Weg zur Interkulturellen Öffnung. *KiTa aktuell Fachzeitschrift für die Leitung von Kindertageseinrichtungen. Ausgabe Baden-Württemberg*, 1, 15–17.

Filtzinger, O. (2013). Interkulturelle Erziehung und Bildung. In Fried, L. and Roux S. (eds). *Handbuch Pädagogik der frühen Kindheit. 3. Aufl.* Berlin: Cornelsen.

Filtzinger, O. and Traversi, M. (eds) (2006). *La scuola dell'accoglienza. Gli alunni stranieri e il successo scolastico.* Rome: Carocci.

Filtzinger, O., Montanari, E. and Cicero Catanese, G. (2011). *Europäisches Sprachenportfolio, Mehrsprachigkeit in der frühkindlichen Bildung wertschätzen und dokumentieren.* Braunschweig: Schubi.

Fthenakis, W.E., Daut, M., Eitel, A., Schmitt, A. and Wendell, A. (2009). *Natur-Wissen schaffen. Band 6: Portfolios im Elementarbereich.* Troisdorf: Bildungsverlag EINS.

Gogolin, I. (2008). *Der monolinguale Habitus der multilingualen Schulen. 2, unveränd. Aufl.* Münster: Waxmann.

Gogolin, I. and Krüger-Potratz, M. (2006). *Einführung in die Interkulturelle Pädagogik.* Opladen: Budrich.

Hofmann, N., Polotzek, S., Roos, J. and Schöler, H. (2008). Sprachförderung im Vorschulalter. Evaluation dreier Sprachförderkonzepte. *Diskurs Kindheits- und Jugendforschung Heft*, 3, 201–300.

Jampert, K., Best, P., Guadatiello, A., Holler, D. and Zehnbauer, A. (2007). *Schlüsselkompetenz Sprache. Sprachliche Bildung und Förderung im Kindergarten. Konzepte-Projekte-Maßnahmen. 2. Aufl.* Weimar: Verlag das Netz.

Jampert K. et al. (2005). *Schlüsselkompetenz Sprache. Sprachliche Bildung und Förderung im Kindergarten. Konzepte, Projekte, Maßnahmen.* Berlin: Verlag das Netz.

Kammermeyer, G., Roux, S. and Stuck, A. (2011). Additive Sprachförderung in Kindertagesstätten. Welche Sprachfördergruppen sind erfolgreich? *Empirische Pädagogik*, 25 (4), 239–461.

Kany, W. and Schöler, H. (2010). *Fokus: Sprachdiagnostik. Leitfaden zur Sprachbestimmung im Kindergarten. 2. Erw. Aufl.* Berlin: Cornlesen.

Klemm, K. (2010). *Gemeinsam lernen, Inklusion leben. Status Quo und Herausforderungen inklusiver Bildung in Deutschland.* Gütersloh: Bertelsmann.

Kolb, A. (2007). *Portfolioarbeit. Wie Grundschulkinder ihr Sprachenlernen reflektieren.* Tübingen: Narr.

Koordinierungskreis 'Ausländische Arbeitnehmer' (ed.) (1979). *Integration der zweiten Ausländergeneration.* Bonn.

Krüger-Potratz, M. (1991). *Anderssein gab es nicht: Auslander und Minderheiten in der DDR.* Münster: Waxmann.

Kühn, H. (1979). *Stand und Entwicklung der Integration der ausländischen Arbeitnehmer und ihrer Familien in der Bundesrepublik Deutschland.* Bonn: Memorandum des Beauftragten der Bundesregierung.

Lengyel, D. (2012). *Sprachstandsfeststellung bei mehrsprachigen Kindern im Elementarbereich.* Munich: Deutsches Jugendinstitut.

Ministerio de Educación, Cultura y Deporte España (2003). *Portfolio Europeo de las Lenguas: Modelo acreditado No. 50.2003 (3–7 años)/European Language Portfolio: Accredited Model No. 50.2003 (3–7 Years).* Madrid.

Ministerium für Bildung, Familie, Frauen und Kultur des Saarlandes (2008). *2 Bände, Mehrsprachiges Aufwachsen in der frühen Kindheit.* Berlin: Verlag das Netz.

Ministero della Pubblica Istruzione (2006). *Portfolio Europeo delle Lingue.* http://archivio.pubblica.istruzione.it/argomenti/portfolio/struttura.shtml [retrieved June 2013].

Prengel, A. (1995). *Pädagogik der Vielfalt: Verschiedenheit und Gleichberechtigung in Interkultureller, Feministischer und Integrativer Pädagogik. 2. Aufl.* Opladen: Leske and Budrich.

Protestantischer Kindergarten Regenbogen and Institut für Bildung im Kindes- und Jugendalter (2010). *Durchgängige Sprachförderung im Kindergarten 'Regenbogen'.* Landau: Empirische Pädagogik.

Reich, H.H. (2007). Forschungsstand und Desideratenausweis zu Migrationslinguistik und Migrationspädagogik für die Zwecke des 'Anforderungsrahmens'. In Bildungsministerium für Bildung und Forschung (ed.), *Anforderungen an Verfahren der regelmäßigen Sprachstandsfestellung als Grundlage für die frühe und individuelle Förderung von Kindern mit und ohne Migrationshintergrund. Bildungsforschung Band 11.* Bonn/Berlin.

Reich, H.H. (2008). *Sprachförderung im Kindergarten. Grundlagen, Konzepte und Materialien.* Weima/Berlin: Verlag das Netz.

Reich, H.H. et al., (2002), *Spracherwerb zweisprachig aufwachsender Kinder und Jugendlicher. Ein Überblick über den Stand der nationalen und internationalen Forschung.* Hamburg: Behörde für Bildung und Sport.

Roux, S. and Stuck, A. (2005). Interkulturelle Erziehung und Sprachförderung im Kindergarten. Forschungsergebnisse. In Roux S. (ed.), *PISA und die Folgen. Sprache und Sprachförderung im Kindergarten.* Landau: Empirische Pädagogik.

Sachverständigenkommission: Zwölfter Kinder- und Jugendbericht (2005). *Bildung, Betreuung und Erziehung von Kindern unter 6 Jahren, Band 1.* Munich: Verlag Deutsches Jugendinstitut.

Tracy, R. (2007). *Wie Kinder Sprachen lernen. Und wie wir sie dabei unterstützen können.* Tübingen: Francke

Vanderheiden, E. and Mayer, C.-H. (ed.) (2014). Handbuch Interkulturelle Öffnung. Grundlagen, Best Practice, Tools. Göttingen/ Bristol: Vandenhoek & Ruprecht.

Wagner, P. (ed.) (2010). *Handbuch Kinderwelten. Vielfalt als Chance-Grundlagen einer vorurteilsbewussten Bildung und Erziehung. 2. Aufl.* Freiburg: Herder.

Chapter 5

The Italian Way for Intercultural Education

Massimiliano Fiorucci

The Presence of Migrants and Groups with Different Cultural Backgrounds in Italy

In recent years, the education systems of the so-called developed countries have taken an:

> increasingly pluralistic form in terms of the origins and cultures of students and families, whether you look at the school at its various levels or make reference to the university. This pluralism comes directly from the intensification of connections and exchanges among countries and peoples, and therefore inevitably involves all the states that have been or currently are the destination of migration flows. (Caritas/Migrantes, 2011: 179)

On the 'international' scene, Italy presents itself with a very particular 'migratory' history. The great migrations of the twentieth century have involved the country from two points of view:

1. As a land of emigration, with around 26 million migrants in 100 years (1876–1976), there are more than 60 million people of Italian origin in the world, and currently more than 4 million Italian workers overseas (Fondazione Migrantes, 2012).
2. As a land of immigration, 1976 was the year in which, for the first time in the country's history, positive net migration was recorded.[1]

There are currently just over 5 million foreign residents on Italian territory, with a small increase (43,000 persons) compared with the 2010 estimate, who account for 8.2 per cent of the resident population. They have more than 190 countries of origin, and the high number of nationalities found in Italy has led some scholars to define Italian society as a sort of 'migratory archipelago' in so far as there are people from almost every country. The top five countries by origin are Romania (997,000 persons), Morocco (506,369), Albania (491,495), China (277,570) and

---

1 More people entered the country (immigrants) than left (emigrants), so this year symbolically marks Italy's transition from a land of emigration to a land of immigration.

Ukraine (223,782), whose nationals together account for half of the migrants present in Italy (Caritas/Migrantes, 2012).

It should be noted, moreover, that there are many linguistic and cultural minorities in Italy (Campani, 2008). According to Ministry of the Interior estimates, about 5 per cent of the population has a mother tongue other than Italian. The Italian Constitution explicitly protects linguistic minorities. Article 6 ('The Republic protects linguistic minorities by means of special provisions') was applied before 1999, especially in some regions with special status (Aosta Valley, Trentino and Friuli Venezia Giulia). Subsequently, through Law 482/1999 concerning 'Provisions for the protection of historical linguistic minorities', the existence of some other (but not all) linguistic minorities was recognised. Article 2 of the law states that:

> In implementation of Article 6 of the Constitution of the Italian Republic and in harmony with the general principles established by European and international bodies, the Republic protects the language and culture of the Albanian, Catalan, German, Greek, Slovenian and Croatian populations and those speaking French, Franco-Provençal, Friulian, Ladin, Occitan and Sardinian.

The law also contains specific provisions for the teaching of minority languages in schools in 12 recognised linguistic communities. According to the law, schools must ensure the teaching of minority languages, and the right of persons to belong to such minorities and to learn their mother tongue is recognised. In particular, Articles 4 and 5 of Law 482 provide for intervention both at the level of individual schools and at the level of the Ministry of Education.

Among the minorities that have been excluded are the native Roma and Sinti groups (Fiorucci, 2011b).[2] In fact, the Roma and Sinti communities are not mentioned either in the *First Report on the Status of Minorities in Italy*, prepared by the Central Office for the Problems of Border Areas and Ethnic Minorities of the Ministry of the Interior in 1994, or in Law 482/1999. Roma and Sinti are the most significant ethnic and linguistic minorities in the European Union (about 10–12 million people), but Italy has no official data on their presence. According to some latest estimates, there are between 120,000 and 160,000 Roma, Sinti and Camminanti in Italy; other sources put the figure at about 150,000. The composition of this population is roughly as follows: 60 per cent are Italian nationals; the remaining 40 per cent come from EU countries (mainly Romania) and non-EU countries (mainly those of the former Yugoslavia). Migration from Romania has been particularly significant in recent years. Rome probably has the largest population of Roma and Sinti, with independent estimates of between 12,000 and

---

2   The term 'native Roma and Sinti' refers to all the communities of Roma and Sinti who have lived in Italy for a long time. It thus refers to Abruzzese and Campanian Roma, Sicilian Camminanti (Gypsies), Italian Sinti and the Kalderasha Roma community from Slovenia living in Italy since the end of World War II.

15,000 living in the city and the surrounding areas (Amnesty International, 2010: 2). The city of Rome is home to a range of communities: from autochthonous communities to communities of foreign origin such as the Roma from the former Yugoslavia and Romania.

It should be noted, however, that in February 2011 the Extraordinary Commission for the Protection and Promotion of Human Rights of the Italian Senate published the results of a survey on the status of these peoples in Italy: *Final Report of the Survey on the Condition of Roma, Sinti and Camminanti in Italy* (Commissione straordinaria per la tutela e la promozione dei diritti umani del Senato della Repubblica, 2011). This is a particularly important document because it was the first time the issue had been given national prominence.

The Main Characteristics of Students with Non-Italian Citizenship and Different Cultural Backgrounds in Schools

This significant migratory flow has had a strong impact on the school system. In about 15 years, the number of foreign students increased more than tenfold, from 59,389 (1996/97 academic year) to 755,939 (2011/12), with the number of children and young people of foreign nationality reaching 8.4 per cent. According to the Ministry of Education's General Directorate for Studies, Statistics and Information Systems – Statistical Service (hereafter MIUR-GDS):

> If one takes into account that the countries of origin are about 200, it is easy to understand the complexity of the phenomenon, especially when it comes to developing initiatives to support the integration of foreign students. (MIUR-GDS, 2012: 3)

The expansive nature of this phenomenon is easily visible if one looks at the distribution of foreign students in different school levels: 20.7 per cent of children attend nursery school; 35.5 per cent primary; 22 per cent lower secondary; and 21.7 per cent upper secondary. In the academic year 2011/12 primary schools – which have always had the highest number of non-Italian students and a higher percentage than other levels of education – registered a historical 'record'. In fact, 268,671 foreign students were enrolled in primary schools, accounting for 9.5 per cent of the total. This was followed by lower secondary schools with 66,043 non-Italian students (9.3 per cent of the total at this level of schooling); upper secondary schools with 164,524 students, equivalent to 6.2 admissions per 100 pupils; and, finally, nursery schools with 156,701 pupils, equal to 9.2 per cent of children attending this type of school.

The presence of students with non-Italian citizenship thus now represents a structural phenomenon, one which, at the same time, is constantly changing both in terms of annual increase and the variables that cause it:

If the increase in the presence of foreigners in Italian schools in the early years was mainly due to immigration, subsequent evolution of the phenomenon has led to an increase in second-generation foreigners compared with new entrants to the country. (MIUR-GDS, 2012: 3)

According to the Foundation for Initiatives and Studies on Multi-Ethnicity (Iniziative e Studi sulla Multietnicità, ISMU):

> Since academic year 2007/08, the Ministry of Education has been recording the place of birth of students with non-Italian citizenship, distinguishing between Italian-born and foreign-born, starting from the consideration that the educational experience of a student who has been educated exclusively in Italian schools is undoubtedly different from that of a student who has just arrived in Italy, without knowledge of the language, rules and functioning of the Italian school system. (MIUR-ISMU 2011: 11–12)

The number of children born in Italy out of the total school population of foreign origin has increased from an average 34.7 per cent in academic year 2007/08 to 44.2 per cent in 2011/12, corresponding to 334,284 students. The incidence is highest in nursery schools (where 80.4 per cent of students with foreign citizenship were born in Italy) and primary schools (54.1 per cent). Next are the lower secondary schools (27.9 per cent) and upper secondary schools, where the incidence is still low (10.2 per cent).

The presence of students with non-Italian citizenship is uneven both in terms of origin and geographical distribution. With regard to origin, the largest migratory flow is from Romania, with 141,050, accounting for 18.7 per cent of the non-Italian school population. This is followed by students from Albania (103,000 or 13.6 per cent) and Morocco (95,912 or 12.7 per cent).

The uneven territorial distribution of students with non-Italian citizenship results in significantly different incidences of foreign presences that, in turn, generates very different school situations concerning organisational and educational aspects related to integration:

> 50% of students with Romanian citizenship attend schools in Lazio, Piedmont and Lombardy. Half of the Albanian students are located in Lombardy, Emilia Romagna and Tuscany, and one-quarter of Moroccan students are in Lombardy [...]. With regard to the distribution of the most foreign nationalities in individual regions, it emerges that the most numerous foreign students in Trentino are Albanian (17.1%); Ecuadorians make up about one-quarter of students with non-Italian citizenship in Liguria; in Emilia Romagna the most present are Moroccans (17.9%) and 18.2% in the Marche region are Albanian. (MIUR, 2012: 5)

Another interesting statistic relating to students with non-Italian citizenship concerns the presence of females, who number 47.6 per cent on average. The highest percentage of girls are in upper secondary schools (49.5 per cent) and the choices fall mainly on former *licei magistrali* (general secondary schools), classical lyceums and then language high schools, while in male-dominated technical and vocational institutes the presence of women is approximately 44 per cent.

Finally, among the students with non-Italian citizenship, the annual report of the Ministry of Education, Universities and Research (Ministero dell'Istruzione dell'Università e della Ricerca, MIUR) also considers so-called 'nomads' (Roma, Sinti and Camminanti),[3] who are distributed almost uniformly in the different geographic areas, with the exception of the north-east where their numbers are lower and amount overall to 11,899. As is known, primary schools are the most attended educational level, with 6,416 pupils. Slightly more than half are enrolled in lower secondary school, while only 134 are enrolled in upper secondary school throughout the entire country.

The Problems and Difficulties of Students with Non-Italian Citizenship in School

MIUR's annual survey describes a situation that is quite critical with regard to students with non-Italian citizenship. It should be noted, however, that there are significant differences between those who were born in Italy and those who arrived a few years earlier:

> In general, at every level of school, students of immigrant origin achieve lower results than Italians in Italian language and mathematics tests and, as has already emerged from previous research, it is mainly the first-generation students who obtain lower average scores and are placed in the lower range of score distribution. Second-generation students show a trend that is more similar to Italians in both Italian language and mathematics tests. (MIUR-ISMU, 2013: 78)

There are, in particular, two obvious areas of concern with regard to students with non-Italian citizenship: the choice of upper secondary school and lagging behind in studies. Overall, in the academic year 2011/12, 2,655,134 students were enrolled at upper secondary school level in Italy: 2,490,610 with Italian citizenship and 164,524 with non-Italian citizenship. As is clear from the available data, the non-Italians mainly attend vocational schools (64,852) and technical institutes (62,981); their attendance is much lower in high schools and former general secondary schools (31,731) and artistic educational institutes (4,960). In terms

---

3   It is not entirely clear why the Ministry insists on defining these students as 'nomads' given that about 95 per cent of them have now been settled for a significant number of years (see Fiorucci, 2011b).

of percentage, professional institutes always have the highest concentration of non-Italians compared with total enrolment. Substantial differences in preferences emerge from the comparison between the educational choices of Italians and non-Italians, which makes the phenomenon of early 'educational channelling' of foreigners even more evident. In fact, foreigners are concentrated in vocational schools (39.4 per cent) and technical institutes (38.3 per cent), followed at a distance by high schools and former general secondary schools (19.3 per cent). On the other hand, Italians prefer high schools and former general secondary schools (44 per cent), technical institutes (33.3 per cent) and, to a lesser extent, vocational schools (18.9 per cent).

The overall picture of the relationship between the chronological age of students with non-Italian citizenship and class of school entry continues to indicate a worrying situation, although there was a slight decrease in 2011/12. The gap between Italians and non-Italians is clear-cut from primary school level and is reinforced at subsequent school levels.

According to data from MIUR (2012), if the average rate of lagging behind for Italian students in the academic year 2011/12 was 10.7 per cent, for non-Italians this figure is close to 40 per cent (Table 5.1); and, although it is already evident in primary schools, it reaches very worrying levels in upper secondary schools (68.9 per cent). As is known, the variables that contribute to determining the lagging behind of non-Italian students are numerous and include decisions concerning the entry class for those arriving in Italy once school terms have started (new arrivals), the territorial mobility of families, language skills and academic success.

Table 5.1   Percentage of students with and without Italian citizenship lagging behind, by school level

	Primary school	Lower secondary school	Upper secondary school	Average
Students with Italian citizenship	0.8	4.8	24.6	10.7
Students without Italian citizenship	17.4	46.0	68.9	39.5

Strategies and Intercultural Educational Practices Adopted in Italian Schools

Faced with such a situation, it is therefore necessary to develop educational responses that are suitable for current problems. The processes of globalisation under way and the multicultural configuration of today's society raise serious questions about the education and training systems which must now aim at training the citizens of the world. From such a point of view, intercultural training of teachers occupies a position of importance: it is only by starting from a correct formulation of educational work in schools that one can hope to diffuse an increasingly necessary 'culture of coexistence'. This is not an easy target: teachers and educators are first called on to question their paradigms of reference in order to attenuate the rate of ethnocentrism in the education system.

In this context, a proposal has been defined for intercultural education that is structured to answer in terms of educational practice the challenges posed by the world of interdependencies. It is an purposeful project that cuts across all fields of study taught in schools and aims to change perceptions and cognitive habits with which we generally represent both foreigners and the new world of interdependencies.

Intercultural education does not therefore have an easy or short-term task, because it implies a review of existing knowledge taught in school and because intercultural education is not a new field of study that is added to others. Rather, it is a point of view, a different perspective from which to look at the knowledge currently taught (Fiorucci, 2008). The origin of intercultural education is linked to the development of migratory phenomena, yet today it has abandoned the field of special education aimed at specific social groups, becoming an innovative pedagogical approach for reforming the school curriculum in general.

Many definitions of 'intercultural education' have emerged in recent years due to the research and experiments conducted in Italian educational contexts (Giusti, 1998, 2012; Catarci, 2006; Gobbo, 2008; Santerini, 2010).[4] It is possible to say, however, that educational research and intercultural practice move substantially along two main axes. In the first place, engaging in intercultural education means working to identify, design and test the *educational and teaching strategies most appropriate for encouraging a positive insertion of foreign students in schools and, therefore, in society* – but schools and social-educational services cannot be left alone in this task (MIUR, 2006). This involves provision of the necessary conditions to ensure that all individuals (natives and immigrants alike) achieve the same rates of academic success (Santerini, 2010). Some areas of work in this direction may be outlined briefly.

Reception: Scholastic Reception Together with Social Reception
(Centro COME, 2011)

This means understanding and being understood – that is, acquiring information and knowledge about the school systems of origin and pupils' prior schooling. It also means providing information on the Italian school system, drawing up

---

4 On definitions of intercultural education see, for example, Chistolini, 1992 and 2007; Susi, 1995; Sirna Terranova, 1998; Damiano, 1999; Gobbo, 2000; Pinto Minerva, 2002; Giusti, 2004; Portera, 2003 and 2013; Favaro, Luatti, 2004; Nanni, Curci, 2005; Zoletto, 2007 and 2012; Santerini, 2010.

a linguistic and cognitive profile of students, and acquiring information about the migratory project of the family. Reception is made up of several aspects: bureaucratic, organisational, affective-relational, educational-learning and cognitive (MIUR, 2006).[5]

Teaching of Italian as a Second Language

This aspect is absolutely central (Tosi, 1995; Vaccarelli, 2001; Favaro, 2002b, 2011; Vedovelli, 2002; Favaro, 2011). Language skills are the basis of any integration process, and it is necessary to teach Italian in a different way for those who are literate in another language. However, that teaching can only be done within normal school classes, avoiding the construction of separate places of learning. Division into groups, for short periods and for specific learning (language laboratories), does not call this choice into question. The central point of school entry is precisely the possibility for foreign students to come into contact with peers from whom, in formal and non-formal ways, they will learn not only the most immediate linguistic forms, but also the various forms of communication and the rules of the host group.

All studies show that complete separation of new students would be detrimental to their ability to fit in with the group-class, at linguistic, communicative, cognitive and cultural levels. Intensive courses (a few hours per week) that strengthen and support learning, especially with increasing age, are obviously different. In fact, as boys and girls gradually become older, intensive courses are more necessary and effective, provided that they are accompanied by a continued relationship with the whole group-class, its activities, its feeling of being 'a group'. The class, in fact, is the meaningful context for every linguistic and communicative expression: that is, the context that gives meaning to the contents – both relational as well as those of learning (Baldacci, 2009).

Enhancement of the Language and Culture of Origin and Multilingualism[6]

This is a complex and structured issue that requires different responses that also depend on the migratory projects of families. The maintenance and reinforcement of the language and culture of origin strengthen the general communication skills of immigrant students, helping to increase self-esteem. And yet here there must be complete freedom, protecting the right of everyone to develop themself from their own starting point. Multilingualism of the individual and of the system must be promoted. In this respect, the considerations made in the document *The Italian Way for the Intercultural School and Integration of Foreign Students* are of great interest: 'The situation of multilingualism that is becoming increasingly common

---

5   See also Demetrio and Favaro, 1996; Pinto Minerva, 2003; Ongini and Nosenghi, 2009; Favaro, 2011.

6   Favaro, 2011; Council of Europe-Italiano Linguadue, 2011.

in schools is an opportunity for all students not just for foreign students.' The action relates to:

- *Multilingualism in schools*, i.e. of the system. Today, two additional European Community languages are taught, which the qualification tables reduce to English, French, German and Spanish, plus Russian. There has to be a rethink of the general offer (not limited to immigrants) of foreign languages, including the languages spoken by the most numerous collectivities depending on the areas of the country and foreseeing the related qualifications. Courses can be organised on the basis of school networks in order to allow the creation of numerous class-groups. In all cases (even in primary schools) teachers can enhance multilingualism by giving visibility to other languages and various alphabets, discovering the 'loanwords' between languages, etc.
- *Individual multilingualism.* Maintenance of the language of origin is a human right, and it is an essential tool for cognitive growth, with positive implications also for Italian as a second language and foreign languages studied in school. The teaching of languages of origin in their standard version can be organised together with Italian and foreign groups and associations, while it will be left to families and communities to expose children to the non-standard varieties spoken by them (Ministero della Pubblica Istruzione, 2007: 13–14).

Common Intercultural Activities

All those activities that contribute to dialogue and mutual understanding should be promoted. These activities (expressive, musical, theatrical etc.) should benefit both the relations between Italian and foreign students in the classroom and relationships with peers outside school time. The quality and quantity of these relationships are important 'indicators of integration' (Favaro, 2008).

In the second axis, because *intercultural education is aimed at everyone, and especially at native people*, taking a perspective with an intercultural connotation means *encouraging receptive habits in Italians*. This can and must be reflected in the review and reform of the schools' training axis, which must aim not only at the formation of the Italian citizen, but also above all at the formation of a global citizen who lives and acts in an interdependent world (Fiorucci, 2008). In brief, this perspective implies that some basic measures should be adopted.

Reinterpretation of knowledge taught at school with an intercultural emphasis and thus the transition to intercultural teaching of fields of study which consists of revising school curricula and teaching programmes (Brunelli et al., 2007; Fiorucci, 2008; Luatti, 2009; Santarone, 2012, 2013). To give a few examples:

- In the teaching of *history*, there should be a revisitation of the issue discovery/ conquest of America (Todorov, 1992; Todorov and Baudot, 1997) and of encounters between peoples in the age of Columbus (Abulafia, 2008); there should be a reconsideration of the story of the crusades also from the point of view of Arab historians (Gabrieli, 1957; Maalouf, 1989); there should be a rediscovery of the history of the 'Mediterranean' as a space of dialogue and encounter among civilisations (Braudel, 1977; Riccardi, 1997). It would be important to reinterpret the close relationship between Europe and Asia (Goody, 2010) and revisit the Italian colonial experience (Di Sapio and Medi, 2009; Tomasello, 2004).
- In the teaching of *geography*, think of the role that could also be played by other cartographic representations of the world such as, for example, the one proposed by Arno Peters (1988; see also Grillotti Di Giacomo, 2008).
- In the teaching of *mathematics* (Cappelletti, 2000a, 2000b; Ascher, 2007; Supino, 2008) and philosophy (Nkafu, 2003; Bernal, 1997), think of the many cultural influences that have determined the development of these disciplines.
- For *music*, think of the intercultural dimension of jazz, blues and 'world music'.
- For *economics*, think of the strong correlations between migration and economic globalisation; and for *law*, to give just one example, think of the issue of 'citizenship'.

Critical analysis of textbooks. School textbooks are the first mediators, and are often carriers of stereotypes and proponents of a Eurocentric and ethnocentric representation (Ministry of Education – General Directorate for Cultural Exchange, Educational Cooperation Movement, 1993).

Intercultural training of teachers. Significant investment is needed to equip them with skills and knowledge of an anthropological, sociological, pedagogical, linguistic, psychological nature and so on; and of themes of great and ancient cultures (such as India or China) and major religions (Sirna Terranova, 1996; Chistolini, 2007; Santerini, 2010).

Intercultural Education and Teaching: Paths and Experiences

Intercultural education is connoted in daily practice with operational strategies characterised by the following basic elements:

- selection of intercultural issues in disciplinary and interdisciplinary teaching, with subsequent revision and integration of school curricula;

- conducting of supplementary interventions for curricular activities, with the contribution of the various institutions and organisations engaged in intercultural activities;
- attention to a climate of openness and dialogue, as well as a reflection on teaching style;
- adoption of targeted strategies in the presence of foreign students with special needs (Favaro, 2002a: 46–7).

In recent years, teachers have adopted different strategies to guide teaching in an intercultural sense, following to guidelines provided by pedagogical theory and empirical and experimental approaches based on self-initiative, individual creativity and the wealth of experience accumulated by schools. Elisabetta Nigris has highlighted the following areas within which to order the best-known and formalised experiences of the intercultural approach:

- teaching of reception
- teaching of Italian as a second language
- teaching for the promotion and comparison of cultures
- teaching for the decentralisation of points of view
- teaching for the prevention of stereotypes and prejudices
- teaching for change of fields of study (Nigris, 2003: 26).

The Teaching of Reception

This may be implemented in the initial entry phase of the foreign student in the school context. Recognising the special needs of foreign children, individual schools have equipped themselves with flexible and operative facilities and pathways to handle the reception of foreign students and their families. Thus, working groups, specific figures and commissions with planning and management tasks in the field of education and intercultural teaching have sprung up. For example, in order to plan effectively the reception of foreign children, a 'reception protocol' can be prepared, bringing together an ensemble of interventions, strategies and operational structures which institutions decide to adopt. These could include primarily: procedures put in place at the time of enrolment; strategies for 'first knowledge'; criteria for assigning students to classes; other reception facilities, such as instruments offered by intercultural documentation centres or allocation of appropriate professional resources.

In this phase it may also be important to collect the personal history of the foreign child, thus also obtaining information on the school system of origin and making a comparison with the Italian system, paying attention to organisational and teaching models as well as levels of preparation required (Nigris, 2003: 27–8).

The procedures for reception that the school puts in place can be divided into bureaucratic-organisational, such as enrolment; informational-cultural, such as the construction of a documentation centre; relational, such as reflection on the mode of reception in a class by children and teachers; or educational-teaching, such as the provision of language laboratories. Such facilities may be more or less effective in promoting the entry of foreign children, depending on the cultural framework and the academic model that they find, as well as the sense of belonging and involvement that these facilities will be able to promote (Nigris, 2003: 30).

Italian as a Second Language

The teaching/learning of Italian as a second language is a targeted strategy implemented in the presence of foreign students with special language needs. One of the priorities in the integration of foreign students is to promote the acquisition of good written and spoken competence in Italian, in the receptive and productive forms, to ensure one of the main factors of academic success and social inclusion. On their arrival, foreign students are faced with two different language needs:

1. Italian in the concrete context, which is essential in everyday life (language for communicating);
2. specific Italian which is required to understand and express concepts, develop learning in various subjects and reflect on the language itself (language for studying).

The language for communicating can be learned in a relatively short period of time which varies according to age, language of origin and use in environments outside school. On the other hand, learning the language for studying may take several years, given that it is a question of specific skills. Study of Italian should be included in the everyday education and school life of foreign students, with language laboratory activities and paths and instruments for its intensive teaching. Learning and development of Italian as a second language must be at the heart of teaching. It is therefore necessary that all teachers are involved, and that appropriate curricula are structured around real needs and monitoring of progress in learning the Italian language, progressively acquired by the foreign student.

Instruments and figures of linguistic facilitation (billboards, alphabet charts, maps, simplified texts, audio-visual or multimedia instruments etc.) can be used in the initial phase, promoting the capacity of the student to develop the language for communicating. Subsequently, particular attention should be paid to learning the language for studying because it represents the main obstacle to the learning of various subjects. As for other original languages – an important resource for cognitive and affective development – for their enhancement it is necessary to assume a polycentric perspective that involves both families and public and private social agencies present on the ground (Vaccarelli, 2001; Favaro, 2002a; Vedovelli, 2002; Baldacci, 2009).

Teaching for the Promotion and Comparison of Cultures

This is undoubtedly the intercultural approach most frequently put in place in recent years by teachers, with the production of activities, courses and teaching materials for students in more or less multicultural school contexts in order to allow the acquisition of skills required to implement a correct perception of other cultures (Nigris, 2003: 31–2). It was the concrete condition of encounters between children and families of different origins that pushed teachers and school directors to offer educational paths aimed at knowledge of the cultural aspects of belonging of foreign children.

The presentation and exploration of aspects of different cultures have thus proved in recent years to be the most immediate ways to put intercultural commitment into practice. Following a first phase of 'emergence', schools have taken steps to introduce educational courses aimed at developing knowledge of diverse cultures into curricula in a stable way. In this sense, topics such as the characteristics of the country, language, social and daily life – feasts, play, school and food – are presented. However, the cognitive approach may involve some risks which are appropriate to point out in order not to impoverish intercultural commitment. In fact, there is the danger of a certain 'transformation into cultural folklore' or of producing a rigid, homogeneous and motionless view of cultures (Susi, 1995: 59–60).

Teaching for the Decentralisation of Points of View

This is a further intercultural approach successfully implemented in recent years by teachers. In this case, specific cultural themes and elements are taken into consideration which are then analysed, starting from different points of view, in order to highlight the existence of a multiplicity of perspectives for the same subject. The ethnocentric attitude is undoubtedly present in all social groups and cuts across all cultures; only a 'critical ethnocentrism' (De Martino, 1977) in its radical sense commits the individual to ethical-political awareness, therefore no longer only logical-cognitive and cultural. In this way, intercultural education means to act on the affective and representational side, as well as on the cognitive and knowledge side, in order to exercise critical comparison and recognition of identities and differences.

Teaching for the Prevention of Stereotypes and Prejudices

This is an approach that also intimately concerns reflection on subject content, prompting teachers to question some of the cultural and epistemological assumptions on which learning itineraries have been constructed to date.

Teaching for Change of Fields of Study

On the other hand, teaching for change of subjects is the most complex approach, and aims to select new and/or revise existing content, starting from the observation that current school curricula exclude certain cultural elements (Fiorucci, 2008). It is a path that necessitates choosing the intercultural perspective as the axis of the entire educational institution, addressing all students.

An Example: Notes for Constructing Educational Courses on Migration Starting from Literature

The issue of migration is one of the fundamental conceptual nodes of intercultural education. According to Elio Damiano, for a topic such as migration the main teaching activity should consist of direct work by students with materials and documentation of various types, for example, newspapers, books or films. A working group under a teacher's guidance is the most suitable because it is necessary to continuously develop the comparison of opinions, given that the relationship with the 'different' implies a psychological involvement that is also influenced by stereotypes and agents external to the school (Damiano, 1998: 466).

A theme such as migration makes it possible to involve many fields of study, especially in literature (Santarone, 2013) where there are now many novels, short stories and poems dealing with this topic; often these works are composed by authors who recount first-hand their own migratory experience. It is possible to start with Moroccan writer Tahar Ben Jelloun and re-read some of his novels with this focus – e.g. *A occhi bassi* (*With Downcast Eyes*) and *Nadia* (1993, 2002) or, conversely, relevant Italian literature. Other examples dealt with by well-known authors are numerous:

- In his 1889 novel *Sull'oceano* (*On the Ocean*), Edmondo De Amicis – best known for his book *Cuore* (*Heart*) – addressed the theme of Italian emigration to Argentina in the 1880s.
- One chapter of Carlo Levi's *Cristo si è fermato ad Eboli* (*Christ Stopped at Eboli*) of 1945 describes emigration from Lucania (today's Basilicata) to the United States during the fascist period.
- In two short stories from 1973, Leonardo Sciascia addresses the issues of Sicilian emigration to Switzerland and Germany (*L'esame/The Examination*) and the United States (*Il lungo viaggio/The Long Journey*).

Equally important is the contribution of Italian writers belonging to historical linguistic minorities. One example is Carmine Abate (2012a, 2012b) – born in

Carfizzi, a small Arbëresh town in Calabria – whose extraordinary works have received major national and international recognition.[7]

Remaining in the field of literature, mention should go to that extraordinary territory that scholars call 'Italian literature of migration', which consists of those texts published directly in the Italian language by foreign authors who have been settled in Italy for a significant number of years.[8] This body of works is now very extensive and of great interest, and is moving from a phase of diaries, testimonies to a phase of real 'literariness' and should be fully counted as part of Italian literature *tout court*.[9]

Within the perspective of intercultural education aimed primarily at Italians, this literary output should be placed in comparison and relation with the Italian literature of emigration – that is, with the letters and literary production of Italian emigrants.[10] The phenomenon of Italian emigration, which has seen about 26 million migrants in a century (roughly from 1870 to 1970), has long been removed from collective memory. However, in recent years, there have been some major signs of revival (Bevilacqua et al., 2001, 2002; Colucci, 2008). And Francesco Durante, journalist and literary critic, besides having translated and edited the works of some Italian-American writers such as John Fante, has been working for a number of years on the relationship of emigrants with their land of departure through the lens of literature (Durante, 2001, 2002, 2005). The places and areas of work are very wide, and the following are some of the main themes concerning the relationship between literature and interculturalism:

- reinterpretation with a cultural emphasis of the authors in our literary tradition;

---

7   In 2012, Carmine Abate won the Campiello Prize for his novel *La collina del vento/ The Hill of the Wind* (in Abate, 2012a).

8   On Italian literature of migration, see Fiorucci, 2006; Portelli, 2001; Gnisci, 1998, 2003, 2004; Bregola, 2002, 2005; Alunni et al., 2001; Rigallo and Sasso, 2002; Fracassa, 2012.

9   To give just two examples, one is thinking here of writers like Igiaba Scego (2004, 2008, 2010) and Amara Lakhous (2006, 2010, 2013).

10   Living between two worlds is something that belongs to all emigrants. There is a love/hate feeling with respect to their country of origin. The ambivalent relationship with their country of origin and with their host country is masterfully expressed in Idria Meacci Vannacci's poem titled 'Due bandiere' (Two Flags). The author is an Italian who emigrated to Argentina in 1948. The text reads: 'Two plump little hands /at a tight flag./ Even my heart tightens, why? … /If the flag is the colour of the sky?/ White clouds, blue of infinity! … / Why?, Why? … /A tear falls, yet another … /and the little one sees! … /Here … take this flag, you can play! … /Yes, my darling, we will play a game/all new! … /To me your flag, to you mine./Clasp it strongly, I clasp yours./Yours white and blue, mine with three sparkling colours./I wish this game would never end./Come on, little one! … /I would like to see the two as one./And the heart resists!/Help me, help me to see/in yours and in all flags,/the one that makes me cry for love!' (in Sbolci, 2001: 69).

- colonialism in Italian literature;
- the representation of the non-Western world in the works of Italian and European writers;
- the theme of Italian emigration;
- Italian literature of migration;
- the contribution of historical linguistic minorities to Italian literature;
- the inclusion of non-Italian authors in literature curricula (Santarone, 2013).

Intercultural Best Practice in the Italian Educational Context: The Way for Intercultural Schools

With reference to the Italian context, after publication of the *Guidelines for the Reception and Integration of Foreign Students* (MIUR, 2006), it is worth noting the important document drawn up by the National Observatory for the Integration of Foreign Students and Intercultural Education: *The Italian Way for Intercultural Schools and Integration of Foreign Students* (Ministero della Pubblica Istruzione, 2007).[11] This is a very advanced document, still relevant and largely yet to be realised. In its first part, the document outlines the essential general principles which have inspired best practice in both schools and in national and local regulations. These principles are:

Universalism

Universalistic criteria for the recognition of children's rights have been adopted since the 1990s, based on two strong, value-related elements:

1. application to the Italian situation of the provisions laid down by the Convention on the Rights of the Child, adopted by the United Nations in 1989, ratified by Italy in 1991 and confirmed in the regulations of those years on the protection of childhood and adolescence;
2. the tradition of the Italian school towards various forms of diversity already developed in the 1970s.

This has meant recognising that:

---

11   The National Observatory for the Integration of Foreign Students and Intercultural Education was established by Ministerial Decree on 6 December 2006 with the aim of identifying effective organisational solutions and useful guidelines for the work of schools. The Observatory was divided into a scientific committee comprising experts from the academic, cultural and social spheres; a technical committee comprising Ministry representatives; and a council of leading research institutions, associations and organisations involved in the integration of foreign students.

- Education is a right of every child, regardless of the position of the parents and also regardless of the presence of the parents in our country.
- School education is at the same time a duty that adults must respect and protect, in particular with regard to compulsory education.
- Everyone should be able to count on equal opportunities in access, educational attainment and guidance. This perspective has been adopted by the European Union, and expressed in its statements and directives. The reference to equal opportunity supports the possibility of some specific actions ('selective policies') for immigrant children, having as its objective the raising of the level of parity and reducing the risks of exclusion (Ministero della Pubblica Istruzione, 2007: 7).

Common School

The Italian school system immediately decided to enrol non-Italian students in common schools, within normal school classes, avoiding the construction of separate places of learning – contrary to what happened in other countries and in continuity with previous guidelines of the Italian school system for the reception of various forms of diversity (gender, disability, heterogeneity of social origin).

It is a question of concrete application of the more general principle of universalism, but also recognition of the positive value of peer socialisation and daily confrontation with diversity. This choice is not challenged by concrete practices of division into groups, usually for short periods and for specific learning, mainly related to study of the Italian language. This principle must now deal with the phenomena of concentration/segregation that are occurring in different contexts and levels of school, and with families' demands for differentiated schools. Reference to Law 62/2000 remains essential, according to which private schools within the public education system should be based on the principles of freedom established by the Constitution and accept school enrolment for all students whose parents so request, provided that these students possess a valid qualification for entry to the class they wish to attend (Ministero della Pubblica Istruzione, 2007: 7–8).

Centrality of the Person in Relation to Others

All contemporary pedagogy, albeit with different emphases, is oriented towards enhancement of the person and the construction of educational projects that are based on students' biographical and relational uniqueness. This approach characterises the regulatory framework of the Italian school; is present in both Law 30/2000 on reform of the school system and the reform Law 53/2003; and is confirmed in the New National Guidelines for nursery schools and for the first cycle of education. It is a principle that is valid for all students, and is particularly significant in the case of children of immigrant origin because it puts the emphasis on attention to diversity and reduces the risks of approval and assimilation. At the same time, attention to a person's relational character can avoid the excesses of the exasperated individualistic approach and help schools recognise the life context of the students, and their family and social biography (Ministero della Pubblica Istruzione, 2007: 8).

Interculturalism

Adoption of the intercultural perspective is made explicit as follows. Italian schools choose to adopt an intercultural perspective – that is, the promotion of dialogue and confrontation among cultures – for all students at all levels: teaching, curricula, pedagogy, fields of study, relations, class life. Choosing the intercultural perspective means, therefore, not being limited to mere strategies of integration of immigrant students, or to compensatory measures of a special nature. Rather, it is a question of taking diversity as a paradigm of the identity of the school itself in pluralism as an opportunity for opening up the entire system to all differences (of origin, gender, social, educational history).

This approach is based on a dynamic conception of culture which avoids both the closure of students in a prison culture and stereotypes or transformation into folklore. In fact, becoming aware of the relativity of cultures does not mean arriving at absolute relativism, which postulates neutrality towards them and thus prevents relationships. Intercultural strategies avoid separating individuals into autonomous and impervious cultural worlds, promoting instead confrontation, dialogue and also reciprocal transformation, to make it possible to live together and deal with resultant conflicts. The Italian way to interculturalism combines the ability to know and appreciate the differences and the search for social cohesion in a new vision of citizenship suited to today's pluralism, in which special attention is paid to building convergence towards common values (Ministero della Pubblica Istruzione, 2007: 8–9).

This is a comprehensive wide-ranging proposal that caters to all students, involving all levels (from teaching to relationships and class life), and which considers all personal, social and educational differences, highlighting the risk of a misunderstood intercultural education (culturalism, trivialisation, transformation into folklore, approval, emphasising differences etc.). Subsequently, the document identifies 10 courses of action that characterise the model of intercultural integration of Italian schools, which can be divided into three main areas.

- *Action for integration* – 1. practices of reception and insertion into the school; 2. Italian as a second language; 3. enhancement of multilingualism; 4. relations with foreign families and orientation).
- *Action for intercultural interaction* – 5. relations at school and in out of school time; 6. interventions on discrimination and prejudice; 7. intercultural perspectives in knowledge and skills.

- *Actors and resources* – 8. autonomy and networks among educational institutions, civil society and territory; 9. the role of school directors; 10. the role of teachers and non-teaching staff.

The document thus represents an essential point of reference on which to agree in proposing an Italian interpretation of 'intercultural education', on which some of the leading scholars of intercultural phenomena have worked and which, for the most part, has yet to be implemented.

Problems and Prospects for Intercultural Educational Orientation in Italy

The analysis carried out considered some aspects of research in the intercultural field; inevitably, however, it had to neglect others. In conclusion, it seems useful to identify by way of example contexts and areas of research which it has not been possible to report on here and on which, however, it would be important to work with even greater determination in the near future:

- from analysis of the contribution of the non-scholastic context to intercultural education, to the role of associations (NGOs, voluntary sector associations, immigrant associations, voluntary organisations etc.);
- from research on paths of integration to identification of clear and shared indicators of integration;
- from critical analysis of Italian school textbooks to education of adult immigrants;
- from continuing and professional education to the academic enrolment of foreign students in upper secondary schools and beyond, to the crucial issue of the so-called 'second generation'.

The adolescents of immigrant origin in Italy experience, in fact, conditions of difficulty because the classic problems of adolescence are compounded – in some cases – by those linked with 'double identity' and 'multiple belonging'. This is a question of a generation that is crucial for the future of Italy, a generation that finds itself between the need for identity and desire to belong and whose exponents are the 'involuntary pioneers of a national identity in transformation' (Ambrosini, 2006: 89).

At the more general level, it should be noted that in the face of enlightened documents and a period of effective interest in the issue, including at the political level, for some years now there has been the progressive reduction of available resources in the field of research and education. The intercultural issue is now considered a matter for specialists, and does not call into question the education system as a whole, which considers it, unfortunately, as just one question alongside others.

Over the last 25 years, as a result of the migratory phenomena under way, the Italian school system has increasingly moved towards a multicultural configuration. In response to these phenomena, since the 1990s the Ministry of Education has been issuing circulars, formulating proposals, drafting documents and producing research reports. In the meantime, over the years throughout the country, educational institutions, evening schools for adults, and voluntary sector associations and organisations have developed a host of responses and proposals, some of them also very advanced, which have remained, however, only the heritage of those who contributed to their preparation.

There has been a serious lack of communication that has made it difficult to circulate and network experiences. In today's situation – in which there are 755,939 students of non-Italian citizenship in Italian schools (corresponding to 8.4 per cent of the total school population) from around 190 countries (MIUR-ISMU, 2013) – it seems necessary to try to put some order into what has been done so far through the establishment of a National Centre for Documentation and Research on Intercultural Education, delegated to the collection, capitalisation and dissemination of the 'best practices' carried out in the different territorial areas. This centre should function as the central 'service' point for the collection, organisation and processing of experiences, and for putting them back into circulation in the network.

The best experiences could be gathered, socialised and eventually transferred, with the necessary adaptations to local context, to other territorial situations. The establishment of such a centre could also facilitate comparison with significant experiences from outside Italy. This centre – equipped with the appropriate human, financial and instrumental resources – could also be seen as a cultural place for:

- promoting and producing research reports;
- carrying out monitoring, studies, research and publications on migratory phenomena and intercultural education;
- making the material collected available and consultable;
- organising and promoting seminars, conferences and follow-up meetings;
- designing and implementing training activities and research;
- launching and consolidating relations with other existing research and documentation centres in Italy (at local level), in Europe and worldwide.

References

Abate, C. (2012a). *La collina del vento*. Milan: Mondadori.
Abate, C. (2012b). *Le stagioni di Hora. Il ballo tondo – La moto di Scanderbeg – Il mosaico del tempo grande*. Milan: Mondadori.
Abulafia, D. (2008). *La scoperta dell'umanità. Incontri atlantici nell'età di Colombo*. Bologna: Mulino.
Alunni, R., De Andrea, R. and Eramo, P.P. (2001). *Scritture e linguaggi del mondo. Narrativa per l'educazione interculturale*. Florence: La Nuova Italia.

Ambrosini, M. (2006). Nuovi soggetti sociali: gli adolescenti di origine immigrata in Italia (pp. 85–104). In Valtolina, G.G. and Marazzi, A. (eds). *Appartenenze multiple. L'esperienza dell'immigrazione delle nuove generazioni.* Milan: Franco Angeli.

Amnesty International (2010). *La risposta sbagliata. Italia: il 'piano nomadi' viola il diritto all'alloggio dei Rom a Roma.* Rome.

Ascher, M. (2007). *Etnomatematica. Esplorare concetti in culture diverse.* Turin: Bollati Boringhieri.

Baldacci, M. (2009). L'educazione interculturale e le classi-ponte. Pedagogia più didattica. *Teorie e pratiche educative*, 2, 33–8.

Ben Jelloun, T. (1993). *A occhi bassi.* Turin: Einaudi.

Ben Jelloun, T. (2002). *Nadia.* Milan: Bompiani.

Bernal, M. (1997). *Atena nera. Le radici afroasiatiche della civiltà classica.* Milan: EST.

Bevilacqua, P., De Clementi, A. and Franzina E. (eds) (2001). *Storia dell'emigrazione italiana. Partenze.* Rome: Donzelli.

Bevilacqua, P., De Clementi, A. and Franzina, E. (eds) (2002). *Storia dell'emigrazione italiana. Arrivi.* Rome: Donzelli.

Braudel, F. (1997). *Il Mediterraneo. Lo spazio. La storia. Gli Uomini. Le tradizioni.* Milan: Bompiani.

Bregola, D. (2002). *Da qui verso casa.* Rome: Edizioni Interculturali.

Bregola, D. (2005). *Il catalogo delle voci. Colloqui con poeti migranti.* Isernia: Cosmo Iannone.

Brunelli, C., Cipollari, G. and Pratissoli, M. (2007). *Oltre l'etnocentrismo. I saperi della scuola al di là dell'Occidente.* Bologna: EMI.

Campani, G. (2008). *Dalle minoranze agli immigrati. La questione del pluralismo culturale e religioso in Italia.* Milan: Unicopli.

Cappelletti A.M. (2000a). *Didattica interculturale della matematica.* Bologna: EMI.

Cappelletti, A.M. (2000b). *Didattica interculturale della geometria.* Bologna: EMI.

Caritas/Migrantes (2011). *Dossier statistico sull'immigrazione 2011. 21° Rapporto.* Rome: Idos.

Caritas/Migrantes (2012). *Dossier statistico sull'immigrazione 2012. 22° Rapporto.* Rome: Idos.

Catarci, M. (2006). L'inclusione dell'altro. Una ricerca sulle strategie di costruzione di una didattica interculturale (pp. 187–213). In Santarone, D. (ed.). *Educare diversamente.* Rome: Armando.

Centro COME (2011). *Accoglienza e inserimento.* http://www.centrocome.it [retrieved June 2013].

Chistolini, S. (1992). *Educazione interculturale. La formazione degli insegnanti in Italia. Gran Bretagna. Germania.* Rome: Euroma-La Goliardica.

Chistolini, S. (ed.) (2007). *Pedagogia della cittadinanza. Lo sviluppo dell'intercultura nella formazione universitaria degli insegnanti.* Lecce: Pensa MultiMedia.

Colucci, M. (2008). *Lavoro in movimento. L'emigrazione italiana in Europa. 1945–57.* Rome: Donzelli.

Commissione straordinaria per la tutela e la promozione dei diritti umani del Senato della Repubblica (XVI Legislatura) (2011). *Rapporto conclusivo dell'indagine sulla condizione di Rom, Sinti e Caminanti in Italia.* Rome.

Council of Europe – Italiano LinguaDue (2011). Guida per lo sviluppo e l'attuazione di curricoli per una educazione plurilingue e pluriculturale. Strasbourg/Milan.

Damiano, E. (ed.) (1998). *Homo migrans. Discipline e concetti per un curricolo di educazione interculturale a prova di scuola.* Milan: Franco Angeli.

Damiano, E. (ed.) (1999). *La sala degli specchi. Pratiche di Educazione interculturale in Europa.* Milan: Franco Angeli.

De Amicis, Edmondo (1889). *Sull'oceano.* Milan: Treves.

De Martino, E. (1977). *La fine del mondo. Contributo all'analisi delle apocalissi culturali.* Turin: Einaudi.

Demetrio, D. and Favaro, G. (1992). *Immigrazione e pedagogia interculturale.* Florence: La Nuova Italia.

Demetrio, D. and Favaro, G. (1996). *Bambini stranieri a scuola. Accoglienza e didattica interculturale nella scuola dell'infanzia e nella scuola elementare.* Florence: La Nuova Italia.

Demetrio, D. and Favaro, G. (2002). *Didattica interculturale. Nuovi sguardi. competenze. percorsi.* Milan: FrancoAngeli.

Di Sapio, A. and Medi, M. (2009). *Il lontano presente. L'esperienza coloniale italiana. Storia e letteratura tra presente e passato.* Bologna: EMI.

Durante, F. (ed.) (2001). *Italoamericana. Storia e letteratura degli italiani negli Stati Uniti (1776–1880).* Milan: Mondadori.

Durante, F. (ed.) (2002). *Figli di due mondi. Fante. Di Donato and C. Narratori italoamericani degli anni '30 e '40.* Cava de' Tirreni: Avagliano.

Durante, F. (ed.) (2005). *Italoamericana. Storia e letteratura degli italiani negli Stati Uniti (1880–1943).* Milan: Mondadori.

Favaro, G. (2002a). Aprire le menti nel tempo della pluralità. In D. Demetrio and G. Favaro. *Didattica interculturale. Nuovi sguardi. competenze. percorsi.* Milan: Franco Angeli.

Favaro, G. (2002b). *Insegnare l'italiano agli alunni stranieri.* Florence: La Nuova Italia.

Favaro, G. (2011). *A scuola nessuno è straniero.* Florence: Giunti.

Favaro, G. (ed.) (2008). *Un passo dopo l'altro. Osservare i cammini di integrazione dei bambini e dei ragazzi stranieri. La sperimentazione del Quaderno dell'integrazione nelle scuole fiorentine.* Florence: Comune di Firenze, Polistampa.

Favaro, G. and Luatti, L. (eds) (2004). *L'intercultura dalla A alla Z.* Milan: Franco Angeli.

Fiorucci, M. (2006). Scritture in movimento. Letteratura e testimonianze delle migrazioni (pp. 215–29). In Santarone D. (ed.). *Educare diversamente. Migrazioni. differenze. intercultura*. Rome: Armando.

Fiorucci, M. (2011a). *Gli altri siamo noi. La formazione interculturale degli operatori dell'educazione*. Rome: Armando.

Fiorucci, M. (2011b). *Per forza nomadi. Problemi. possibilità e limiti delle politiche di integrazione sociale per i Rom e Sinti a Roma*. Rome: Aemme.

Fiorucci, M. (ed.). (2008). *Una scuola per tutti. Idee e proposte per una didattica interculturale delle discipline*. Milan: Franco Angeli.

Fondazione Migrantes (2012). *Rapporto Italiani nel Mondo 2012*. Rome: Idos.

Fracassa, U. (2012). *Patria e lettere. Per una critica della letteratura postcoloniale e migrante in Italia*. Rome: Giulio Perrone.

Gabrieli, F. (1957). *Storici arabi delle crociate*. Turin: Einaudi.

Giusti, M. (1998). *L'educazione interculturale nella scuola di base*. Florence: La Nuova Italia.

Giusti, M. (2004). *Pedagogia interculturale. Teorie. metodologia. laboratori*. Rome-Bari: Laterza.

Giusti, M. (2012). *L'educazione interculturale nella scuola*. Milan: Rizzoli.

Gnisci, A. (1998). *Creoli meticci migranti clandestini e ribelli*. Rome: Meltemi.

Gnisci, A. (2003). *Creolizzare l'Europa. Letteratura e migrazione*. Rome: Meltemi.

Gnisci, A. (2004). *Via della Decolonizzazione europea*. Isernia: Cosmo Iannone.

Gobbo, F. (2000). *Pedagogia interculturale. Il progetto educativo nelle società complesse*. Rome: Carocci.

Gobbo, F. (ed.). (2008). *L'educazione al tempo dell'intercultura*. Rome: Carocci.

Goody, J. (2010). *Eurasia. Storia di un miracolo*. Bologna: Il Mulino.

Grillotti Di Giacomo, M.G. (2008). Per una didattica interculturale della geografia (pp. 158–74). In Fiorucci M. (ed.). *Una scuola per tutti. Idee e proposte per una didattica interculturale delle discipline*. Milan: Franco Angeli.

Lakhous, A. (2006). *Scontro di civiltà per un ascensore a piazza Vittorio*. Rome: edizioni e/o.

Lakhous, A. (2010). *Divorzio all'islamica a viale Marconi*. Rome: edizioni e/o.

Lakhous, A. (2013). *Contesa per un maialino italianissimo a San Salvario*. Rome: edizioni e/o.

Legge n. 482 del 15 dicembre 1999. 'Norme in materia di tutela delle minoranze linguistiche storiche'. Gazzetta Ufficiale del 20 dicembre 1999, n. 297.

Levi, C. (1945). *Cristo si è fermato a Eboli*. Turin: Einaudi.

Luatti, L. (ed.) (2009). *Educare alla cittadinanza attiva. Luoghi. metodi. discipline*. Rome: Carocci.

Maalouf, A. (1989). *Le Crociate viste dagli arabi*. Turin: SEI.

Ministero dell'Interno (1994). *Primo rapporto sullo stato delle minoranze in Italia*. Rome: Ufficio centrale per i problemi delle zone di confine e delle minoranze etniche.

Ministero della Pubblica Istruzione (2007). La via italiana per la scuola interculturale e l'integrazione degli alunni stranieri. Rome: Osservatorio nazionale per l'integrazione degli alunni stranieri e per l'educazione interculturale.

Ministero della Pubblica Istruzione – Direzione Generale per gli Scambi Culturali, Movimento di Cooperazione Educativa (1993). *Interculturalismo e immagine del mondo non occidentale nei libri di testo della scuola dell'obbligo.* Brussels: I Quaderni di Eurydice.

MIUR (2006). *Linee guida per l'accoglienza e l'integrazione degli alunni stranieri.* Rome: Fondazione ISMU.

MIUR-Direzione Generale per gli Studi, la Statistica e per i Sistemi Informativi – Servizio Statistico (2012). *Gli alunni con cittadinanza non italiana nel sistema scolastico italiano. Anno scolastico 2011–2012.* Rome: Fondazione ISMU.

MIUR-ISMU (2011). *Alunni con cittadinanza non italiana. Verso l'adolescenza. Rapporto nazionale Anno scolastico 2010–2011.* Milan: Fondazione ISMU.

MIUR-ISMU (2013). *Alunni con cittadinanza non italiana. Verso l'adolescenza. Rapporto nazionale Anno scolastico 2010–2011.* Milan: Fondazione ISMU.

Nanni, A. and Curci, S. (2005). *Buone pratiche per fare intercultura.* Bologna: EMI.

Nigris, E. (ed.) (2003). *Fare scuola per tutti. Esperienze didattiche in contesti multiculturali.* Milan: Franco Angeli.

Nkafu, M. (2003). *Aprire la filosofia all'intercultura.* Bologna: EMI.

Ongini, V. (2011). *Noi domani. Un viaggio nella scuola multiculturale.* Rome-Bari: Laterza.

Ongini, V. and Nosenghi, C. (2009). *Una classe a colori. Manuale per l'accoglienza e l'integrazione degli alunni stranieri.* Milan: Vallardi.

Peters, A. (1988). *La nuova cartografia.* Rome: Asal.

Pinto Minerva, F. (2002). *L'intercultura.* Rome-Bari: Laterza.

Portelli, A. (2001). Le origini della letteratura afroitaliana e l'esempio afroamericano. *L'ospite ingrato*, 3, 69–86.

Portera, A. (2006). *Globalizzazione e pedagogia interculturale.* Trento: Erickson.

Portera, A. (2013). *Manuale di pedagogia interculturale.* Rome-Bari: Laterza.

Portera, A. (ed.). (2003). *Pedagogia interculturale in Italia e in Europa. Aspetti epistemologici e didattici.* Milan: Vita e Pensiero.

Riccardi, A. (1997). *Mediterraneo: Cristianesimo e Islam tra coabitazione e conflitto.* Milan: Guerini.

Rigallo, D. and Sasso, D. (2002). *Parole di Babele. Percorsi didattici sulla letteratura dell'immigrazione.* Turin: Loescher.

Santarone, D. (2012). *Didattica e intercultura.* Rome: Armando.

Santarone, D. (2013). *Le catene che danno le ali. Percorsi educativi tra didattica intercultura e letteratura.* Florence: Le Lettere.

Santarone, D. (ed.) (2006). *Educare diversamente. Migrazioni. differenze. Intercultura.* Rome: Armando.

Santerini, M. (2010). *La qualità della scuola interculturale. Nuovi modelli per l'integrazione.* Trento: Erickson.

Sbolci, A. (2001). *Amore di terra lontana. Storie di emigranti attraverso le loro lettere (1946–1970)*. Florence: Le Lettere.

Scego, I. (2004). *Rhoda*. Rome: Sinnos.

Scego, I. (2008). *Oltre Babilonia*. Rome: Donzelli.

Scego, I. (2010). *La mia casa è dove sono*. Milan: Rizzoli.

Sciascia, L. (1973). *Il mare colore del vino*. Turin: Einaudi.

Sirna Terranova, C. (1998). *Pedagogia interculturale. Concetti. problemi. proposte*. Milan: Guerini.

Sirna Terranova, C. (ed.) (1996). *Docenti e formazione interculturale*. Turin: Il Segnalibro.

Supino, P. (2008). Per una didattica interculturale della matematica. In Fiorucci, M. (ed.). *Una scuola per tutti. Idee e proposte per una didattica interculturale delle discipline* (pp. 204–17). Milan: Franco Angeli.

Susi, F. (1995). *L'interculturalità possibile. L'inserimento scolastico degli stranieri*. Rome: Anicia.

Todorov, T. (1992). *La conquista dell'America. Il problema dell' 'altro'*. Turin: Einaudi.

Todorov, T. (2009). *La paura dei barbari. Oltre lo scontro delle civiltà*. Milan: Garzanti.

Todorov, T. and Baudot, G. (1997). *Racconti aztechi della conquista*. Turin: Einaudi.

Tomasello, G. (2004). *L'Africa tra mito e realtà. Storia della letteratura coloniale italiana*. Palermo: Sellerio.

Tosi, A. (1995). *Dalla madrelingua all'italiano*. Florence: La Nuova Italia.

Vaccarelli, A. (2001). *L'italiano e le lingue altre nella scuola multiculturale*. Pisa: ETS.

Valtolina, G.G. and Marazzi, A. (eds) (2006). *Appartenenze multiple. L'esperienza dell'immigrazione delle nuove generazioni*. Milan: Franco Angeli.

Vedovelli, M. (2002). *Guida all'italiano per stranieri*. Rome: Carocci.

Zoletto, D. (2007). *Straniero in classe. Una pedagogia dell'ospitalità*. Milan: Raffaello Cortina.

Zoletto, D. (2012). *Dall'intercultura ai contesti eterogenei. Presupposti teorici e ambiti di ricerca pedagogica*. Milan: Franco Angeli.

Chapter 6

Intercultural Education in the Spanish Context

Teresa Pozo Llorente, Jordi Vallespir Soler and Lidia Cabrera Pérez

Immigration and the Educational Response to Cultural Diversity in Spain

Migratory Movements

The current economic recession affecting some countries of the European Union (EU) is leading to the decision by a large sector of immigrants to return to their countries of origin. At the same time, the shortage of jobs and low pay in some of these countries, such as Spain, is bringing about an emigration process, especially among highly qualified young people. Although migratory movement continues, the period of intense immigration flows may have come to an end, indicates Pajares (2011). A change in the production model will require a change in the immigration model, or at least changes in the dynamics, the intensity and the characteristics of immigration flows.

It is worth remembering that around 216 million people (3.15 per cent of the world's population) do not reside in their country of birth. Spain is one of the

Table 6.1   Top migrant destinations

Country	Immigrants
USA	42,788,029
Russian Federation	12,270,388
Germany	10,758,061
Saudi Arabia	7,288,900
Canada	7,202,340
United Kingdom	6,955,738
Spain	6,900,547
France	6,684,842
Australia	5,522,408
India	5,436,012

Source: http://peoplemov.in [retrieved June 2013].

countries with the highest volume of immigrants. It occupies the seventh position, as shown by Table 6.1.

Despite the steep drop in immigration since 2009, in Spain the number of foreigners with residence permits was as high as 5,363,688 (as of 30 September 2012), according to the country's Permanent Observatory on Immigration (OPI, 2013). These are the official figures, although other sources put the number of immigrants at 6,900,547, which represents 14.84 per cent of Spain's total population (46,505,963).[1] Returning to the OPI data, if we look at the immigration legislation applicable to these foreign residents, 48.97 per cent (2,626,503) of them are subject to Spain's Community Immigration laws (*Régimen Comunitario*),[2] while 51.03 per cent (2,737,185) are subject to the General Immigration legislation (*Régimen General*).[3]

Visas for entering Spain are classified by the reason for entry: transit, short stay and residence. The majority of visas granted are for short stays (tourism), while the most relevant here are residency visas. In 2009 these visas registered a drop of 45.3 per cent with respect to the preceding year, according to the OPI. This decrease is in what can be called legal immigration, as it involves people who have been given authorisation to enter the country. As for the place of origin of the foreigners with valid residency permits in Spain, Europe is the continent that contributes the most residents (Pajares, 2011: 28ff.). Overall, the most numerous nationalities are Romanian and Moroccan, which together represent just over 23 per cent of the total number of foreign residents. It should be noted also that of the 15 nationalities with the most presence, seven belong to the EU: Romania, the United Kingdom, Italy, Bulgaria, Portugal, Germany and France (Table 6.2).

Looking at the figures for each Autonomous Region (Community), Catalunya has the largest population of residents from other countries (1,228,754), followed by Madrid (909,042), Valencia (689,011) and Andalusia (688,258). Together these regions account for 65.57 per cent of the total number of resident aliens.

These data reveal that migratory flows are not the same throughout Spanish territory, either in numbers of immigrants or in their countries of origin. At the

---

1   See, for example, http://peoplemov.in, which uses World Bank data; and http://datos.bancomundial.org.

2   *Régimen Comunitario* is the Spanish law applicable to foreign nationals and their families from other EU member states and from countries belonging to the European Free Trade Association (EFTA) – comprised of Iceland, Liechtenstein, Norway and Switzerland – and also to nationals of third countries who are related to Spaniards (*Real Decreto 240/2007, de 16 de febrero, sobre entrada, libre circulación y residencia en España de ciudadanos de los Estados miembros de la Unión Europea y de otros estados parte en el Acuerdo sobre el Espacio Económico Europeo*).

3   *Régimen General* is the Spanish legislation applicable to nationals of third countries, unless they are subject to the *Régimen Comunitario* as relatives of EU citizens (*Ley Orgánica 4/2000, de 11 de enero, sobre derechos y libertades de los extranjeros en España y su integración social y Reglamento de Desarrollo de la LO 4/2000 aprobado por RD 557/2011, de 20 de abril*).

Table 6.2   **Principal nationalities of immigrants in Spain**

Country	% (rounded)
Romania	12
Morocco	11
Ecuador	8
United Kingdom	6
Colombia	5
Argentina	5
Bolivia	4
Germany	4
France	4
Peru	3
Others	39

Source: Permanent Observatory on Immigration, 2013.

same time, it is interesting to note that listing the host regions according to their percentage of immigrant population causes the order to change considerably, with the Balearic Islands having the highest immigrant population (Table 6.3).
Source: Permanent Observatory on Immigration, 2009.

Table 6.3   **Percentage of immigrants in Spain with regard to native population, immigrant population and native population**

	Immigrant population (%)	Native population (%)
Catalunya	14	86
Madrid	14	86
Valencia	12	88
Andalusia	8	92
Balearic Islands	18	82

Source: Permanent Observatory on Immigration, 2009.

People from Romania (913,405;34.78 per cent), the UK (246,533; 9.39 per cent) and Italy (189,841; 7.23 per cent) represent over half (51.39 per cent) of the total number of foreigners to whom Spain's Community Immigration legislation is applicable. Meanwhile, Morocco has the highest number of residents subject to

General Immigration legislation (822,923; 30.08 per cent), followed by Ecuador and Colombia with 358,437 and 219,632 residents respectively.

In eight of the 15 nationalities with the most residents subject to General Immigration legislation – Ecuador, Colombia, Bolivia, Peru, the Ukraine, the Dominican Republic, Argentina and Brazil – drops have been observed with respect to the preceding quarter, although the decreases are less than 2 per cent. On the other hand, it must be noted that the nationalities with growing percentages include India, Pakistan, Paraguay and Senegal.

The population records kept at the municipal level, and the statistics derived from them, reflect migratory movement more precisely because they include the entire immigrant population, whether legal or not. According to these records, the migration balance grew steadily until 2007 (721,560), dropped considerably in 2008 (460,221) and then fell drastically in 2009 (51,505).

Immigration in Times of Crisis

As mentioned briefly above, the current economic crisis is affecting, in various spheres and very directly, both host countries and countries of origin, especially in terms of the employment situation. Faced with great difficulties, non-EU migrants and their families have had far fewer options for dealing with the situation, and often find themselves forced to return to their countries of origin.

The Economically Active Population Survey (EAPS) corresponding to the first quarter of 2012 shows that in Spain as a whole the unemployment rate for foreigners is considerably higher than it is for the population of Spanish nationals: 36.95 per cent compared to 22.21 per cent (a difference of almost 15 points). However, the activity rate of foreigners is much higher than that of the Spanish population, 75.84 per cent as opposed to 57.77 per cent (just over 18 points). This difference is due mainly to the age pyramid.

Additionally, in 2011 a negative migration balance was observed, and this trend continued through the first half of 2012. In overall figures for Spain as a whole, 195,530 persons settled there during the first six months of 2012, while 269,515 left. Of those who left, 40,625 were of Spanish nationality and 228,890 were foreigners. For the first time in many years it was evident – although caution must be exercised in interpreting the data – that more people were leaving than were coming in; emigration was higher than immigration.

For some years now, different studies have revealed that only the massive immigration of people from other continents will make it possible to maintain the current balanced population, both in the EU and in the US. Data from Eurostat (2011), especially the figures regarding birth rates and rising life expectancy, indicate that in Spain and most other EU countries there should be no doubt as to the immigration policy to follow. The only discussion would centre on the type of immigration; that is, the type of training and qualifications that immigrants should have. As Pajares (2011) points out, what has to be foreseen is that the need to attract qualified workers will not diminish in EU countries. The higher educational level of the young people who enter the job market for the first time, the continuing increase in women's employment and the training of unemployed people so as to facilitate their reincorporation into the job market are all factors that will mitigate the need for qualified workers from other countries – but they will not cancel it out (Llistar, 2009).

The future of Spain, and of the rest of the EU, continues to be filled with immigration, although to successfully weather the current crisis, the production model in place over the last decade needs to be re-examined (Pajares, 2011: 127–8). Much-needed immigration, paradoxically, has been accompanied by an increase in negative attitudes towards immigrants, as illustrated in the 2011 report by the Spanish Observatory on Racism and Xenophobia (Cea and Valles, 2011). It is well known that in times of economic crisis clichés about immigration become more prevalent. In people's everyday language, stereotypical, and therefore false, expressions start taking hold, such as: *we are being invaded; with so many immigrants, Spain is a more dangerous place; they commit crimes out of need, they arrive with nothing and start stealing; they receive more economic benefits; they are saturating the country's social services* etc. (Carretero, 2009). Also gaining strength are negative stereotypes regarding school performance (Carabaña, 2012) or the level of training that immigrants tend to have (Vallespir and Morey, 2004).

Spain's Immigration Policies

Government attention to cultural diversity in Spain is in the hands of the country's 17 Autonomous Regions, because authority in this matter is held by regional government, which logically acts in agreement with the guidelines established by the national government. National law in turn reflects the legislation adopted by the European Union.

The foundations for the treatment of immigration issues at the European level were laid in the mid 1980s. In the context of the EU, the goal of creating an internal market – the 1986 Treaty on European Union (also known as the Maastricht Treaty) – contributed to immigration being considered a question that had to be dealt with at the European level. At the Tampere European Council (Finland, 16–17 October 1999) European leaders addressed the need to build a common immigration policy as a priority for 1 May 2004.[4]

Despite declarations of this type, specific actions by EU member states in the area of migration have not had the benefit of clear guidelines and such actions have even been contradictory at times. It is reasonable to state that there is no common European policy regarding immigration, despite the repeated references that appear in official EU documents: Schengen, 1990; Amsterdam, 1997; Nice, 2001; Seville, 2002; The Hague, 2004; Lahti, 2006 etc. According to Delgado (2002), immigration is addressed more and more frequently in EU political discourse, but there have been no significant advances.

---

4   http://www.eumc.eu.int.

It appears that most progress has been made in the area of common policy related to so-called illegal immigrants. This has resulted in what has been called a framework of 'institutional discrimination' (Pajares, 2011) which leads to the social exclusion of immigrants. The missing element, in the opinion of Ilies (2009), has been ways to combat illegal immigration.

Looking at the specific initiatives set up by the Spanish government, mention must be made of the Global Programme for the Regulation and Coordination of Foreign Citizens and Immigration (*Programa Global de Regulación y Coordinación de Extranjería e Inmigración* or GRECO), which was passed in March 2001 for the period 2001–04. The introductory section indicated that this document was 'the first initiative taken in this country to address the topic of foreign nationals and immigration in all of its aspects'. According to the Dirección General de Integración de Inmigrantes/Directorate General for Immigrant Integration (2007), GRECO's main lines of action can be summarised as follows:

- the global and coordinated treatment of immigration as a necessary and desirable phenomenon for Spain, within the framework of the EU;
- the integration of resident aliens and their families, who contribute actively to the country's growth;
- the promotion of policies regulating migrant flows so as to guarantee peaceful coexistence in Spanish society;
- maintenance of the system that protects refugees and displaced persons.

The Plan for the Social Integration of Immigrants (*Plan para la Integración Social de los Inmigrantes* or PISI), was approved by the government in December 2004. This plan was intended to serve as a 'reference framework for Spain's central government, as an action proposal for the Autonomous Regions and local governments, and as a channel for active participation by civil society towards the integration of the immigrant population'. PISI was the first attempt to address the matter using a global approach, following EU guidelines: 'Integration requires that immigrants be considered in their totality, not just as workers but as citizens, with needs and requirements in the fields of education, culture, health care, relations with other populations and their participation in society.'

Without doubt, PISI was the point of departure for regional governments to start drawing up plans for the integration of the immigrant population. It also led to the creation of the Forum for Social Integration of Immigrants and the Permanent Observatory on Immigration.

Regulations concerning the rights, freedoms and social integration of foreigners in Spain (*Reglamento sobre derechos y libertades de los extranjeros en España y su integración social*), passed in December 2004, are among the pillars of Spain's current immigration policy. These regulations, which are also known as *Reglamento de extranjería*, are of an administrative nature, meaning they do not directly affect integration processes. However, according to the Directorate General for Immigrant Integration (2007), they do have beneficial effects on integration in that they facilitate immigration by legal channels and combat irregular hiring practices.

The Strategic Plan for Citizenship and Integration (*Plan Estratégico de Ciudadanía e Integración 2007–2010*) aimed to complete the process of public intervention for the integration of immigrants, and at the same time it took a new approach to immigration management (Directorate General for Immigrant Integration, 2007). The plan targets all citizens, both native and immigrant, because integration concerns all members of society, and it is based on the premise that integration policies must be addressed in a global or holistic fashion. Although some of the smaller plans comprising the Strategic Plan focus mainly on education, the majority respond to a wide array of matters, in accordance with European and national guidelines, with a view to achieving the desired integration of immigrants: employment, health, housing, social services, awareness, education, reception etc.[5]

As explained in the Strategic Plan for Citizenship and Integration, there are a number of general principals that define the philosophy of these plans:

- *equality*: rights, duties and opportunities must be the same for both the native population and the immigrant population;
- *comprehensiveness*: the entire set of issues that directly affect integration must be addressed;
- *transversality*: issues related to integration must be incorporated into all types of public intervention;
- *normalisation*: all immigrants must be included in all services provided by the government to its citizens;
- *interculturality*: cultural diversity must be considered in all interventions undertaken by the public sector;
- *participation*: the process of drawing up, implementing and evaluating the plans must involve all relevant actors, including associations of immigrants;
- *co-ordination*: the actions of central government and regional government must be coordinated, as must the actions of local bodies with those of social organisations;
- *decentralisation*: it is important to facilitate the participation of local governments and social organisations in the development of the plans (Directorate General for Immigrant Integration, 2007: 107–8).

It is also worth mentioning that many municipalities are putting in place complementary actions along these same lines. The Spanish Federation of Municipalities and Provinces has a database listing the municipalities of over 20,000 inhabitants that have an integration plan.[6]

The measures adopted by the Autonomous Regions to respond to the educational needs of immigrant children have been quite varied. According to the

---

5   http://www.aulaintercultural.org.
6   La Federación Española de Municipios y Provincias, http://www.femp.es.

information furnished by the regional governments themselves, the characteristics of these measures can be synthesised as follows (CIDE, 2009):[7]

a. The intercultural focus of education: practically all the Autonomous Regions highlight the multiculturality of their schools and the value of cultural pluralism. They also state that intercultural education should be used to strengthen attitudes of tolerance and respect. In general, it is believed that programmes should target all schoolchildren and not just immigrant pupils. Some Autonomous Regions highlight that action must be taken within the General Plan for Attention to Diversity (e.g. Asturias, Cantabria, Madrid, Navarra), while others promote programmes involving *compensatory education* (Castilla y León, Galicia, Rioja, Basque Country).

b. Reception of immigrant pupils: in general, schools in all the Autonomous Regions have reception programmes; in some cases they are included in the General Plan for Attention to Diversity (Asturias, Cantabria, Catalunya) but in most cases they are reception programmes that specifically target immigrant students (Andalusia, Balearic Islands, Canary Islands, Basque Country).

c. Organisational and curriculum-related measures: the implementation of the programmes often entails curricular adaptations and also modifications to the way schools are organised: *specific compensation actions* (Murcia, Valencia, Rioja), *intercultural workshops* (Castilla-La Mancha), *extracurricular activities* (Andalusia, Balearic Islands, Extremadura). They also receive additional human and material resources.

d. Responding to linguistic and cultural diversity: every Autonomous Region has made it a top priority to teach Spanish and, if it has one, the region's own language. Some have created a *regional linguistic and cultural plan* (e.g. Canary Islands, Catalunya, Basque Country) and practically all of them have *reception classrooms* or *linguistic support classrooms* for recently-arrived immigrant pupils. Some Autonomous Regions even have programmes in which immigrant pupils can continue learning their native language and culture (Andalusia, Aragon, Asturias, Valencia).

e. Attending to the needs of families: in general, all the Autonomous Regions have put in place two types of measures. On the one hand, emphasis is placed on receiving immigrants and helping them access the educational system, by means of *informative brochures* or meetings at the schools (Asturias, Galicia, Madrid, Basque Country, Rioja, Valencia); on the other hand, steps are taken to encourage the integration of the pupils' families in the schools (Aragon, Balearic Islands, Extremadura, Catalunya, Navarra). Various Autonomous Regions have also started a service involving *interpreters*

---

7   Centro de Investigación y Documentación Educativa (Centre for Eductional Research and Documentation).

and/or *intercultural mediators* to facilitate communication with families (Balearic Islands, Andalusia, Valencia, Catalunya, Madrid, Murcia).

f. Teacher training: all the Autonomous Regions have expanded their activities in intercultural education training, targeting both initial and ongoing training programmes. Most of them also organise events, conferences, lectures and seminars on responding to cultural diversity in schools (Andalusia, Balearic Islands, Canarias, Catalunya, Galicia).

g. Other resources: most of the Autonomous Regions have some type of special funding for the preparation of extra didactic materials to support immigrant students. Another interesting resource created by some regions are observatories focused on immigration (Galicia, Madrid, Valencia).

It must be noted that the vast majority of these measures are heavily conditioned by the ideologies of the political parties in power in the different regional governments, and that frequently the measures are little more than statements of intent, as insufficient funds have been allocated to them. Also, according to Mijares (2009), most of the specific programmes put in place by the Regional Ministries of Education continue to be based on compensatory measures, and language policies are still dominated by the deficit theory.

Immigrant Pupils in the Spanish Education System

The total number of non-Spanish pupils, not including university students, during the 2011–12 academic year was 781,446, according to the document *Evolution and Current Situation of Foreign Students in the Spanish Educational System (2011–2012)* published by the National Centre for Educational Innovation and Research (CNIIE). The difference with regard to the preceding year is insignificant (305 pupils), continuing the trend towards stabilisation in the foreign student population that began two academic years earlier, after 10 years of significant increases (see CIDE, 2013).

The evolution shown by this group of pupils, however, is not homogeneous. In primary education there has been a decrease of 13,314 pupils (4.7 per cent) and in compulsory secondary education the drop has been of 4.658 (2.1 per cent). In contrast, the number of foreign children enrolled in preschool education (age 3–6) has grown by 13,387 (10 per cent). The number of foreign pupils has also increased by 5.8 per cent at the level of post-compulsory secondary education and 9.8 per cent in *Bachillerato* (baccalaureate) programmes (pre-university secondary level).

As for the geographical area of origin, the predominance of students from Central and South America continues (36.9 per cent), followed by those from other European Union countries (30.3 per cent) and Africa (25 per cent). The countries that stand out are Morocco with 154,529 pupils, Romania with 96,914, Ecuador with 80,306 and Colombia with 49,215 pupils.

According to the preview data on education, there are also significant differences between Autonomous Regions and cities (Table 6.4): those with the highest percentage of foreign pupils are Rioja (16.3 per cent), the Balearic Islands (14.6 per cent) and Catalunya (13.6 per cent). The one with the lowest rates is Extremadura (3.3 per cent). It must also be pointed out that the percentage of foreign pupils in schools varies depending on the type of school, with the public school system having 11.33 per cent – more than twice the percentage of private schools (5.52 per cent).

Table 6.4 • Percentage of immigrant students in Spanish Autonomous Regions and cities

Area	% (rounded)
Andalucía	6
Aragón	13
Asturias (Principado de)	5
Balears (Illes)	15
Canarias	9
Catabria	7
Castilla y León	8
Castilla La Mancha	10
Cataluña	14
Comunidad Valenciana	11
Extremadura	3
Galicia	4
Madrid (Comunidad de)	14
Murcia (Region de)	12
Navarra (Comunidad Foral de)	10
País Vasco	8
La Rioja	16
Ceuta	4
Melilla	8
Total	10

Source: Spanish Ministry of Education, Culture and Sports, 2012.

In the school context, most European policies have focused primarily on acquisition of the official languages, in order to facilitate school and social integration.

Research into Cultural Diversity at School: Topics, Challenges, Concerns, Approaches and Methodological Biases.

Interculturality: A Research Topic

Interculturality in education first became a popular research topic in the 1990s, when pupils from other countries began to have significant presence in Spanish schools. For Rodríguez Izquierdo (2009), the ever-greater presence of these pupils in Spanish classrooms turned intercultural education into a fashionable subject and a social necessity. As pointed out by García Castaño et al. (2008: 23), 'it was around these schoolchildren that the discourse of interculturality took shape in Spain'.

This situation awakened a logical interest not only in citizens and the media, but also in scientists, due to both the novelty of the phenomenon and the pace at which it was evolving; and the need to analyse and understand everything related to cultural diversity (Pérez Yruela and Rinken, 2005).

Prior to this time, the only studies on intercultural education in Spain had examined the process of incorporating the Roma community into the basic education system. This group, which arrived in Spain from India around 1425, has suffered the negative effects of repeated attempts throughout Spain's history to homogenise the culture of its inhabitants. In this regard, important work has been done by Fresno Garcia (1994), Muñoz Sedano (1993), Fernández Enguita (1995), García Castaño (1995) and others. It would be unfair not to also acknowledge the rigorous work of different associations, NGOs and collectives before anybody was talking about intercultural education in Spain. Associations such as Enseñantes con gitanos, Secretariado General Gitano, Presencia Gitana[8] and many others have contributed considerably to the progress made in educational research on diversity and ethnic minorities in Spain (Murillo et al. 1995; García Castaño et al., 2008).

In the 1990s research into intercultural education became richer and more diverse, shaped as it was by a new reality: the mass arrival of people from all corners of the planet. Scientific work on this subject started to appear in various national and international databases (e.g. ERIC, Eudised, Eurybase, Dissertation Abstracts, ISOC, Teseo) and in numerous monographs. Conferences and scientific forums took place; interdisciplinary research teams were formed to study interculturality (Laboratorio de Estudios Interculturales, Colectivo INTER, Colectivo IOÉ, Grup de Recerca en Educació Intercultural, TEIM etc.); and government studies were funded and published. The policy-makers in charge of the Ministry of Education at the time gave high priority to this field, which became one of the lines of strategy of the Ministry's Centre for Educational Research and Documentation. Four events then deepened academic interest in intercultural education.

1. The first was the seminar on interculturalism and education organised by the Ministry of Education and Science in 1987. Its objective was to

---

8   See http://aecgit.pangea.org; http://www.gitanos.org; http://www.presenciagitana.org.

present the results of the Council of Europe's widely known 'Project 7' initiated in 1980, which over a period of five years studied the educational interventions taking place with the children of immigrants.

2. The second landmark event took place in 1992. It was the presentation, by the Ministry of Education and Science, of the *Report on Intercultural Education in Spain*, the response to the commitment that the European Commission had made one year earlier to all member states.

3. The third event – the 10th National Conference on Pedagogy, which also took place in 1992 and was devoted to this topic ('Interculturalism and Education in the European Perspective') – also reflects the growth of academic interest in this area.

4. The fourth event, and the one that would light the flame of institutional attention to this area of research in subsequent years, was the inclusion of this theme in the priority areas of the National Competitive Process for Educational Research Project Funding, which the Ministry of Education and Science announced in 1992 through its Centre for Educational Research and Documentation (CIDE).

Scientific Production, Advances, Challenges and Methodological Approaches in Intercultural Education Research

The scientific production related to intercultural education from the early 1990s to the present can be grouped into four large blocks by theme:

1. The schooling of immigrant children: academic development, school organisation models, teacher training, intervention models, educational proposals and the dissemination of best practices in the area of responding to diversity in inclusive classrooms.

2. The design and evaluation of specific programmes and resources aimed at providing guidance and support.

3. Bilingualism and language diversity at school.

4. Values and attitudes.

The sense of citizenship and civic values, identity and intercultural competence. The aims of these studies, and the methodological approaches used in them, have been quite varied. The very earliest studies sought to describe in statistical terms the migratory phenomenon in relation to schools and to explain, using an exploratory perspective, what was happening with these 'new schoolchildren' when they joined the school system (García Castaño et al., 2008: 24). Shortly thereafter other somewhat more ambitious studies made timid contributions to improving praxis: studies focusing on the implications arising from the incorporation of these schoolchildren into the education system; analysis of the educational practices carried out in such a context; teaching–learning methodologies; language teaching; attitudes with regard to diversity and their repercussion on the academic performance of these children. Of special importance are the works by Muñoz Repiso (1992); Martín Domínguez (1993); Calvo Buezas (1993, 1997); Bartolomé (1994); Colectivo IOÉ (1992, 1994); Mesa Franco and Sánchez (1994); Merino Fernández (1994); Díaz-Aguado and Baraja (1993); García Parejo (1994); Giménez Romero (1996); Salazar González (1996); García Castaño (1995), among others.

As Bartolomé (2004) indicates, the purpose of these studies was to provide arguments and strategies for moving towards an intercultural educational model and to offer critiques of the different policy models (assimilation, recognition, integration and pluralistic tolerance) and their possible repercussions on educational institutions. For Rodríguez Izquierdo (2009: 3), these studies revealed:

> the monocultural nature of Spanish schools and the need to address, through educational research, the design of school curricula, the skills and competencies of the educators, the creation of the best possible resources and policies for responding to the needs of all boys and girls, regardless of their cultural and ethnic origin.

In addition, it became clear that schools were responding to the challenge of multiculturality with an assimilationist and compensatory approach, since their intention was that minority cultural groups would become part of a dominant majority culture and because intervention was focused on solving specific learning problems rather than promoting integration. The intercultural focus of education, which by then had made a timid appearance in official texts, was barely perceptible in school practices (Bartolomé, 1992; Merino Fernández, 1994; Colectivo IOE, 1992b, 1995; Soriano, 1997, 1999).

The research conducted during this first period uncovered both successes and failures by schools and policy-makers in their efforts to respond to cultural diversity in the classroom. This led to the development of new lines of research and to consolidation of the idea that research should help clarify the situation and put forward ways that would help the education system fulfil the functions that society has assigned to it (Murillo et al., 1995). Some of the situations detected by these early studies included:

- the high correlation between immigration and marginality;
- the high rates of underachievement shown by these students;
- the insufficiency of resources;
- the inadequate training given to educators to help them respond to diversity while respecting identity;
- the socio-family situation of these pupils;
- ignored bilingualism and the poor command by immigrant students of the teaching language.

These issues thus became topics of new research conducted at the end of the 1990s. Rodríguez Izquierdo (2009: 18) points out that in these studies there is a great deal of 'theoretical discourses about what interculturality or multiculturality should be when it serves as a modifier of the concept of education'. Indeed, this is the purpose of the works of many authors: Grañeras Pastrana et al. (1995a); Sandín (1996), Salazar González (1996); García Castaño et al. (1996); Sales (1996); Aguado Odina et al. (1996); Mesa Franco and Sánchez Fernandez (1996); Gimenez Romero (1996); Sánchez et al. (1997); Soriano and Fernández Prados (1997); Aguirre Martínez (1997); Sánchez Fernández and Mesa Franco (1997); García Parejo (1997); Díaz-Aguado and Andrés (1997); Montes del Castillo (1998), among others.

At the beginning of the twenty-first century, scientific production on this subject grew exponentially, and at the same time the studies became more critical. Recurring themes in these studies include: the process of getting immigrant children enrolled at school; educational intervention models; didactic proposals; teaching/learning methods; the training of educators; bilingualism, prejudices and stereotypes; equity and social inclusion. During the first 10 years of this century, there were increasing numbers of studies about the attitudes of Spaniards towards foreigners; the development of ethnic identity in children and adolescents in a multicultural context; the condemnation of segregating educational practices; the construction of an intercultural and democratic citizenry; and the socio-educational situation of second-generation immigrants.

Currently, new subject areas are being explored in intercultural education, in studies whose aims are to:

- evaluate the programmes, schools and resources designed and their implementation;
- dismantle the stereotypes and the discursive debate related to the consequences or effects that the presence of immigrant children in schools might cause;
- argue that some of the labels – such as 'problems in relation to the schooling of immigrant children' – are in fact problems connected to schooling in general that existed in Spain's classrooms before the arrival of the so-called 'new schoolchildren';
- prove that success/failure at school can only be explained through multicausal models;
- justify the need to break with the uniformisation tendency present in studies that consider all immigrant children to be in the same 'collective';
- offer suggestions about how to work on intercultural competencies in the classroom, with proposals for effective and efficient intervention aimed at all pupils;
- ensure that the education system not only facilitates the incorporation of all children into the compulsory stages of education, but also that it allows all students to enjoy the same kind of experience at school and have the same chances of continuing to secondary education. Some studies now being conducted aim to develop new visions of the meaning of educational

achievement in the classroom, while others describe and analyse a variety of school experiences.

- establish commonly agreed indicators of the satisfaction (here meaning well-being) felt by the different immigrant groups present in classrooms;
- contribute relevant information to selecting indicators with which to evaluate educational policy and practice, from the perspective of intercultural education;
- guide decision-making in educational policies and practices to ensure that they are coherent with an intercultural focus.

Other topics addressed in the most recent studies undertaken in Spain include: the gender perspective; relationships among intercultural education, attention to diversity and inclusive schooling; and defence of the right to be different. Of particular importance here are works by Bartolomé (2000, 2004); Bartolomé and Cabrera (2003); Martín Rojo et al. (2003); Santos Rego (2003); Naval (2003); Montes Pérez (2004); Buendía, González and Pozo (2004); Soriano (2004); Brunet et al. (2005); Carbonell et al. (2005); García Castaño and Pulido (2005); Marín Díaz (2006); Pérez Sola (2006); Essomba (2006); Ponce Solé (2007), Sánchez (2007); Ortiz Cobo (2006); Cabrera Pérez (2008); Dietz et al. (2007); García-Cano et al. (2008, 2010); Aguado Odina (2011); Pozo et al. (2011); Rebollo (2012); Márquez Lepe et al. (2012); and Aguado Odina and Ballesteros (2012), among others.

These studies have been presented at a number of different conferences and events organised by highly prestigious national associations in the field of social sciences and, more specifically, education. The Spanish Society of Pedagogy and the Interuniversity Association of Research in Pedagogy are two of the organisations that have embraced this topic and have promoted exchange between researchers at their conferences and in their scholarly journals.

As indicated above, that intercultural education has become a matter of institutional interest and concern is evident through its place in national and regional programmes for the funding of educational research and in it being considered a preferential field of research and innovation by successive policy-makers leading the Ministry of Education over the past two decades. In this regard, we would like to draw attention to the Centre for Educational Research and Documentation (CIDE) and the National Centre for Educational Innovation and Research (CNIIE) – attached to the Ministry of Education, Culture and Sports – for their efforts in disseminating scientific production.

The economic and ideological crisis that Spain is currently experiencing is, without doubt, a turning point in the treatment and protagonism that this theme has received over the past 20 years or so. The budget-slashing policies of Spain's current administration is having an enormous impact and is causing very significant regression, not just in the social and educational rights to which all citizens – including these collectives – are entitled but also in the commitment and ability of schools to respond to the diversity of people, groups and languages and to make use of cultural and language plurality as a valuable educational resource.

Now more than ever this line of research must continue, and it must defend the argument that interculturality is the best possible approach for defining educational proposals, rising above the vision that many schools have of diversity as a problem, associating it with deficiencies that must be overcome and compensated (Aguado and Ballesteros, 2012).

A wide range of research methodologies has been used in these studies. Methodological developments have been heavily conditioned by the incorporation of social epistemology into educational research, with the consequence of greater presence of social, cultural and historical factors in scientific production (Colás, 2001). As suggested by Murillo (2004), research into intercultural education in Spain has grown hand in hand with educational research.

Most studies on intercultural education conducted in Spain prior to the 1990s followed the methodologies of descriptive and correlational research. Therefore, survey-based research, quasi-experimental studies and *ex post facto* studies played a leading role in these research efforts. However, over the last two decades there have been more and more projects looking at the socio-educational situation from a global and comprehensive perspective, using a wide array of techniques and methods. This has resulted in research in the field showing a tendency towards complementarity, while at the same time more qualitative methodologies – and others based on interaction, observation, consultation and discussion – have also gained strength. Ethnographic studies, evaluative research, action research, case studies, participatory research and descriptive studies on development are the approaches comprising the methodological panorama in this field. Discussion groups, observational registries, ethnographic interviews and life stories are some of the strategies most commonly used for gathering information. Fortunately, there are fewer and fewer studies that restrict their exploration to the information provided by a single instrument, as it is increasingly recognised that such studies have a limited ability to make useful contributions to decisions that seek to improve the situation in schools.

García Fernández (2006) points out that research in intercultural education has its own set of difficulties that are derived from the conceptual and methodological limitations inherent in the field. The ambiguity of the concept of intercultural education; the disparity of criteria used to characterise the research aim; the ideological and cultural bias affecting many researchers in their studies; and the difficulty of accessing the target population due to its particular situation (mobility, irregular legal status etc.) are some of the problems present in these studies, making it necessary, as García Fernández points out, to exercise great caution both epistemologically and methodologically.

Administrative Regulations, Programmes and Resources for Responding to Cultural Diversity in Schools: Innovations, Reproductions and Best Practices

When the percentage of immigrant children in Spanish schools became significant, the cultural and linguistic reality in schools changed, generating a new context that required specific responses. A brand new educational panorama thus arises which, as discussed in the previous section, is the object not only of a great deal of research but also of numerous administrative and technical regulations – some more fortunate than others – the purpose of which is to respond to two situations in need of an educational response:

1. to attend to students having specific educational needs due to their recent incorporation in Spain's education system;
2. to give all students new competencies that will foster harmonious coexistence in today's intercultural schools and society.

These educational needs are the foundations for the intercultural education policies and practices that have gradually been put in place in the Spanish education system, as will be explained below. The measures were implemented little by little but they now comprise a large package of educational principles, actions, teaching resources, organisational models, bibliographies etc. and configure the Spanish model of intercultural education.

Educational Responses to Culturally Diverse Students and Students Recently Incorporated into the School System

In this area of action we find two groups of students, or measures according to the target population: a) educational measures for students with specific needs for support as a consequence of their recent incorporation (children who have never before attended school; disparities between the education system in Spain and the country of origin; emotional maladjustment etc.); and b) educational measures for immigrant students new to Spanish schools, to encourage their speedy integration.

Educational measures for students with specific needs are included in the decrees and orders that each Autonomous Region issues in its endeavour to respond to the cultural diversity of the student body. In some regions, these needs are attended following the same protocol as is followed for other students in need of specific support to help them reach the educational objectives corresponding to their grade, while other regions have established specific protocols for attending to needs derived from cultural diversity. In all cases, an array of rules and regulations dictate the procedures for the early detection of needs, for making diagnoses and for implementing measures – which may be ordinary (within the classroom), extraordinary (curricular adaptations) and in some cases even exceptional (such as enrolment in special schools or programmes). In general, the measures consist of educational support and reinforcement.

The second type of measures, which target all immigrant pupils, are often provided in combination with the preceding ones; and at other times they are provided within intercultural education programmes targeting all students, both foreign-born and native. It is this second group of measures that includes the greater part of the actions targeting immigrant students, the measures that each school must include in its 'Attention to Student Diversity Plan'. These measures tend to focus on the reception of immigrant students and on providing information and support to families unfamiliar with the Spanish education systems and community resources, etc.

Because Spain is divided into Autonomous Regions, not all regions or all schools have adopted the same measures, although a series of actions can be found throughout them, as some reviews have shown (CIDE, 2005; Grañeras Pastrana and Díaz-Caneja, 2010). The actions common to the majority of the Autonomous Regions are described below:

a. *Reception programmes* These are sometimes put in place by the Regional Ministry of Education and at other times by the schools themselves. They include information for families, the printing of informative brochures in different languages, actions designed to enhance the family–school relationship, the assignment to each new student of 'student-guides' who accompany the newcomers during their first few weeks at the school, etc.

b. *Teaching of the host country language* Although there are differences among the Autonomous Regions, these classes pursue the same objectives in all cases: to give new students the skills in the school's teaching language that they need to take part in regular classes. In some places other public administrations also provide language reinforcement for students and their families, outside of school hours.

c. *Teaching of the native language and culture* These activities take place outside of school hours, and target children from countries with which the Spanish government has signed an agreement. Examples are the 'Portuguese language and culture programme', offered through cooperation with the government of Portugal, and the 'Arabic language and Moroccan culture programme', in cooperation with Morocco. Some Autonomous Regions are considering the possibility of these subjects becoming part of the elective curriculum, and the construction of curricular materials in different languages.

d. *Education programmes* These allow specific actions to be designed for foreign-born students, practically at the individual level. Such actions may include: flexibilisation of school enrolment procedures, organisation of curricular support groups until the student achieves the competencies corresponding to their grade, etc.

e. *Teacher training programmes* A great deal of effort has been devoted to this type of measure. Training has followed two paths: specific training and advisory services for educators who have direct contact with foreign-born students in their classrooms; training for educators who have voluntarily started intercultural education programmes at their schools and who are involved in the reception of immigrant students and their families, and in the design, development and coordination of activities and their evaluation.

f. *Incorporation of other types of professionals* In many Autonomous Regions, with local government support, different kinds of professionals are joining the school, such as reception counsellors or interculturality coordinators, teachers of native languages and cultures and, particularly, intercultural mediators. Their role is to facilitate awareness and communication among all members of the educational community; provide direct guidance to immigrant students; to help reach consensus and establish rules for harmonious coexistence; to inform and receive new families at the school, promoting knowledge of basic cultural guidelines, translation and reinforcement of material in the native language etc. Intercultural mediation has been instrumental in fomenting attitudes of inclusion and respect for cultural diversity.

g. *Resource centres* These have appeared with the goal of supporting educators and furnishing the materials they need. They are usually part of the teacher training and guidance centres put in place by educational authorities and of the specific web platforms of each Autonomous Region. In parallel, web platforms have been started by research groups and collectives concerned about intercultural education. Of special interest in this area are the forums and platforms devoted to best practices in intercultural education. These developments will be discussed in greater detail in the sections devoted to resources.

h. *Different ways to organise schools* These are measures adopted by the regional education authorities to facilitate the integration of immigrant children. The most relevant are: plans to facilitate the school enrolment of immigrant children soon after their arrival in Spain; the promotion of normalised incorporation into schools and improved accessibility; the prevention of absenteeism and the promotion of permanence; the balanced distribution of immigrant students among the classes; flexibilisation of age requirements for entering different grades; increased admissions in areas with high demand; reserving spaces and funds according to forecasts for new immigrant students expected to arrive throughout the academic year; reduction of class sizes for students who have educational compensation needs. In some Autonomous Regions more specific measures have been adopted, such as the incorporation of curricular content adapted to these needs; the creation of special schools with singular educational activity in areas with a predominance of such needs; the hiring of teaching support staff etc. Finally, also worth highlighting are efforts to encourage participation by immigrant families in all school representation bodies, such as school councils, guidance departments, parent associations and other groups active at the school. Other measures of this type that seek to respond to school diversity include coordination and exchange of experiences among and between schools and external institutions or initiatives.

i. *Community measures aimed at the families of immigrant children and at minorities* These measures are put in place by other government bodies or by local organisations, sometimes in collaboration with schools and sometimes in parallel. The content of such measures ranges from language support to guidance regarding relevant educational, health, work and social resources and legislation etc.

Specific Programmes Designed to Give Students New Competencies that Will Foster Harmonious Coexistence in Today's Intercultural Schools and Society

Intercultural education programmes in schools began to appear alongside the migratory phenomenon, and the purpose of all such programmes is two-fold: first, to raise positive awareness regarding immigration, viewing it as more of an opportunity than a disadvantage; and second, to foment in all students (majorities and minorities) competencies conducive to intercultural interaction, based on respect for and tolerance of difference.

There has been a wide range of programme modalities and modes of organisation, such as funding and support. The most common are the programmes that the schools themselves put in place, with incentives and specific funding from the education authorities; and those put in place by other government branches and local associations in collaboration with the schools. In some Autonomous Regions these programmes form part of the 'General Plan on Immigration' designed by each regional government.

The themes most commonly addressed by these programmes have been the educational and social inclusion of immigrant students and their families; the eradication of racism, xenophobia and any other type of exclusion present in schools as a by-product of cultural diversity; and the promotion of the values and attitudes that are necessary in interculturality. All have the three-fold aim of educating in the values of equality, justice and social equity; preventing conflicts derived from cultural differences; and deepening the educational community's knowledge about the cultures of origin of the students at the school.

Material Resources

Parallel to the creation of policies that responded to the new needs at schools, and to the design of theoretical models that justified the implementation of certain educational actions, an infinite number of didactic materials have been developed to guide and support intercultural education. These have been created with the involvement of the regional or national educational authorities, the schools themselves – through various groups and teachers' associations – and research groups in different disciplines.

As a result of this proliferation of material, new physical and virtual spaces have been created to compile and house all these educational resources; to make them available to teachers and intercultural schools, and to forums for debate and experience sharing. All Autonomous Regions have specific resource centres and web portals whose purpose is to inform and support the work of teachers. Among these resource centres, the following deserve special mention because they function at the national level and are of significant magnitude: Resource Centre for Attention to Cultural Diversity in Education,, Intercultural Workshop Portal; Network of Intercultural Schools (Spanish Education and Popular Culture League).

Resource Centre for Attention to Cultural Diversity in Education/Centro de recursos para la atención a la diversidad en educación (CREADE)

This centre was created by the Spanish Ministry of Education through CIDE as part of its specific line of action initiated in the area of intercultural education. It aims to offer resources to support educators and to encourage research and innovation in intercultural education. It has funded, promoted and conducted studies and reports related to the educational response to the cultural diversity of students. This web portal compiles material prepared by the ministry and by other bodies, and has specific areas for each Autonomous Region showing regulations and specific actions.

Intercultural Workshop Portal

This is a project undertaken by the Federation of Teachers (FETE-UGT) with participation of and funding by the Directorate General for Immigrant Integration of the Spanish Ministry of Labour and Immigration; the European Fund for Integration (EFI); and the European Union and the Institute for Teacher Training, Research and Innovation (IFFIE) of the Spanish Ministry of Education. It appears in different languages and has a forum through which users can interact and share experiences. It has an outstanding digital library organised by subject matter, and a specific area devoted to teaching tools to help teachers in their work in the classroom.

One of the most relevant actions of the Intercultural Workshop has been the publication of the 'White Paper on Intercultural Education', with the participation of countless professionals from different sectors of the political and educational spheres. The book makes proposals regarding: a) educational policies to foment and improve intercultural education, such as research, groupings of schools and resources, different modalities of coordination between Autonomous Regions and schools etc.; b) strategies to follow in teacher training; and, c) research- and experience-based action in schools. Some of these lines of action propose increasing the autonomy of the educational community; making language issues part of the Educational Project that each school must develop; using ICT (especially for multilingual computer-based resources) to help close the communication gap; carrying out actions of solidarity involving educational support for populations in socially and culturally disadvantaged populations; evaluating the actions of schools and teachers in terms of inclusivity and interculturality; making academic counselling a core element of individualised learning throughout the compulsory stages of education; and also different actions in the community and with families.

Network of Intercultural Schools

This is attached to the NGO Education and Popular Culture League, comprised primarily of educators interested in contributing to a participatory and egalitarian society. Among its actions and projects is the *Network of Intercultural Schools*, which was created not only to promote and support intercultural programmes and actions, but also to give more visibility to the successful practices being put in place in schools to respond to cultural diversity. Besides exchanging materials and experiences, the network formulates joint action proposals and organises training sessions. This project is funded by the European Fund for Integration and the Directorate General of Immigrant Integration.

This network also has an interesting publication, 'Network of Intercultural Schools: Basic Proposals'. To draw up these proposals three basic principles were kept in mind: a) the importance of a sense of citizenship and civic values above any other socio-cultural considerations; b) the global and transversal nature of intercultural education; and c) interrelations among all the actions and all the people involved in the educational community. The most relevant proposals include:

- The tasks involved in the interculturalisation of the school should be distributed among the school's entire educational staff.
- All languages of origin present at the school should be recognised and respected.
- Interaction and exchange between schools and people from other segments of the community, other regions and other countries should be promoted.
- Education in values and in education for citizenship and civic values should be planned with more awareness and monitoring in relation to interculturality projects.
- The knowledge and life experiences of each child should be included in the teaching and learning process.
- The linguistic, cultural and political plurality of Spain and its Autonomous Regions should be recognised and valued.

This network's relevance lies in the fact that it is comprised of active professionals in the field of education, and the materials are prepared using successful experiences in schools. One example is the publication 'Best Practices: Schools and

Intercultural Co-Existence', which was published in 2006 with the participation of various educators from schools in Madrid, Málaga and Murcia. They also recently published the book *Interculturality and Citizenship: Network of Intercultural Schools* (2010), which suggests some keys to achieving an intercultural school, based on analysis of past experiences. The major challenges of intercultural education, as indicated in the authors' discourse, is that intercultural education must be neither a pedagogical project on attention to immigrants nor a school discourse. Instead, it should be a social and political project on human relationships between people who are socially and culturally differentiated and who live in democratic, pluralistic and multicultural contexts (López Cuesta et al., 2010).

Therefore, actions that are conducive to intercultural education are those that promote coexistence and acceptance of others with their differences, and those that ensure that 100 per cent of the student body acquire the competencies considered basic and indispensable. In consequence, the best practices in intercultural education are those that target all students and involve all teachers, through all the different curricular areas, and in which the entire educational community takes part. These actions must be present in all school documents (the Educational Project that each school must have, its plan to achieve harmonious co-existence, diversity plans, immigrant student reception plans etc.). The activities must not be performed in a decontextualised manner, as if following the individual steps of a recipe. Finally, another key to achieving intercultural education is that these values must be present in all decisions regarding school organisation (groups, teaching staff, support services, complementary activities etc.), and they must be based on a thorough analysis of the situation and the needs of everyone involved.

Other Educational Resources

At a more specific level, both geographically and thematically, research groups, associations and collectives have been formed to work in the area of intercultural education. Such groups often give rise to virtual spaces with the same aims: to share resources and create forums for debate. They include:

- GREDI, at the University of Barcelona, with vast experience in intercultural research. Their publications are available on their website.[9]
- INTER, a group associated with the National University of Distance Education (UNED), comprised of researchers and Spanish and non-Spanish educators. This group carries out research and is also involved in training and cooperation activities with other institutions.
- HUM-665, of the University of Almería. This pioneering group in the research and evaluation of intercultural education has forums and annual conferences where experiences are presented and analysed.

---

9 http://www.ub.edu/gredi.

- Amani, a collective of teaching professionals, is known for its methodological proposals for intervention and its attention on peaceful co-existence and conflict management.
- EduAlter. This network covers current topics on education for peace, development and interculturality, and is funded by various educational bodies in Catalunya. This web portal offers resources and information, including intercultural education, in the form of books, games, videos, didactic materials etc. This space offers educational resources organised by subject matter, such as learning about other cultures, discrimination and racism, migration, working with families, language learning etc.

Other resources considered 'best practices' because of their contribution to intercultural education have been: *intercultural mediation*, which has helped achieve peaceful co-existence among groups; *translation and interpretation services*, which have facilitated communication and interaction between schools and immigrant families; cooperation programmes with families, which have proven to be very influential in improving the academic performance of immigrant pupils; and *community programmes and actions* that promote interculturality.

Successes and Failures in Research and Intervention in Intercultural Education in Spain

The conceptual and practical evolution of intercultural education in Spain cannot be understood without first understanding the relationship between research, action and legislation. One of the aims of research in this field has been to guide decision-making in educational policies and practices with an intercultural focus. However, some of the political decisions taken in Spain have responded more to political and ideological beliefs than to research findings, which has led to measures that in some cases are incoherent and inappropriate.

At the EU level, there has been a great interest in creating a common immigration policy, and emphasis has been placed on the need to attend to immigrants from a global perspective, using a comprehensive approach. However, the actions taken by the member states reveal that such a common policy is far from becoming reality, one reason being the diversity of the member states. For example, Spain has had to submit to legislation that focuses more on border control than integration because controlling borders is considered by many to be the dominant need in Europe as a whole. However, in recent decades Spain has joined the group of countries with the highest percentage of foreigners. It has thus had to develop its own distinct migratory policy, which has not always coincided with the needs and interests of the rest of Europe.

At a more specific level, Spain is differentiated from many other countries in that in a relatively short period it has had to design measures that allowed and facilitated the incorporation, attention and integration of immigrants into its society. These measures are reflected generically both in Spain's national plans and in those of all its Autonomous Regions.

Apart from the principles and philosophy of the strategic plan on citizenship based on the EU principles adopted in 2004, in our opinion one of the most interesting ideas to be developed in Spain has been to give immigration plans a comprehensive structure. And at the school level, current legislation requires appropriate measures for addressing students with special educational needs, obviously including those from cultures different from native ones.

While generally speaking the political and administrative decisions of the various Autonomous Regions have followed this line, a certain inequality between them has been perceived. This comes not just from the inequality of sensibilities and resources devoted to the integration of the immigrant population, but also from the distribution of immigrants in national territory, as some areas have been sites of concentration and others of only slight presence.

After analysing more than two decades of research on intercultural education and political, administrative and professional responses to diversity in schools, we can now confirm that this subject garners great interest, and that what used to be an emerging theme has become a main line of strategy of the various government administrations that have been in power in Spain over the past decades, and a very important presence in these administrations' research agendas.

In Spain, governmental responses (at national, regional and local level) to the changes occurring in the educational context were slow in coming, in part due to the mistaken idea transmitted by the European Union that these migrations were transitory. These responses soon became the object of study. It was evident, in some cases, that interventions had not taken the best approach, treating intercultural education as a set of actions exclusively for the immigrant population and considering 'difference' to be a deficit in need of compensation. The earliest institutional responses were assistance-oriented and left wide gaps that had to be covered by social collectives and organisations.

It is true that the research itself (its aims, methodology, sources of information etc.) contributed in part to a mistaken conceptualisation of intercultural education. Yet it would be unfair not to acknowledge the intense activity of various research groups in trajectories marked not just by voluminous scientific production referred to above, but also by the activist role they performed, denouncing and criticising the compensatory nature of most of the intervention measures put in place (e.g. transition classes, specific groupings, language reinforcement); measures that do not affect the curriculum, the school or the decisions made there, but rather only foreign-born immigrants and their ethnic or cultural group. These research groups showed great interest in breaking with the uniform vision often used to analyse diversity. They were also intent on providing tools that would help people look at others from different perspectives so as to understand how they think and feel. The prevailing idea was that only by respecting diversity could benefits be had by all schoolchildren and their families, and at all schools.

These criticisms, derived from the research conducted, have also been made with respect to the sources of information used. It is widely acknowledged that statistical studies on the migratory phenomenon must be improved, since their tendency to rely solely on educational authorities as sources is not good practice. As pointed out by García Castaño et al. (2008: 47), the educational authorities are 'sources with which we should be more critical, and we would be if we really knew how such authorities construct their data'. It is vital that other sources be taken into account, sources that do not carry erroneous interpretations such as concentrations of immigrant pupils or the almost inevitable classification of pupils by nationality. Research has demonstrated that these statistical studies can be used as methodological resources, but not as elements that will make a difference or that can explain inequality.

The experience of immigrant pupils at school and the essential role of teachers as primary actors in understanding and making the most of the multicultural and plurilingual nature of schools are some of the most recurrent themes in studies conducted. The most common aims include diagnosis of the educational system in relation to specific cultural groups and suggesting specific proposals that schools can use to respond to the cultural and linguistic diversity of their students. Increasing numbers of studies focus on the evaluation of specific programmes and mechanisms put in place to respond to diversity in schools. Their purpose is not so much to determine their efficiency, effectiveness, success or failure as to understand their real effects and impacts on the academic lives of the boys and girls who have been touched by them. Research into the acquisition of the teaching language by immigrant pupils is shifting to a new focal point. Instead of examining the degree of language acquisition by these pupils it is now looking more at the uses given to their languages by children in different areas of communication and interaction, of which the school is but one example.

Among concerns now being debated and investigated in Spain are how to build a sense of citizenship and civic value in a situation of ethnic and cultural diversity; and how to generate a feeling of identity and community belonging in the face of different and sometimes contradictory cultural realities (Pozo et al., 2011).

Certainly one of the successes in Spain with regard to research in intercultural education has been the support not only from the government but also from social organisations and collectives. Although briefly mentioned above, it is necessary to underline that a major shift is occurring in terms of governmental support for research, development and innovation in intercultural education. It may be that the current economic downturn – marked by policies of passivity and social, economic, cultural and educational cutbacks – will bring about a recession in the subject at hand that proves very difficult to overcome. Yet the prediction is that Spain will continue to receive immigrants, and at the same time will continue to see many of its nationals leave for other parts of the world, for which they will need intercultural competencies.

As discussed earlier, the measures and programmes put in place to respond to cultural diversity in schools have been quite varied. Of particular interest are the reception-related measures such as Catalunya's 'reception counsellors', 'special classrooms' and 'workshops to facilitate the adaptation and learning of basic instrumental concepts', or Andalusia's 'temporary classrooms for language adaptation'. While these measures initially fulfilled an important purpose, over time some of them have been redefined while others have been phased out, to be replaced by new initiatives and resources calling for different types of practice. Today's practices must aim to provide an education that gives everyone the opportunity to decide their own lives; to use their own abilities; to take care of themselves and others; to maintain high expectations and interests; and to enjoy full social and political participation (Aguado and Ballesteros, 2012).

The greatest shortcoming of the various programmes implemented over the decades has been the concept that they transmit of culture and interculturality, which focuses attention almost exclusively on others (Gómez Lara-Colectivo Amani, 2010). Although educational principles have been based on integration and mutual enrichment, the targets of the intercultural education have often been only immigrants or foreigners. The educational policies have had as a core concept knowledge of cultural diversity as a means to mutual enrichment; but, as demonstrated by García-Cano et al. (2008: 159), 'this is more an expression of the social desirability of peaceful co-existence than of comprehension and acceptance of how, in situations of equality between different groups, culture rebuilds itself and changes, giving rise to new ways of acting that affect both groups'. These drawbacks have been hotly debated and have led to countless theoretical documents that review existing models of intercultural education and contribute new ones (Aguado, 2003; Agrela and Gil Araujo, 2005; Besalú, 2002; Carrasco, 2003; Dietz, 2003; Essomba, 2006; Jordán and Castella, 2001; Soriano and Osorio Méndez, 2008, among others).

At this time, the national movements most committed to intercultural education are encouraging schools to revise their educational principles in such a way that intercultural education does not act as an element of socialisation that transmits a single culture, but rather as something that helps us understand the world we live in and be prepared to face its challenges, and for this we need to be told things from another point of view, not just from our own ethnocentric perspective (Gómez Lara-Colectivo Amani, 2010).

Despite the government's current apathy and diminished activity, two decades of hard work have had the effect of extending, in practice, the culture of attention to diversity and training in intercultural education. Moreover, with the research findings and progress made in this field, intercultural education has gradually come to be understood as one of the few arms available to society to promote – not just at the theoretical and legislative level but also in practice – the values of tolerance, equality and solidarity, responding to cultural diversity in a way that recognises the different identities in a collective space (Banks, 2004).

We therefore need more of these educational practices: practices that transform isolated actions into everyday actions; practices that are embedded within curricula and aimed at all pupils; educational practices involving innovative actions that contribute to research, transfer and betterment of the educational act; practices based on the principles and values of best practices in intercultural education, which are all those practices based on recognition of human diversity as normality and the assumption of equality as an ethical undertaking for educators (Aguado and Ballesteros, 2012). In consequence, best practices in research will be those that address this phenomenon in all its complexity, and not just as the expression of an immediate event.

References

Agrela Romero, B. and Gil Araujo, S. (2005). Constructing otherness. The management of immigration and diversity in the Spanish context. *Migration: European Journal of International Migration and Ethnic Relations*, 43–4.

Aguado Odina, M.T. (1996). *Educación Multicultural, su Teoría y su Práctica*. Madrid: Universidad Nacional de Educación a Distancia (UNED).

Aguado Odina, T. (2003). *Pedagogía intercultural*. Madrid: McGraw-Hill.

Aguado Odina, T. (2010). *Diversidad e Igualdad en Educación*. Madrid: UNED.

Aguado Odina, T. (2011). *Diversidad cultural y logros de los estudiantes en educación obligatoria*. Madrid: Ministerio de Educación.

Aguado Odina, T. and Ballesteros, B. (2012). Equidad y diversidad en la Educación Obligatoria. *Revista de Edcación*, 358, 12–17.

Aguirre Martínez, M.C. (ed.) (1997). *Estudio comparativo entre la adquisición del español como primera lengua y la adquisición del español como segunda lengua para su aplicación metodológica a la enseñanza del español a inmigrantes*. Unpublished document. Madrid: CIDE.

Bartolomé, M. (1992). *Diagnóstico de las diferencias étnicas y de los procesos desarrollados en la Educación Primaria*. Unpublished document. Madrid: CIDE.

Bartolomé, M. (2000). *La construcción de la identidad en contextos multiculturales*. Madrid: MEC.

Banks, J.A. (2004). Teaching for social justice, diversity and citizenship in a global World. *Educational Forum*, 68, 289–98.

Bartolomé, M. (1997). *Diagnóstico a la Escuela Multicultural*. Barcelona: Cedecs.

Bartolomé, M. (2004). Identidad y ciudadanía: hacia una sociedad intercultural. *Bordón*, 56 (1), 65–79.

Bartolomé, M. (ed.) (1994). *Diagnóstico de las diferencias étnicas y de los procesos desarrollados en la Educación Primaria*. Unpublished document. Madrid: CIDE.

Bartolomé, M. and Cabrera, F. (2003). Sociedad multicultural y ciudadanía. Hacia una sociedad y ciudadanía interculturales. *Revista de Educación*, special issue, 169–89.

Besalú, X. (2002). *Diversidad cultural y educación*. Madrid: Síntesis.

Brunet, I., Pastor, I. and Belzunegui, A. (2005). *El calidoscopi de la immigració. La inserció educativa dels immigrants al Camp de Tarragona.* Barcelona: Portic.

Buendía, L., Gonzalez, D. and Pozo, M.T. (2004). *Temas fundamentales en la investigación educativa.* Madrid: La Muralla.

Cabrera Pérez, L. (ed.) (2008). *La integración cultural y social de inmigrantes latinoamericanos. Inquietudes y sugerencias para políticas de cambio.* Madrid: Universitas.

Calvo Buezas, T. (ed.) (1993). *Igualdad de oportunidades respetando las diferencias. Encuesta escolar.* Unpublished document. Madrid: CIDE.

Calvo Buezas, T. (1997). *Racismo y solidaridad de españoles, portugueses y latinoamericanos. Los jóvenes ante otros pueblos y culturas.* Madrid: Ediciones Libertarias.

Comunitat Autònoma de les Illes Balears (CAIB) (2005). *II Plan Integral de Atención a las Personas Inmigradas de las Illes Balears.* Palma: Govern de les Illes Balears. http://dgimmi.caib.es [retrieved 1 February 2013].

Carbonell, J., Simó, N. and Tort, A. (2005). *Magrebíes en las aulas. Municipio, escuela e inmigración: un caso a debate.* Barcelona: EUMO-Octaedro.

Carabaña, J. (2012). *Concentración de inmigrantes y resultados escolares. Una falsa alarma.* http://www.realinstitutoelcano.org [retrieved 1 February 2013].

Carrasco, S. (1997). Usos y abusos del concepto de cultura. *Cuadernos de Pedagogía*, 264, 14–18.

Carrasco, S. (2003). La escolarización de los hijos e hijas de inmigrantes y de minorías étnicoculturales. *Revista de Educación*, 330, 99–136.

Carretero, N. (2009). *Inmigración: desmontando tópicos. Ocho mentiras que nos hacen xenófobos.* http://www.sinanimodenada.blogspot.com [retrieved 1 February 2013].

Cea, M.Á. and Valles, M.S. (2011). *Evolución del racismo y la xenofobia en España.* Informe 2011. Madrid: Ministerio de Trabajo e Inmigración.

CIDE (2005). *La atención al alumnado inmigrante en el sistema educativo español.* Madrid: Ministerio de Educación y Ciencia.

CIDE (2009). *La atención al alumnado inmigrante en el sistema educativo en España.* Madrid: Ministerio de Educación y Ciencia.

CIDE (2013). *Evolución y situación actual del alumnado extranjero en el sistema educativo español (2011–2012).* Madrid: Ministerio de Educación y Ciencia. http://www.mecd.gob.es/cniie/investigacion-innovacion/educacion-intercultural/informes.html [retrieved 1 February 2013].

Colás, P. (2001). Educación e investigación en la sociedad del conocimiento: Enfoques emergentes. *Revista de Investigación Educativa (RIE)*, 19, 2, 291–313.

Colectivo IOE (1992a). *Estadísticas oficiales sobre extranjeros en España.* Unpublished document. Madrid: CIDE.

Colectivo IOE (1992b). *La educación intercultural en España.* Unpublished document. Madrid: CIDE.

Colectivo IOE (1994). Extraños, distintos, iguales o las paradojas de la alteridad. Discursos de los españoles sobre los extranjeros, *Revista de Educación*, 307, 17–51.

Colectivo IOE (1995). *La pluralidad cultural en el sistema educativo. Posibilidades de una educación intercultural desde los valores y actitudes de los agentes del proceso educativo*. Unpublished document. Madrid: CIDE.

Díaz-Aguado, M.J. and Baraja, A. (1993). *Interacción educativa y desventaja sociocultural. Un modelo de intervención para favorecer la adaptación escolar en contextos interétnicos*. Unpublished document. Madrid: CIDE.

Díaz-Aguado, M.J. and Andrés, MT. (1997). *Educación intercultural y aprendizaje cooperativo en contextos heterogéneos*. Unpublished document. Madrid: CIDE.

Dietz, G. (2003). *Multiculturalismo, interculturalidad y educación. Una aproximación antropológica*. Granada: Universidad de Granada y CIESAS.

Dietz, G., García-Cano, M., Márquez, E., Ruiz, F. and Pozo, M.T. (2007). *Las competencias bilingües y biculturalesde los niños y niñas trasnmigrantes Hispano-alemanas. Estudio de caso en Granada*. Editorial Laboratorio de Estudios Interculturales. Universidad de Granada.

Delgado, L. (2002). *La inmigración en Europa: realidades y políticas*. http://www.iesam.csic.es/doctrab2/dt-0218.pdf [retrieved 1 February 2013].

Dirección General de Integración de Inmigrantes (2004). *Plan para la Integración Social de Inmigrantes*. Madrid: Secretaría de Estado de Inmigración y Emigración.

Dirección General de Integración de Inmigrantes (2007). *Plan Estratégico de Ciudadanía e integración 2007–2010*. Madrid: Secretaría de Estado de Inmigración y Emigración.

Essomba, M.A. (2006). *Liderar escuelas interculturales e inclusivas. Equipos directivos y profesorado ante la diversidad cultural y la inmigración*. Barcelona: Graó.

Essomba, M.A. (2008). *Díez ideas clave. La gestión de la diversidad cultural en la escuela*. Barcelona: Graó.

Eurostat (2011). *Estadísticas de migración y población migrante*. http://www.epp.eurostat.ec.europa.eu/statistics_explained/index.php/ … /es [retrieved 1 February 2013].

Eurydice (2009). *Integrating Immigrant Children into Schools in Europe*. Brussels: Eurydice. http://www.eurydice.org [retrieved 1 February 2013].

Fernández Enguita, M. (1995). *La escolarización del pueblo gitano*. Granada: Laboratorio de Antropología de la Universidad de Granada.

Fresno García, J.M. (1994). *Evaluación de la incorporación de los niños y niñas gitanos a la enseñanza básica*. Unpublished document. Madrid: CIDE.

García-Cano, M., Márquez, E. and Agrela, B. (2008). Cuándo, por qué y para qué la educación intercultural. *Discursos y praxis de la educación intercultural*. Papers, 89, 146–67.

García-Cano, M., González, E., Márquez, E., Ruiz, F., Dietz, G. and Pozo, M.T. (2010). Estrategias Bilingües e interculturales en familias transmigrantes. *Revista de Educación y Ciencia*, 352, 289–308.

García Castaño, F.J. (1995). *Investigación, intervención y evaluación para la integración lingüística de inmigrantes*. Granada: Laboratorio de Estudios Interculturales, Universidad de Granada.

Garcìa Castaño, F.J. and Pulido, R. (2005). Extranjeros y escolares. Formas de construir la diferencia en el ámbito de la educación formal en Andalucía mediante la llamada educación intercultural. In Vera Vila, J. (ed.), *Educación Intercultural. Diversidad e inmigración*. Madrid: Fundación Santa María.

García Castaño, F.J. et al. (2006). Integración educativa. In Barañano, A. et al. (eds), *Diccionario de relaciones interculturales*. Madrid: Universidad Complutense de Madrid.

García Castaño, F.J., Rubio Gómez, M. and Bouachra, O. (2008). Población inmigrante y escuela en España: un balance de investigación. *Revista de Educación*, 345, 23–60.

García Fernández, J.A. (2006). *La investigación sobre educación intercultural en España. Evolución temática, metodológica, necesidades y tendencias futuras*. http://weib.caib.es/Documentacio/jornades/Web_I_Cong_Medit/PDFs/investiga2.pdf [retrieved 4 September 2013].

García García, M., García Corona, D., Biencinto López, C. and Asensio Muñoz, I. (2012). Medidas eficaces en atención a la diversidad cultural desde una perspectiva inclusiva. *Revista de Educación*, 358, 258–81.

García Parejo, I. (1994). *Enseñanza/aprendizaje de la lengua e integración. Una propuesta educativa centrada en el inmigrante adulto sobre la base de datos relativa a la Comunidad Autónoma de Madrid*. Unpublished document. Madrid: CIDE.

García Parejo, I. (ed.) (1997). *Enseñanza-aprendizaje de la lengua e integración. Una propuesta educativa centrada en el inmigrante adulto sobre la base de datos relativos a la Comunidad Autónoma de Madrid*. Unpublished document. Madrid: CIDE.

Giménez Romero, C. (ed.) (1996). *Variables claves en la integración sociocultural en la escuela. Un análisis del contexto educativo desde la antropología social*. Unpublished document. Madrid: CIDE.

Gómez Lara, J.-Colectivo Amani (2010). Lo ético en la escuela intercultural. In López Cuesta, B. et al., *Interculturalidad y ciudadanía. Red de escuelas interculturales*. Madrid: Liga española de la educación y cultura popular.

Gordo López, J.L. and Molinuevo Santos, J. (1998). *Catorce años de investigación sobre las desigualdades en educación en España*. Unpublished document. Madrid: CIDE.

Grañeras Pastrana, M. (ed.) (2000). *Las desigualdades en la educación en España* (II). Madrid: CIDE.

Grañeras Pastrana, M., Lamelas Frías, R., Segalerva Cazorla, A., Vázquez Aguilar, E. and García Castaño, F.J (1995). *La escolarización de niñas y niños inmigrantes en el sistema educativo español: estudio comparado entre diferentes provinciasespañolas de la situación en las escuelas de los hijos inmigrantes extranjerosdesde la perspectiva de la antropología social*. Unpublished document. Madrid: CIDE.

Grañeras Pastrana, M. and Díaz-Caneja, P. (2010). Hacia unas políticas educativas inclusivas. El binomio inmigración-educación intercultural. In López Cuesta, B. et al., *Interculturalidad y ciudadanía. Red de escuelas interculturales*. Madrid: Liga española de la educación y cultura popular.

Ilies, M. (2009). *La política de la Comunidad Europea sobre integración irregular. Medidas para combatir la inmigración irregular en todas sus fases*. http://www.realinstitutoelcano.org [retrieved 1 February 2013].

Jordán. J.A. and Castella, E. (2001). *La educación intercultural, una respuesta a tiempo*. Barcelona: Universitat Oberta de Catalunya.

Liga española de la educación. *Red de escuelas interculturales. Propuestas básicas*. Madrid: Liga española de la educación, Fondo europeo para la integración y Ministerio de empleo y seguridad social. http://www.escuelasinterculturales. eu/spip.php?article1 [retrieved November 2012].

Llistar, D. (2009). *Anticooperació. Interferències Nord-Sud. Els problemes del Sud Global no es resolen amb més ajut internacional*. Barcelona: Icària.

López Cuesta, B. et al. (2010). *Interculturalidad y ciudadanía. Red de escuelas interculturales*. Madrid: Liga española de la educación y cultura popular.

Marín Díaz, V. (2006). Niños de inmigrantes en los niveles de infancia y primarios de la educación. In Adam, M.D. and Jiménez, G. (eds), *La educación y la formación profesional de los inmigrantes*. Córdoba: Servicio de Publicaciones de la Universidad de Córdoba.

Márquez Lepe, E. and García Cano Torrico, M. (2012). *Educación intercultural y comunidades de aprendizaje*. Madrid: Catarata.

Martín Domínguez, A. (1993). *Diversidad cultural y conflictos nacionales en el mundoactual. Diseño y experimentación de una propuesta didáctica para la etapa docedieciséis años*. Unpublished document. Madrid: CIDE.

Martín Rojo, L., Alcalá Recuerda, E., Garí Pérez, A., Mijares, L., Sierra Rodrigo, I. and Rodríguez, M.A. (2003). *¿Asimilar o integrar? Dilemas ante el multilingüismo en las aulas*. Madrid: Ministerio de Educación y Ciencia.

Merino Fernández, J.V. (1994). *La educación de niños inmigrantes extranjeros en los centros escolares de la Comunidad de Madrid*. Unpublished document. Madrid: CIDE.

Mesa Franco, C. and Sánchez, S. (1994). *Exploración de la situación bilingüe en los escolares de Melilla. Propuestas y estrategias de intervención educativa*. Unpublished document. Madrid: CIDE.

Mesa Franco, M.C. and Sánchez Fernández, S. (1996). *Educación y situaciones bilingües en contextos multiculturales. Estudio de un caso: Melilla*. Granada: Laboratorio de Estudios Interculturales, Universidad de Granada.

Mijares, L. (2009). *Políticas europeas de integración del alumnado inmigrante. Una mirada comparativa*. Madrid: FETE-UGT.

Ministerio de Educación y Ciencia (1992). *La educación intercultural en España*. Madrid: CIDE.

Montes del Castillo, A. (ed.) (1998). *Evaluación del impacto de la incorporación de la población inmigrante al sistema educativo. El caso de los inmigrantes marroquíes y la Educación de adultos en la región de Murcia*. Unpublished document. Madrid: CIDE.

Montes Pérez, C. (2004). Educación, modelos familiares y antropología. Retos para una sociedad multicultural en la comarca del Bierzo. In Espina, A.B. (ed.), *Familia, educación y diversidad cultural*. Salamanca: Universidad de Salamanca.

Muñoz-Repiso, M. (ed.) (1992). *Las desigualdades en la educación en España (I)*. Unpublished document. Madrid: CIDE.

Muñoz Sedano, A. (ed.) (1993). *La educación multicultural de los niños gitanos de Madrid*. Unpublished document. Madrid: CIDE.

Murillo, J. (2004). Un marco comprensivo de mejora de la eficacia escolar. *Revista Mexicana de Investigación Educativa*, 9 (21), 319–59.

Murillo, J.. Grañeras, M.. Segalerva, A. and Vázquez, E. (1995). La investigación española en Educación Intercultural. *Revista de Educación*, 307, 185–97.

Naval, C. (2003). Orígenes recientes y temas clave de la educación para la ciudadanía democrática actual. *Revista de Educación*, special issue, 169–89.

Navarro Barba, J. (undated). *La interculturalidad en el medio escolar. Mitos, retos y realidades*. http://www.educa2.madrid.org/principal [retrieved November 2011].

Observatorio Permanente de la Inmigración-OPI (2013). *Extranjeros residentes en España a 30 de septiembre de 2012. Principales resultados*. http://extranjeros.empleo.gob.es/es/index.html [retrieved 1 February 2013].

Ortiz Cobo, M. (2006). Escuelas e inmigración. Gestión de la diversidad lingüística. *Revista Docencia e Investigación*, 16, 279–308.

Ortiz Cobo, M. (2012). Efectos escolares de la inmigración. Discursos sobre concentración. *Revista Iberoamericana de Educación*, 59 (1).

Pajares, M. (2011). *Inmigración y mercado de trabajo. Informe 2010*. Madrid: Ministerio de Trabajo e Inmigración, Observatorio Permanente de la Inmigración.

Pérez Sola, N. (2006). La respuesta del sistema educativo a la escolarización de los menores inmigrantes. Una aproximación a la situación de la escolarización en Jaén. In *Jornadas de Expertos sobre la inmigración en la provincia de Jaén*. Jaén: CES de Jaén.

Pérez Yruela, M. and Rinken, S. (2005). *La integración de los inmigrantes en la sociedad andaluza*. Madrid: CSIC.

Ponce Solé, J. (2007). *Segregación escolar e inmigración. Contra los guetos escolares: derecho y políticas públicas urbanas*. Madrid: Centro de Estudios Políticos y Constitucionales.

Pozo Llorente, M.T. and Gallardo Vigil, M.A. (2011). Las técnicas narrativas y de consulta en investigación en educación intercultural. Casos prácticos. In

Amador, L. and Musitu, G. (eds), *Exclusión social y diversidad*. México, DF: Trillas.

Rebollo, M.A., Piedra de la Cuadra, J., Sala, A., Saavedra, J. and Bascón, M. (2012). La equidad de género en educación: análisis y descripción de buenas prácticas educativas. *Revista de Educación*, 358, 129–53.

Rodríguez Izquierdo, R.M. (2009). La investigación sobre la educación intercultural en España, *Archivos Analíticos de Políticas Educativas*, 17 (4).

Salazar González, J. (ed.) (1996). *Los principios de comprensividad y diversificacióncomo respuesta a la diversidad en una escuela multicultural dentro de la Enseñanza Obligatoria*. Unpublished document. Madrid: CIDE.

Sales, M.A. (1996). *Educación intercultural y formación de actitudes. Propuesta deprogramas pedagógicos para desarrollar actitudes interculturales en EducaciónPrimaria y Secundaria*. PhD thesis, Universidad de Valencia.

Sanchez, A. (2007). *Influencia de la inmigración en la elección escolar*. Barcelona: Institut d'Economia de Barcelona.

Sánchez Fernández, S. and Mesa Franco, M. (1997). *Actitudes hacia la tolerancia y lacooperación en ambientes multiculturales*. Unpublished document. Madrid: CIDE.

Sandín, M.P. (1996). *Desarrollo de la identidad étnica en adolescentes desde una perspectiva intercultural: evaluación participativa de un programa de accióntutorial*. PhD thesis, Universidad de Barcelona.

Santos Rego, M.A. (2003). *La inmigración en un país de emigrantes. El desafío de la escuela intercultural en Galicia*. Madrid: MEC.

Soriano, E. (1997). Análisis de la educación multicultural en los centros educativos de la comarca del poniente almeriense. *Revista de Investigación Educativa*, 15 (1), 43–67.

Soriano, E. (ed.) (1999). *La escuela almeriense. Un espacio multicultural. Evaluación de los valores del alumnado inmigrante y autóctono*. Almería: Servicio de Publicaciones de la Universidad de Almería, Instituto de Estudios almerienses.

Soriano, E. (2003). La escolarización de alumnos y alumnas inmigrantes en los centros educativos almerienses. In Serra, L. (ed.), *Inmigración extranjera en Andalucía*. Granada: Dirección General de Coordinación de Políticas Migratorias.

Soriano, E. (2004). La construcción de la identidad cultural en contextos multiculturales. Presentationa at the *XIII Congreso nacional y II Iberoamericano de Pedagogía*. Valencia.

Soriano, E. and Fernández Prados, J.S. (1997). Realidad multicultural en las escuelas de la comarca del Poniente Almeriense. *Boletín del Instituto de Estudios Almerienses*. Letras, 15, 191–200.

Soriano, E. and Osorio Méndez, M. (2008). Competencias emocionales del alumnado autóctono e inmigrante de Educación Secundaria. Bordón. *Revista de Pedagogía*, 60(1), 129–48.

Vallespir, J. and Morey, M. (2004). *La recerca en educació intercultural. La multiculturalitat en el context de l'educació primària a les Illes Balears.* Presentation at the *IV Congreso sobre la Inmigración en España*, Girona. http://www.udg.edu/congres_immigracio/ESP/index.htm [retrieved 1 February 2013].

Chapter 7

Intercultural Education in Europe: The Greek Experience

George P. Markou and Christos Parthenis

Introduction

In contemporary Greek society, the presence of individuals or groups of people from a linguistic and culturally diverse background (i.e., returning Ethnic Greeks, foreign immigrants, Greek Roma, Greek Muslims from Thrace) presents fundamental challenges not only for the scientific conceptualisation of the consequences of such a presence, but also for the formation of policies and the adoption of practices which address the problems that emanate from the inclusion of such diverse individuals in Greek social and political institutions, particularly considering that in the 1991 census 95 per cent of the population was linguistically, ethnically and religiously homogeneous (National Census, 1991).

The rejection of the assimilation model in several countries, at least at a theoretical level, led to the adoption of the intercultural model and the realisation of an 'inclusive society' in which people from linguistic and culturally diverse backgrounds are able to pursue and attain economic, political and social rights and are equally able to equitably access the same institutions within the host country as the rest of the population. At the level of policy practice regarding the inclusion of immigrants, rejection of an assimilation policy is linked with the granting of citizenship to immigrants who in turn are placed in a position to accept the political culture of the host country, the development of specialised institutions and the implementation of specific measures which facilitate integration. On the part of the immigrant, there are the following requirements:

- acceptance of the host country's fundamental constitutional principles;
- knowledge of the host language, history and culture;
- the development and fostering of relationships with the host population;
- participation in social and civic networks; and
- the development of a subjective sentiment of 'co-belonging' with the host society.[1]

---

1 Despite individual differences, the integration of migrant populations in many European host countries is fundamentally pursued through their institutions for the inclusion of all citizens by laterally creating new and specialised institutions for its facilitation. In

In this chapter, the significance of *intercultural education* is linked with the wider process of integration of people from migrant backgrounds in Greek society, since the typology of integration policies adopted define the framework from which all intercultural based interventions are developed. Intercultural integration therefore means the recognition of the cultural diversity of the society and the concurrent pursuit of interaction and cooperation while supporting the right of all social groups to preserve aspects of their culture they deem relevant and which contribute to the general culture of the host society. It also means the promotion of intercultural dialogue and the building of public trust and shared cultural development, with a particular emphasis on the reform of public institutions and services so that they are in a position not only to respond to the new challenges but also meet the needs of all citizens.

Within the process of intercultural integration, the uniqueness of the so-called 'purity' of each culture and the need for its preservation is not stressed. There is no exaggeration of cultural differences and divisionary lines between the various cultural groups that make up a given society. Above all, there is no support for the notion that these differences should be protected by the laws and institutions of the state. The adoption of policies which accentuate differences is considered to lead to rivalries, conflict and segregation among cultural groups in their attempt to gain increasing share of power, often resulting in the isolation, ghettoisation and exclusion of particular groups, with all the known consequences both for the said groups and for society as a whole (Markou, 2010).

The aim of this chapter is to present the basic elements of intercultural policies for the integration of people from migrant backgrounds over the last two decades in Greece. It is important to note that the central structure of the Greek state bestows on the state itself a dominant role in formulating such policies and allows it to perceive integration as a process that can and should be guided by a policy of intervention.[2]

Policies of Intercultural Integration and Social Cohesion

Integration policies in Greece address the following social groups:

- foreigners (immigrants and refugees)[3]

---

the past, the acquisition of citizenship and the expansion of social and civil rights (to the working class, women etc.) were key institutional parameters for integration which had remarkable results in European capitalist societies. Societal inclusion through citizenship has historically constituted a fundamentally traditional mechanism (Marshall, 1950).

2   Greek integration policy is expressed in the sanctioned laws that have been voted in over time for the integration of returning ethnic Greeks and foreign immigrants, and in numerous projects that have been developed to guide the integration policies.

3   The term 'foreigner' is defined as 'any natural person who does not have Greek citizenship or nationality' (Law 2910/2001, Article 1). The term foreigner, which was

- 'Ethnic Greeks' from countries of the former Soviet Union and Albania[4]
- returning Greek emigrants.

Greece as an Immigrant Country

The collapse of the former Soviet Union and the end of the Cold War are marked with the movement of significantly large numbers of immigrants from Eastern to Western Europe. In Greece, there was a significant influx of immigrants – mainly from Albania, but also from Russia, Ukraine and Georgia – many of whom are acknowledged as Ethnic Greeks, recognised by the state and accorded preferential treatment. It was during this period that migration issues and immigration policies in Greece were given political priority and, for the first time and acknowledgement of the need to adopt specific measures in the integration of immigrants into Greek society.[5] During the last decade and notably since 2005, there have been major changes regarding the origin of immigrants: significantly reduced numbers from countries such as Albania, Russia and Georgia; and increasing rates from Asia, Africa and the Middle East. This is despite the serious obstacles faced by the Greek State, the recent economic crisis afflicting Greek society and the Dublin II Regulation.

Despite its relatively recent migration experience in comparison with other European countries and the absence of a strong tradition in the integration of immigrants, Greece has maintained a particularly strong debate on migration and immigration policy in recent years, in light of the ongoing and largely unregulated influx of immigrants in search of the 'Promised Land' in EU countries. One point

---

adopted by the National Statistics Service, is in itself problematic since the differentiation of data on citizenship (ethnic Greek – foreigner) does not lend itself to the understanding of the integration process. There is no data differentiation, for example, between successfully integrated foreigners and non-integrated foreigners. Similarly, in the case of ethnic Greeks, who are naturalised almost automatically, it is difficult to identify within the data their problems of integration. We believe that this could be resolved by adopting terms which would allow differentiation between foreign nationals, for example: naturalised Greeks born in Greece, Greeks with a Greek parent, Ethnic Greeks etc.

4   The term 'Ethnic Greek' (*homogeneis*) refers to any person who claims Greek descent and shares common cultural elements with Greeks – such as language, religion, traditions and national consciousness – but without Greek citizenship. Ethnic Greeks are nationals of countries outside the European Union (EU) originating initially from Greece and migrated from countries outside Greek territory or territory once annexed to Greece which continued to accept the influence of Greek culture. This particular group of people feel (or consider themselves to feel) that they are returning to the 'homeland'. In this chapter we refer exclusively to Ethnic Greeks from countries of the former Soviet Union and Albania. Their case can be described as something akin to the German *Aussiedler*.

5   State interest is expressed through the establishment of the Migration Policy Institute (IMEPO). The first recipients of the integration measures are Ethnic Greeks from the former Soviet Union.

of difference in comparison with other European countries, particularly those of the north, is that, in a very short period of time, Greece was transformed from a country of emigrants (outbound migrants) to a recipient of immigrants (incoming migrants) without having the necessary infrastructure both at institutional level and in terms of social consciousness.[6] The massive nature of this migration is directly linked to the fact that Greece is considered the 'gateway' to European territory.

Notably though, during the first decade of the twenty-first century, while there was a reduction in migration rates to northern European countries and a shift in political- and scientific-based interest in inclusion and integration policies, in Greece there was a continuous and unregulated influx of immigrants, igniting a heated debate over the feasibility of permitting economic immigrants to remain in the country. Several politicians consider and assert that migrant stay should be temporary, while others question whether the country is in a position at all to accept the permanent settlement of 'illegal' immigrants from Asia, Africa and the Middle East. Proposals emanating from left-wing parties and trade union movements advocate for the permanency and inclusion of immigrants in Greek society. Nevertheless, the government is endeavouring to repatriate many illegal immigrants. The government deems necessary stringent measures to reduce the numbers of immigrants while at the same adopting inclusion measures for those immigrants with legal residence status. The formulation of a controlled and planned immigration programme through strict reduction measures, such as those adopted in other EU member states, whilst implementing integration measures in Greek society for legal and long-term immigrants, is the nexus upon which all efforts to shape Greek migration policy in recent years is based (Bagavos and Kapsalis, 2008).

Demographics and Immigration

According to the 2001 Census (the 2011 results were still pending at the time of writing), there were 797,093 foreigners (without citizenship) registered as living in Greece, representing 7.3 per cent of the total population (10,964,080). The majority of immigrants registered by nationality were from Albania, constituting 57.0 per cent (438,036) of the total immigrants in Greece, 76–86 per cent of whom lived in the regions of Epirus, Thessaly and Western Macedonia. Immigrants from Bulgaria followed with a considerable difference at 5 per cent of the total

---

6   However, within the space of a few years – comparing the time it took northern European countries with long experience of immigration, such as Germany – Greece can rightly boast of the rapid adaptation of its society and its citizens to the unprecedented conditions created by immigration. This adaptation concerns both the institutions that incorporated all relevant EU Directives and the labour market where, despite high unemployment rates generally, unemployment among immigrants is lower than that of native Greeks. It should be noted here that a considerable degree of immigrants' access to the labour market refers to undeclared work (see Robolis, 2011).

Table 7.1　Immigrants with legal status in 2012 and distribution of immigrants according to the 2001 Census

Country of Origin	Immigrants with Legal Status	Distribution of Immigrants
Albania	284,367	438,036
Bulgaria	–	35,104
Romania	–	21,994
Pakistan	12,393	11,130
Ukraine	15,911	13,616
Poland	–	12,831
Georgia	12,940	22,875
India	10,394	7,216
Egypt	10,359	7,448
Philippines	7,774	6,478
Moldova	8,816	5,716
Syria	5,672	5,552
Russian Federation	12,262	17,535
Bangladesh	4,760	4,854
Iraq	565	6,936
Armenia	4,678	7,742
Yugoslavia	3,165	3,832
Nigeria	1,339	2,015
Ethiopia	4,760	1,163
Other Countries	16,869	129,740
Total	417,028	761,813

Source: Greek Ministry of Interior Affairs, 31 December 2012; National Statistic Services (NSS), 2001. The absence of data from Bulgaria, Romania and Poland is due to the fact that immigrants are not included as foreign nationals but as nationals of EU countries.

distribution in Greece, Georgians at 3 per cent and Romanians equally at 3 per cent of the total foreign population. There was an overall gender balance of total registered immigrants: 415,552 (54.5 per cent) men and 346,639 (45.5 per cent) women. However, certain groups of immigrants had highly skewed percentages; for example, immigrants from Asian countries (Pakistan, Bangladesh, India) and from Syria and Egypt were almost exclusively male (over 80 per cent).

Table 7.1 gives a preliminary yet differentiated picture of the distribution of legal status immigrants in Greece, by country of origin, according to the most recent data (end of 2012) from the Ministry of Interior Affairs juxtaposed with the 2001 Census. These figures recorded a strong tendency for repatriation to their countries of origin by migrants from Albania, Russia and Georgia, while at the same time there was an increase in numbers of immigrants from Asia, Africa and the Middle East.[7]

Of special note is the data relating to the basic characteristics of the immigrant population resulting from further analysis of the 2001 Census with reference to foreign immigrants and relating to the following areas.

Place of settlement (location in Greece)
The range of immigrant population densities and regions of settlement are associated with patterns of migrant economic integration. Almost half of the immigrant population (48.6 per cent) is located in the Attica region, followed by Central Macedonia at 13.1 per cent. The Peloponnese, Crete, Central Greece, Western Greece and Thessaly employ 25 per cent of the total immigrant population, and the remaining percentages are allocated to the islands of the northern and southern Aegean (1.37 per cent and 3.7 per cent) respectively, Eastern Macedonia and Thrace (2.6 per cent), Epirus (2.0 per cent) and Western Macedonia (1.2 per cent). Notably, more than 80 per cent of immigrants choose to settle in urban areas and of these more than 60 per cent settled in Attica and Central Macedonia. The remaining regions have a ratio of 60 per cent urban and 40 per cent rural settlement (National Statistic Services, 2001: Table1).

Population dynamics
Approximately 80 per cent of immigrants are involved in productive labour (are of working age), with more than half aged 25–44. This corresponds to 45.6 per cent of the total immigrant population, while for the general Greek population the percentage is only 28.9 per cent. Only 3.5 per cent of immigrants are over 65, in contrast to 18.1 per cent of Greeks (National Statistic Services, 2001: Table 3).

Level of education
Nearly a quarter (23.3 per cent) of immigrants have completed primary school education; 28 per cent are graduates of secondary education; 17.9 per cent have

----

7   It should be emphasised that a significant number of foreigners in Greece belong to the category of 'illegal immigrants'. Although it is impossible to know the exact number of immigrants residing without authorisation, estimates range between 400,000 and 500,000, with Attica and Thessaloniki being the main regions of attraction, primarily due to employment opportunities and migrant networks. It is estimated that 1 in 10 Greeks has a migrant background. Similar difficulties are encountered regarding the accurate number of Ethnic Greeks from the former Soviet Union and Albania. Various sources put the figure at about 65,000 by the mid-1990s, while estimates for the total population by around 2005 range between 150,000 and 200,000 (see Lianos et al., 2008; Kanellopoulos et al., 2011; Maroukis, 2011; Robolis, 2008).

completed compulsory education; and 8.3 per cent have a tertiary diploma or post-graduate degree. Immigrants with the highest levels of education are from the former Soviet Union (Russia, Ukraine, Georgia), Poland and Romania. Relatively low educational levels are observed in immigrants from Albania, Bulgaria and Pakistan (National Statistic Services, 2001: Table 4).

Reason for migration and length of residence in Greece
From the total registered immigrant population, more than half (54.2 per cent) declared that finding a job was the major reason for migrating to Greece, 13 per cent for family reunion and 7 per cent for repatriation. A relatively high percentage (21.5 per cent) reported reasons that did not fall within the main categories of the Census. Regarding the length of stay of those who declared that they migrated for work, only 12.2 per cent were in the first year of residence in Greece; 46.8 per cent had been in the country for 1–5 years; and 41 per cent had been resident for over 5 years (National Statistic Services, 2001: Tables 6 and 7).

Employment
Around 90 per cent of immigrants were salaried workers (13 per cent of the total salaried employment in Greece) and 6.5 per cent were self-employed (there were differentiated ratios of men and women). Over two-thirds (66 per cent) of immigrants said that they worked as unskilled manual labourers, technicians, small tradesmen and operators of transport vehicles; 10 per cent worked in the service sector and as vendors in shops and flea markets; and 7 per cent said they worked as agricultural or livestock farmers etc. With reference economic sector, 25 per cent worked in the construction industry, 20 per cent in primary production, 12.5 per cent in industry, 16.0 per cent in the trade, hotel/restaurant sector and 20.5 per cent in other services (National Statistic Services, 2001: Tables 8 and 9).

The Integration of Immigrants into Greek Society

In any given society, citizenship constitutes the basis for the integration of individuals into its institutions.[8] The acquisition of citizenship forms the necessary condition for immigrants to achieve a sense of 'co-belonging' in the host society,

---

8   The concept of citizenship, beyond its clear legal term, has a social and cultural dimension. It is both a medium and a means of social restriction, since contemporary nation-states perceive themselves as and derive their legitimacy from serving the interests of specific social groups. A typical example is the inaccessibility of non-citizens to voting rights. According to Brubaker, citizenship policies relate primarily to those who belong to the nation. The national state, in addition to national and demographic dimensions and institutional arrangements, is a way of thinking and validating political and social membership. This is why discussions on the provision of citizenship to immigrants are largely about the nation and what 'co-belonging' should mean (Brubaker, 1992: 180).

and contributes in many ways to their active civil involvement and participation. This has in turn a positive impact on the immigrants' capability and desire to be integrated, since they feel accepted and acknowledged as members of a civil community (Vermeulen, 2001). In Greece, as in the case of other European countries, until the first decades of the post-war period the term 'nationality' was inextricably linked to a privilege reserved only for those who had ethnic ancestral origins.[9] The key political player in this area, usually a government, worked in the past within the parameters of Greek tradition. The National Authority of Citizenship, which constitutes Greek tradition, proved to be a major obstacle to the naturalisation of foreigners (immigrants – refugees).

Citizenship and Integration

Until the passing of Law 3838/2010, existing citizenship policy referenced the formation of the Greek nation state two centuries earlier with the conceptualisation of 'nation' based on the principle of homogeneity. Deviations from linguistic, religious, ideological and regional norms were perceived as threats to the State's social and political cohesion. The concept of nation was based on the creation of a common language and a common culture. Nationality corresponded to citizenship and national integration was sought through the status of citizenship and education primarily constituting the key institution for achieving national integration. Over time, there were efforts to integrate Ethnic Greeks from the Diaspora in areas annexed to Greek territory into the Greek nation. This was predominately attempted through citizenship status and public education. Acquisition of Greek citizenship, formulated on the logic of the 'right of blood' (*ius sanguinis*) differentiates Greeks from foreign nationals with the exception of the defined category of Ethnic Greek foreign nationals who are perceived as sharing a common origin, language, culture and religion. The naturalisation of foreigners was acceptable and traditionally resolved only in exceptional cases and with very low rates (Kontis, 2009: 21–69). These exceptional cases were led by the principle that naturalisation should be the end product of the whole integration process and not the medium to achieve integration, or at least an important step in the process of integration.

It is worth noting that debates surrounding the status of citizenship in Greece are predominately stereotypical, often ignoring the non-static and historically variant concept of nation as a basis for the concept of citizenship. This is largely because for many decades the Greek State supported a 'national myth' which was based on great achievements of the past, with no emphasis on the present, which was more often than not stigmatised by poor performance compared to previous eras. A bonding mechanism between past and present seemed to be that of origin, on which the identity of the Modern Greek citizen was based. By the turn of the

---

9   The term 'nationality' comes to mean the public law right of the individual to bond with a particular country and to a particular people with whom they feel they belong (Krispi-Nikoletopoulou, 1965: 18, 36, 53).

century, there was an apparent shift from a national to a more political concept of citizenship and attempts were made to connect it to the formation of a new national consciousness based on a new democratic political structure and a new model of economic development.[10]

The reform process which took into account the gradual shift from the hitherto dominant principle of *ius sanguinis* to the principle of *ius soli* (right of the soil/ land) occurs through the inclusion of the mode of acquisition of Greek citizenship in the Foreigners' Act (Law 2910/2001, Law 3446/2003 and Law. 3284/2004), linking the granting of citizenship to social and political integration, initially to Ethnic Greeks (Law 2790/2000, Law 3013/2002) and later to foreign immigrants (Law 3838/2010).

The change in the perception of the nation and of citizenship in Greece is a result of accumulative factors over time that exerted pressure for change. Some of the most significant factors are outlined below.

- *In the intellectual sector and in the political world in general* the effect of the deconstruction of the concept of nation as a result of extreme nationalism by the Nazi totalitarian regime and the crimes committed by the Nazi troops on the occupied Greek people during the Second World War. Additionally, the nationalist concept of nation that dominated during the days of the Colonels and the restoration of constitutional legality based on the political principle of the Western world since the fall of the Junta Regime in 1974. But more recently, the significant rise of the racist (in the sense of race) political party, Golden Dawn and its representation in Greek Parliament.
- *Greece's entry into the European Union* marked a new historical phase: a period of redefining the basic principles of the Constitution and its social structures. The Greek Constitution adapted significantly to the new European context (in terms of demographic, social and economic parameters), hence affecting the convergence of Greeks and foreigners at the level of individual, social and political rights (access to public health services, education, social security, political participation etc.).[11]

---

10   The new sense of the national identity is dictated by the need to avoid undermining the collective consciousness and the need for social cohesion. Those who believe in 'constitutional patriotism' – interpreted as identification with the nation state due to constitutional rules, laws and commitment to democratic institutions – look forward to a new national consciousness based on principles of a democratic society and institutions governed by equality and justice which all citizens can identify with.

11   In the report on the constitutionality of certain provisions of the Bill, 'Current provisions for Greek citizenship and political participation of Ethnic Greeks and legally residing immigrants and other regulations', which Conservative MPs had reported as unconstitutional during the debate in Parliament, the Scientific Council ruled in favor of the constitutionality of these provisions of the Bill making reference to specific articles of the constitution that prove their compatibility with the economic, social and political

- *Migration as a subject of political debate and as a field of implementation of state policy* had a particular influence on the further development of the concept of nation and the institution of citizenship. Political parties, associations, unions, migrant organisations, lawyers, intellectuals, journalists and many others have initiated debates on the need to change the law on citizenship. These discussions ultimately included the concept of nation and the nation state, as they constitute the main obstacle to immigrant integration. Many argued that *ius soli* should be added to the principle of descent so as to facilitate naturalisation.[12]

Naturalisation Policy and Integration

Law 2910/2001 effected an initial change in the acquisition of Greek citizenship. The significance of this change is that, for the first time, elements of *ius soli* were incorporated in the *ius sanguinis* process of naturalisation of immigrants. From this law's basic requirements it can be inferred that only those foreigners who lead an 'honest life' for many years and who have a satisfactory knowledge of Greek language, history and culture may acquire Greek citizenship through naturalisation. More specifically, the law sets certain conditions for the naturalisation of foreign immigrants. Applicants must:

- have a total of 10 years' legal residence in Greece during the last 12 years before their application;
- be at least 18 years old;
- have no pending expulsion decision or any convictions under the criminal code;
- have sufficient knowledge of the Greek language, Greek history and Greek culture in general.

These conditions – especially 10 years' legal residence, participation in Greek lifestyle, knowledge of the language, history and culture (and the certification of this knowledge required for the interview process of the applicant before the Naturalisation Committee –) show the State's intention to preserve the basic notion that sees the issue of Greek citizenship by naturalisation to be the last act of a long process of integration, hence the sealing with the oath taken by the applicant: 'I swear to guard faith in this homeland, show obedience to the Constitution and laws of the State and discharge conscientiously my duties as a Greek citizen.'[13]

---

participation of immigrants in Greek society (Greek Parliament, Directorate B Scientific Studies – Department of Legal Drafting and Bill proposals, 2010).

12   As characteristically referred to in the Explanatory Memorandum of Law 3838/2010, 'it detaches Greek Citizenship from the stifling exclusive anchorage of the 'right of blood' (ius sanguinis)'.

13   Law 2910/2001, article 62: 'Entry and Stay of Foreigners in the Greek Territory. Acquisition of Greek Citizenship by naturalisation and other provisions.' Of interest is the

The naturalisation of second-generation immigrants depends solely on the naturalisation status of first-generation immigrants. Children whose parents are Greek citizens automatically become Greek citizens at birth, and children with parents without Greek citizenship can obtain it only on the condition that they are born in Greece and have come of age. The naturalised foreign immigrant may retain the citizenship of the country of origin and has full legal status as with native Greek citizens.

The point of differentiation in the naturalisation policy concerns those who are recognised as Ethnic Greeks. In their case, naturalisation is seen as a fundamental means of accelerating their integration into Greek society through additional 'fast-track' measures. This is especially apparent in the case of Ethnic Greeks from the former Soviet Union and Albania.[14] Specifically, in Law 2790/2000 and 3013/2002 regarding granting Greek citizenship to Ethnic Greeks from countries of the former Soviet Union, there were distinct provisions and regulations in place for resettlement and community integration support.[15] Integration into society was predominately promoted through institutional infrastructure: by providing appropriate housing, employment and vocational opportunities as well as teaching

---

emerging logic of decentralisation through the law, which essentially indicates that there is awareness that integration has also a local implication. This is apparent in legal provisions where, although Greek citizenship is accorded by ministerial decision, the substantive part of the naturalisation process is entrusted to two decentralised institutions of the region: a) Naturalisation Committee, which through interviews assesses the personality of applicants for Greek citizenship, confirming their real interest and conferring an opinion on the Minister regarding the granting or denial of citizenship; b) Committee on Migration, which consists of two employees from the Immigration Department and a representative of the Police Authority, for examining the validity and thoroughness of the applicants' supporting documentation and formulating an opinion on the granting of Greek citizenship.

14   We note here the distinction between 'Northern Epirus' Ethnic Greeks from Albania and 'Pondion' Ethnic Greeks from the former Soviet Union regarding the legalisation process. Pondion Ethnic Greeks are recognised as 'repatriated/returning Greeks' and treated as refugees – something similar to those from Asia Minor in 1922 – who could benefit from low interest rate housing loans, land concessions and other benefits not covered by other immigrant groups. Conversely, the Northern Epirus group, not recognised as refugees, did not enjoy the privileges of the Pondions except for the special identity card which enabled unrestricted renewal of residence and work permits. This difference is related to the assessed necessity of the presence of Ethnic Greeks in Albania in light of bilateral Greek–Albanian relations.

15   Apart from the possibility of acquiring Greek citizenship, this particular group may alternatively choose to be granted a 'Special Identity Card for Ethnic Greeks Abroad'. This is essentially provided in cases where the acquisition of Greek citizenship involves loss of citizenship of the country of origin in accordance with the provisions of the local law of that country (Law N.2790/2000). The Special Identity Card for Ethnic Greeks serves as a residence and work permit, permitting Ethnic Greeks to remain in Greece as foreign nationals yet enjoying the rights and benefits of returning Ethnic Greeks with Greek citizenship.

and learning support for the children of these immigrants in the education system. Law 3386/2005 (art. 65) promotes the social integration of immigrants through:

> the granting of civil rights to non EU citizens, which not only safeguard equitable participation in the economic, social and political life of the country, but also reiterate the obligatory respect for the fundamental laws and values of the Greek society [...] while preserving at the same time their ethnic identity.

To a greater extent, this particular law was able to deal with issues regarding the possibility of securing permanent residency, the right of family reunion and the right to work by decentralising the process of granting residency permits from the Regional Foreigners and Migration Offices to the Offices of the Regional Decentralised Administration Directorates (since the passing of Law N.3852/2010 the Regional Directorate of the Decentralised Administration is now the responsible authority). Law 3386/2005 also included relevant EU directives regarding family reunion, the right of stay and the granting of residency permits to those immigrants deemed 'long-term residents'.[16] According to Article 66 of the same law, the integration of an immigrant into Greek society can be considered successful on the provision that there is:

• certified knowledge of the Greek language and the successful completion of history, Greek culture and lifestyle courses;
• evidence of inclusion in the Greek workforce and active community participation.

For these purposes, a National Committee for the Social Integration of Immigrants was established whose main task was to put forward proposals and actions for the social inclusion of immigrants to the Interministerial Commission. An 'Integrated Action Plan' (Programme ESTIA 2007–2013) was also developed, which included specific programmes for access to the workforce, education, health, housing, cultural activities and other public sectors; for services and counselling of immigrants; for combating racism and xenophobia; and for community awareness (Law 3386/2005: art. 66; Law 3536/2007; Opinion No. 165/16.01.2007). This integrated plan also includes several other subprogrammes and intervention measures whose outcomes at both macro social and economic level will not be analysed at length here. We can however stress that the fundamental principles underpinning the Integrated Action Plan are indicative of efforts to integrate into Greek migration legislation all those European directives on human rights relating

---

16   The right to family reunification is regulated by European legislation which has been incorporated into Law 3386/2005. Family reunion is a key factor in facilitating the integration of immigrants into the local community.

to migrants, and that the results of the activities developed within this programme are not completely ineffective.[17]

Despite the magnitude of the endeavours for integration policy transformation, the main conclusion drawn from the overall activities of the State by around 2005 is that Greece still remains irresolute in front of a fundamental issue: the exclusion of a substantial proportion of its population from their basic civil rights, as implied in terms of democratic legitimacy. As a consequence, there emerge fundamental contradictions where on the one hand the State expresses its intent for the integration of immigrants, and on the other it seeks to preserve their national identity without making it clear how it intends to facilitate this preservation.[18] Within the specific understanding of the legislation, inclusion is defined as also incorporating the perspective of reproducing the ethnic minority, since the aim is the integration and the lateral maintenance of ethnic identity.[19] However, the evidence so far is in the direction of a policy of assimilation, since integration is interpreted here as the full adaptation to Greek lifestyle conditions and the State refuses to give minority status to migrant groups.

The granting of Greek citizenship to foreign people who were born and educated in Greece (i.e. second-generation and long-term residents) and who have no criminal court case involvement was outlined in Law 3838/2010, almost 10 years after the first attempt to address the problem of the naturalisation of immigrants. This respective law weakens significantly the bond between ethnicity and nationality, and attempts to shift the emphasis from the principle of 'right of blood' (*ius sanguinis*) to the principle of 'right of soil' (*ius soli*). Hence, in turn, it is able to shape those fundamental conditions necessary for the integration of foreign immigrants into the institutions of Greek society by providing a comprehensive set of policies and social rights.[20] According to Law 3838/2010 Greek citizenship can be acquired:

---

17   This becomes evident when one compares the results in Greece with results of similar activities in other countries – members of the European Union (see Harmovitis, 2011).

18   Unless, for this purpose, it can be considered sufficient within the statement of the law in which according ministerial approval may regulate 'matters for optional teaching of the mother tongue and culture where there is a sufficient number of students who are interested, as part of support measures offered by Ministry of National Education and Religious Affairs and to determine the employment relationship and the qualifications of teachers who teach the mother language and culture of their country of origin (Law 3386/2005: art. 72).

19   The explanation that can be given here is that the policy-makers have not thought out or adequately analysed this issue and have failed to recognise the need to formulate a clear policy of integration. It also seems that there is no attempt to openly acknowledge their intent to seek integration in the sense of assimilation, and they therefore choose ambiguity.

20   The Greek Citizenship Code (Law 3284/2004), modified by the new law (3838/2010) based on *ius sanguinis*, under which a person can acquire citizenship through a Greek parent automatically at birth, regardless of place of birth. This was dictated by the need for Greek migrants abroad and their children to maintain the bond with their homeland.

- *ipso jure* (automatically at birth) by children whose foreign immigrant parents were born in Greece, live permanently and have legal resident status in Greece (art. 1);
- by foreign immigrant children born and living in Greece, whose parents have legally resided in Greece for at least seven consecutive years (art. 1);
- by foreign immigrant children who have successfully completed at least six grades of schooling in Greece and have lived permanently and legally in the country since the completion of their six years of study. A precondition is that both parents must reside permanently and legally for at least seven years in Greece. The prerequisite length of residence is reduced to three years for immigrants from EU Member States, spouses of Greek nationals, those having legal parental authority over children with Greek citizenship, foreign nationals of Ethnic Greek background, officially recognised political refugees, stateless people etc. (art. 3).

Foreign immigrants who wish to be naturalised as Greek citizens should:

- have knowledge of the Greek language and should be successfully integrated into the economic and social life of the country;[21]
- actively participate in the civil activities of the country.[22]

The fulfillment of these requirements is attested through a special test conducted before the Committee on Naturalisation (Ethnic Greeks are exempted). Table 7.2 shows naturalisation figures for foreign immigrants for the period 2000–12 from the Directorate of Citizenship (Ministry of Interior Affairs).

The law also refers to the right of Ethnic Greeks and foreign immigrants to participate in prospective primary elected bodies in local government, that is,

---

But there were elements under *ius soli* in which Greek citizenship can be acquired by persons born in Greece, provided that they do not acquire at birth, *ipso facto*, the nationality of another country for the purpose of limiting the cases of statelessness.

21   Consideration is given to familiarity with Greek history and culture; business and economic activities; any public or charitable activities; possible attendance at Greek educational institutions; participation in social organisations or collective bodies whose members are Greek citizens; any kinship and bond through marriage to a Greek citizen; the fulfilment of taxation obligations and duties towards social security authorities; the acquisition/ownership of real estate and overall general asset situations. Special weight is given to recommendations made by Greek citizens regarding the applicant's social and professional life (Law 3838/2010: art. 4).

22   Consideration is given to sufficient familiarity with the institutions of the democratic Greek polity and the political life of the country as well as basic knowledge of Greek political history and recent political events. Special emphasis is also given to the participation in collective organisations, political associations or unions involving Greek citizens, and prior involvement of the applicants with primary election authorities (Law 3838/2010: art. 4).

Table 7.2 Naturalisation data of Ethnic Greeks and foreign immigrants for the period 2000–12

Naturalisation Data for the Period 2000–12

Year	Ethnic Greeks	Foreign Immigrants (N.3838)	Foreign Immigrants	Article 13 Law 4018/11	Total	Denials Ethnic Greeks	Denials Foreign Immigrants	Pending Ethnic Greeks	Pending Foreign Immigrants
2000	464	543			1,007				
2001	690	1,084			1,774				
2002	445	1,696			2,141				
2003	528	1,368			1,896				
2004	464	806			1,270				
2005	545	1,313			1,858				
2006	570	1,348			1,918				
2007	5,823	1,071			6,894	24	101		
2008	9,946	898			10,844	66	66		
2009	12,354	612			12,966	18	46		
2010	6,162	375			6,537	30	42		
2011	6,551	827	103		7,481	26	97		
2012	5,199	590	558	13	6,360	61	256		
Total	49,741	12,531	661	13	62,946	225	608	3,000 active	5,000 active

participation in the political process of the country. The right to vote is accorded Ethnic Greeks and foreign immigrants with permanent and legal residence status of five consecutive years only in the event of local government elections. Nowhere in the law is there reference to participation in national elections. The right to be elected is granted to registered voters on special lists permitting them to submit their candidature for the office of councillor, for consultant of municipal departments and of local councils provided that they are at least 21 years of age, and with the additional condition that they have sufficient knowledge of the Greek language for the performance of their duties (Law 3838/2010: art. 14).

The new law on citizenship and the legal status of the citizen reflects a new concept towards the nation. It was only natural that this new concept would spark intense confrontations during parliamentary debates, with 'conservative' opposition MPs raising the issue of the unconstitutionality of the law. The main opposition party at the time, the New Democracy Party, raised strong opposition to the new regulations and was persistent about the retainment of the prerequisites as set by then the current applicable laws granting Greek citizenship to foreign immigrants. They maintained that political 'mass naturalisations' jeopardise the national and social cohesion of the country as it becomes a draw card for the massive entry of illegal immigrants, resulting in extensive unemployment and increased insecurity and deprivation for all. They consider the multicultural approach as an 'ideological construct which is collapsing everywhere', since 'it proclaims that all cultures can live together in harmony, even though this has been disproved, as cultural elements that cannot coexist' (Press Office of the New Democracy Party, 2010b). They also maintain that the integration of immigrants is understood as meaningful if there is acceptance of the culture and norms of Greek society:

> We want immigrants who choose to take root in our country, to leave behind elements of their culture which are incompatible with our own, to join our society, to feel Greek, to become Greek through our own education. We do not wish that they simply receive their legal papers through fast track processes and then generate into different ghettos. (Press Office of the New Democracy Party, 2010b)

The aforementioned position by the New Democracy Party is particularly interesting as it clarifies for the first time the party's position on the necessary preconditions for the granting of Greek citizenship and on the social integration of immigrants. It casts off therefore the up until then ambiguity in Law 3836/2005 which expressed the State's desire for social integration of immigrants with the parallel preservation of their national identity. In essence, this stance supports the notion of the assimilation of immigrants – that is, that immigrants need to feel Greek, to become Greek – which it considers a means of averting the development of separate migrant communities and, hence, the spawning of ghettos. To this accord then was the insistence on 10 years' legal residence during the 12 years prior to application for naturalisation. For the children of immigrants, it is proposed that the right to Greek citizenship should be acquired at the onset of adulthood provided that they have completed the compulsory 10 years of education (Press Office of the New Democracy Party, 2010a). The New Democracy Party continues to see the granting of citizenship to foreign immigrants as an end result of successful integration into Greek society.

However, the official policy in Greece since the mid-1990s has been the intercultural approach and not the multicultural approach (Law 2413/1996). Supporters of the intercultural approach argue that social cohesion, a prerequisite in democratic societies, is best assured when there is recognition of the civil rights of people from diverse linguistic and cultural backgrounds and participation in local and national elections is achieved. In this manner, people from diverse language and cultural backgrounds are able to connect with the local community, hence reducing any tension, violence and crime. Supporters of the intercultural approach, in turn, do not accept (and therefore reject) the basic premise of the multicultural approach regarding the uniqueness of each culture, and more so the notion of the State's obligation to defend the dividing lines between the different cultural groups that make up society. The intercultural approach emerges only in democratic states whose democratic preservation and reinforcement are promoted through a democratic culture and the rule of law (Markou, 2010).

School Education and Integration

Up until the mid-1990s, the number of returning Ethnic Greeks and foreign immigrant students in Greek schools was limited. However, during the decade 1995–2005 there was notably a sharp increase in enrolment of students from migrant backgrounds: from 8,455 students in 1995, this number rose to approximately 130,114 in 2004, representing 8.9 per cent of total enrolment (8 per cent in kindergarten, 9.5 per cent in primary schools, 10.3 per cent in junior secondary, 4 per cent in senior secondary and 8.4 per cent in technical vocational education). Students from Albania comprised 71.5 per cent of the total from a migrant background, followed by those from the former Soviet Union at 15.9 per cent (Dretakis, 2001; Gotovos and Markou, 2004).

According to Law 2910/2001 (art. 40.1), 'Foreign minors residing on Greek territory are subject to the requirement of the minimum schooling as their counterpart nationals.' The same law also regulates free access to all levels of schooling and education by immigrant children by following the same procedure: 'The foreign minors studying at all levels of education have unrestricted access to school or educational community activities' (art. 40.2). In fact, it obliges the school administration to enrol immigrant and political refugee children even in the event of 'insufficient documentation', hence viewing access to and participation in schooling by immigrant and refugee children as independent from the residence permit status of their parents. The same law sets the terms and conditions for the recognition and accreditation of educational qualifications gained in the country of origin. It also provides the framework for the possibility of the teaching of the immigrant students' mother tongue together with cultural aspects of their country of origin, on a voluntary basis, after school hours (Law 3386/2005: art. 72). Conjunct to this, Law 2413/1996 envisages the adoption of intercultural education and the adjustment of the school curriculum to the new social, cultural and educational needs generated in multicultural environments (arts. 34 and 35).

According to the present legislation, returning Ethnic Greeks and foreign immigrant children living in Greece must be integrated into the regular school programme.[23] The indicative duration of studies in kindergarten is two years with only the second year deemed compulsory. Children from the age of four years become eligible for entry into kindergarten. The importance of early childhood education for later and successful attendance in primary school has been established sufficiently. For continuation into primary school, students are enrolled in June following graduation from kindergarten. Foreign immigrant students can however enrol outside this time frame. The duration of studies at primary school is six years and three years for junior secondary school; hence a 10-year compulsory education. Graduates have the opportunity to continue their studies in a senior secondary school or in technical vocational training schools. Those over the age of 18 who have not completed compulsory education are able to attend Second Chance Schools, as legislated by Law 2525/1997.

The safeguarding and facilitation of free access to public education covering the full spectrum of the education system – that is, from kindergarten to university – are considered key factors of the integration process through which opportunities for social mobility are offered. The integration of returning Ethnic Greeks and foreign immigrant students into regular public schooling is a conscious choice by the State. It is for this reason that enrolment in public schools is possible irrespective of the legal residence status of the parents; that is, even in the event that parents are deemed illegal immigrants. Schooling not only provides the opportunity for the development of the students' cognitive ability but also provides the opportunity for the acquisition of knowledge about the host country culture and the development and expansion of information and social networks. 'Cultural integration' also includes the notion of internalisation of values, norms, attitudes and the shaping of beliefs – and in which language plays a key and essentially significant factor. It is sequential then, that immigrant children included in the Greek educational system are in a position to receive the appropriate socialisation influences through the holistic functioning of the school.

---

23 Exceptions to this rule are the named 'National-Ethnic Schools' for Polish and Armenian students, in which core subjects are taught in the mother tongue. The reasoning behind this decision (measure) was to avoid problems associated with temporary residence in Greece. It is difficult to understand the logic that dictated the establishment of these separate (separatist) schools; perhaps it has to do with the logic of 'minoritorisation' or with the logic and practice of the Labour Rotation System (in the case of the Greek Ethnic Schools in the Bavarian region of Germany).

Table 7.3 Distribution of foreign immigrant students in Greek state schools across regions for the academic year 2012/13

Region	Preschool Education/ Kindergarten			Primary Education			Junior and Senior Secondary Education			TOTAL
	M	F	Total	M	F	Total	M	F	Total	
Eastern Macedonia/ Thrace	206	296	402	805	699	1,549	394	335	729	2,680
Central Macedonia	1,501	1,390	2,891	4,989	4,531	9,520	2,758	2,369	5,127	17,538
Western Macedonia	148	135	283	554	537	1,091	324	292	616	1990
Epirus	235	185	420	789	699	1,488	524	425	949	2857
Thessaly	622	520	1,142	1,973	1,725	3,698	1,250	1,118	2,368	7,208
Ionian Islands	345	322	667	1,144	1,055	2,199	655	610	1,265	4,131
Western Greece	498	463	961	1763	1867	3,630	906	816	1722	6,313
Central Greece	668	569	1,237	2,142	1,919	4,061	1,285	1,180	2,465	7,763
Attica	3,423	2,965	6,388	14,096	12,488	26,584	8,822	7,698	16,520	49,492
Peloponnese	928	722	1,550	2,698	2,474	5,172	1,341	1,162	2,503	9,225
Northern Aegean	204	181	385	530	503	1,033	305	266	571	1989
Southern Aegean	522	469	991	1,784	1,538	3,322	1007	936	1943	6,256
Crete	786	759	1,545	2,719	2,508	5,227	1,143	1008	2,151	8,923
Total for the country	10,086	8,976	18,862	35,986	32,543	68,574	20,214	18,216	38,929	126,365

Source: Ministry of Education, Religious Affairs, Culture and Sports; Department of Primary Education and Department of Secondary Education.

Table 7.4   Distribution of returning Ethnic Greek students in Greek state schools across regions for the academic year 2012/13

Region	Preschool Education/ Kindergarten			Primary Education			Junior and Senior Secondary Education			TOTAL
	M	F	Total	M	F	Total	M	F	Total	
Eastern Macedonia/ Thrace	50	48	98	414	332	746	189	198	387	1,231
Central Macedonia	175	138	313	771	706	1477	606	579	1,185	2,975
Western Macedonia	3	4	7	18	16	34	26	18	44	85
Epirus	–	–	–	26	27	53	27	20	47	100
Thessaly	6	5	11	23	23	46	14	11	25	82
Ionian Islands	2	3	5	24	15	39	6	11	17	61
Western Greece	3	1	4	22	16	38	11	14	25	67
Central Greece	6	7	13	14	7	21	13	14	27	61
Attica	192	200	392	627	608	1235	287	241	528	2,155
Peloponnese	1	1	2	59	49	108	9	8	17	127
Northern Aegean	–	–	–	9	8	17	2	7	9	26
Southern Aegean	3	1	4	23	10	33	13	15	28	65
Crete	27	24	51	81	61	142	27	26	53	246
Total for the country	468	432	900	2,111	1,878	3,989	1,230	1,162	2,392	7,281

Source: Ministry of Education, Religious Affairs, Culture and Sports; Department of Primary Education and Department of Secondary Education.

The most recent data (2013) regarding enrolment of students from a migrant background in Greek schools reinforce the need for sustainability and constant appraisal and readjustment of interventions required in school settings. This is because the figures show that, despite the economic crisis and the repatriation of immigrants from Albania, Russia and Georgia, there is a stronger than ever presence of immigrant children in Greek State schools (Table 7.3 and 7.4).

School Education and Learning Support Measures

Education policy has also had to undergo extensive changes incorporating within its framework of educational approach an intercultural education, defined as *an approach* which promotes the appreciation of cultural diversity, solidarity and tolerance, the fostering of mutual respect, ethnorelative thinking as a means of avoiding stereotyping and prejudice; and as *a strategy*, focusing on the reformation of the school curriculum, of its established practices, of its procedures and structure as a means of reducing the impact of the disablement of students from different language and cultural backgrounds (Markou, 2010: 74; Banks and Banks, 1993: 9).

The reduction of barriers that inhibit student progress due to language, cultural and family background differences which students from migrant backgrounds bring into the school setting constitute the main intervention parameters not only in ensuring successful learning and peer acceptance but also successful school and wider community inclusion both for the students and their families. In order to meet the needs of these students and as a general response to the challenges posed by the multicultural synthesis of the student population evident in Greek schools, the Greek State has, over time, developed and implemented a series of measures identified either as *general measures*, directed towards all school students, or as *specialised measures* directed for implementation in specific schools with significantly high numbers of students from migrant backgrounds, for the purpose of facilitating school inclusion.

General Support Measures

An intercultural approach in education, as a means of school improvement, is fundamentally about raising student achievement through focusing on the teaching–learning process and the conditions which support intercultural understanding and communication. Therefore, any strategies developed should focus on improving the school's capacity for providing quality education for all students in times of change:

Remedial teaching
As with all students experiencing learning difficulties and poor school results, students from migrant backgrounds can equally attend remedial support classes. This compensatory teaching and learning activity forms part of a broader

framework of State initiatives designed to raise the quality of education and promote equal opportunities.

Intercultural interventions

A series of interventions have been implemented over the years within the Greek education system with the aim of introducing the intercultural dimension. Amongst others, these, include:

- the redesign and reconstruction of school curricula and textbooks to adhere to the principles of intercultural education;
- the establishment of an interdisciplinary approach to analyse issues related to multiculturalism, European identity, globalisation and the daily lives of citizens;
- the establishment of partnerships between Greek and foreign schools;
- the integration of intercultural education into the curricula of university teacher education departments;
- intercultural education training and development seminars for teachers in primary and secondary schools;
- programmes for intercultural intervention at school level.

Specific Support Measures

In addition to the general measures adopted to facilitate the successful integration of students from a migrant background into Greek schools, and which are implemented in *all schools*, the Greek State has taken specific measures to ensure the successful integration and participation of these students in the learning process when and wherever necessary. The key educational intervention measures adopted have as a focus:

- emphasis on the prevention of school failure
- early intervention for struggling learners
- professional development and training in specialised support measures for teachers.

At the level of implementation, these short-term measures are in the form of additional or complementary lessons, usually under the auspices of the Ministry of Education or the responsibility of designated University Teacher Education Institutions. These measures make reference to the following areas.

Reception classes

The establishment and function of reception classes in Greece were first legislated in 1983 in Law 1404/1983 and Ministerial Decree 494/1983 for the children of Ethnic Greeks returning from countries in Europe, from North America and Australia. Experience gained from these classes, and specifically during the wave of migration mainly from the former Soviet Union in the decade that followed, urged the re-examination of their operational framework. Reception classes are usually divided into two phases. During Phase I, students attend separate classes for intensive instruction in Greek and other language-based subjects of the curriculum. In subject areas where Greek language skills are less demanding (such as music, gymnastics, art and another foreign language), immigrant students are integratedwith mainstream students. The maximum period in Phase I classes is two years and close cooperation between school and family is expected.

During Phase II, students are mainstreamed into the school curriculum and participate in regular classes with their peers but receive additional support in the form of individualised instruction. In this revised form, students are no longer isolated in autonomous parallel classes but are integrated into the mainstream school with participation in support classes. It is generally a flexible institutional and instructional intervention at school level for the purpose of supporting successful integration of returning Greek and foreign immigrant children in Greek schools. For the establishment of reception classes in schools, there needs to be a minimum of nine students (maximum 17) and approval of the teachers' school body. Students who continue to experience learning difficulties in mainstream classes due to language deficiencies usually attend Phase II of reception for up to another academic year following evaluation by the teachers' body; the student is then completely integrated in the mainstream. Lessons are usually entrusted to teachers qualified in teaching Greek as a second language. Usually, further optional support continues in afterschool classes.

Afterschool tuition
Students from a migrant background in state schools who need further support attend small afterschool classes (three–eight students) which provide curriculum-specific language support. These usually cater for students who have completed both phases of reception class support. It is worth noting that these types of learning support are solely funded by the State without any fees for the parents and without any involvement or financial support from the students' countries of origin. The support teachers are usually mainstream staff from the same school. One can comment that over the years the State has recruited and remunerated many teachers for this purpose. In all support measures, teachers' intercultural knowledge and competencies are taken into consideration during their selection process. Additionally, teacher training seminars are also organised by school administrators and counsellors.

Intercultural schools/classes
According to Article 35 of Law 2413/1996, new or designated existing schools or classes with significant numbers of students from linguistic and/or culturally diverse backgrounds can be deemed Intercultural Schools. The law foresees the establishment of these schools by local authorities, religious institutions and other nonprofit organisations. Without altering the basic purpose of the integration of

Table 7.5 Distribution of immigrant students and country of origin in Greek Schools of Intercultural Education (SIE) for the academic year 2012/13

Regional	Country of Origin	Primary Education			Secondary Education			Total		
		M	F	Total	M	F	Total	M	F	Total
Africa	Egypt	19	9	28				19	9	28
	Ethiopia	4	2	6				4	2	6
	Nigeria	12	34	46	3	3	6	15	37	52
	Tanzania	0	3	3				0	3	3
	Kenya	3	0	3	1	0	1	4	0	4
	Syria	16	14	30	4	4	8	20	18	38
	Ghana	2	0	2	0	2	2	2	2	4
	Morocco	0	1	1	1	0	1	1	1	2
	Algeria	0	1	1				0	1	1
	Libya				1	0	1	1	0	1
	Seychelles	0	1	1				0	1	1
	Eritrea				0	1	1	0	1	1
	Congo				3	0	3	3	0	3
	Ivory Coast				—					
	Senegal				0	1	1	0	1	1
	Somalia				3	0	3	3	0	3
	Sudan				1	0	1	1	0	1
	Guinea	2	0	2	4	0	4	6	0	6
Asia	Bangladesh	3	1	4	1	2	3	4	3	7
	India	3	3	6	6	1	7	9	4	13
	Philippines	8	2	10	5	1	6	13	3	16

Asia continued	Pakistan	5	2	7	9	2	11	14	4	18
	Sri Lanka	0	1	1				0	1	1
	South Korea	0	1	1				0	1	1
	China	2	0	2	10	13	23	12	13	25
	Palestine				1	1	2	1	1	2
	Afghanistan	10	8	18	35	9	44	45	17	62
	Lebanon	0	1	1				0	1	1
	Turkey	1	0	1	3	0	3	4	0	4
	Armenia	4	3	7	1	2	3	5	5	10
	Iran				3	2	5	3	2	5
	Uzbekistan	0	1	1	1	3	4	1	4	5
	Kazakhstan				2	1	3	2	1	3
Balkans	Albania	109	78	187	79	53	132	188	131	319
	Romania	4	2	6	11	11	22	15	13	28
	Bulgaria	7	8	15	18	17	35	25	25	50
	Serbia-Herzegovina	1	2	3	2	1	3	3	3	6
	FYRof Macedonia				5	1	6	5	1	6
Eastern Europe	Moldavia	2	2	4	13	7	20	15	9	24
	Georgia	21	17	38	35	38	73	56	55	111
	Poland	4	2	6	7	5	12	17	7	18
	Ukraine	4	2	6	6	7	13	10	9	19
	Russia	8	6	14	6	10	16	14	16	30
	Lithuania	0	1	1				0	1	1
	Belarus	0	1	1				0	1	1

Table 7.5 Distribution of immigrant students and country of origin in Greek Schools of Intercultural Education (SIE) for the academic year 2012/13 continued

Regional	Country of Origin	Primary Education			Secondary Education			Total		
		M	F	Total	M	F	Total	M	F	Total
Central/Western Europe	Italy	0	2	2	1	0	1	1	2	3
	Portugal	0	1	1				0	1	1
	Belgium				0	1	1	0	1	1
	Germany				1	0	1	1	0	1
	Greece				12	7	19	12	7	19
North/ South America	USA	6	6	12				6	6	12
	Canada	2	2	4				2	2	4
	Santa Dominica	1	0	1	0	1	1	1	1	2
	Cuba	1	0	1				1	0	1
	Brazil				3	3	6	3	3	6
	Venezuela	1	0	1				1	0	1
	Total	265	220	485	297	210	507	562	430	992

Source: Ministry of Education, Religious Affairs, Culture and Sports. Figures were not available for the Ivory Coast.

this category of students, it is possible to enrich the school curriculum and general operational framework with intercultural activities in an attempt to best meet the needs of the students. The composition of the student population varies from school to school, and teachers are chosen for their knowledge of intercultural teaching and learning skills. From 1996 until today 26 Schools of Intercultural Education operate across the country: 13 primary, 9 junior secondary and 4 senior secondary (of which 10 are in Macedonia-Thrace, 13 in Attica, 2 in Epirus and 1 in Crete).[24]

Table 7.5 illustrates the countries of origin and the distribution of students of migrant background who attended Schools of Intercultural Education (SIE) during the academic year 2012/13. Experience to date from the functioning of these schools does not enable us to make generalisations regarding their positive contribution to the successful integration of children from linguistic and culturally diverse backgrounds. This is because there are significant differences between them relating to one of the outcomes of intercultural education, namely the effects and opportunities related to the interaction between Greek and foreign immigrant students. There are, for example, SIEs with exclusively foreign immigrant student populations, due to either the laxity of the State or because the schools failed to convince Greek parents of the quality of the intercultural education provision to allow their children to attend these schools.

The Programme for the Education of Returning Ethnic Greek and Foreign Immigrant Children

As a means of promoting intercultural educational measures and the integration of migrant children in the Greek school system, the Ministry of Education proceeded in 1997 to develop and implement three intervention programmes:

a. The Education of Returning Greek and Foreign Immigrant Children
b. The Education of Roma Children
c. The Education of the Greek Muslim Minority Children of Thrace.

These programmes, which are co-funded by the State and the EU's Social Structural Fund, form the bases for innovation in Greece and contribute significantly both at

---

24   It should be noted that the establishment and functioning of reception and tuition classes either through the Ministry of Education staffing allocations or through external programme funding constitutes a financial burden concerning teachers' salaries, training and professional development, school infrastructure, teaching resources etc. Schools of Intercultural Education are considered 'expensive' because the small number of students per classroom, the enriched programme with additional subjects and activities, the extended teaching programme and, most importantly, student transportation by bus from various parts of the city constitute a financial burden that far exceeds the average expenditure per student in other public schools.

the level of scientific discourse on intercultural education and of school-based aspects of interculturalism.

The Programme for the Education of Returning Greek and Foreign Immigrant Students has been developed and implemented primarily by the Centre for Intercultural Studies of the University of Athens and partly by the University of Thessaloniki. This programme was due to end in 2013 but there is increased probability for its continuation in the coming years. The programme has an established extensive network of partners covering all administrative regions in Greece through which centrally developed activities can be effectively and successfully implemented at school level. These activities include:

1. the examination of the social, pedagogical and psychological factors and school conditions conducive for the integration of migrant children into the education system;
2. the development and implementation of coordinated intervention measures which promote inclusion and reduce forms of exclusion of migrant children in the educational system and eliminate the barriers which prevent students from diverse cultural and linguistic backgrounds from reaching their full learning potential;
3. the development of a framework for re-examining those barriers in terms of changes in the learning environment;
4. improving support structures and networks for the inclusion of students from diverse linguistic and cultural backgrounds in schools and their community as a whole;
5. the development of a coordinated professional development programme for teachers and educational policymakers and members of the wider educational community on issues relating to intercultural education;
6. the design and development of appropriate teaching materials and methods which allow all students to become involved in learning processes;
7. the promotion of activities which ensure school achievement and foster respect for cultural diversity, international understanding and the interaction between school and society.

All these dimensions of the programme are directly related to the general aim of the State to enhance the quality of Greek school educational provision, the promotion of equal opportunities and the creation of conditions that foster understanding and cooperation. Intercultural inclusion activities developed and implemented aim to prevent the alienation of children from linguistic and culturally diverse backgrounds from their family environment while at the same time facilitating their intercultural integration into the school and wider community.

The teaching of the mother tongue and culture
With regard to the teaching of the students' mother tongue, lessons can be offered after school hours on a voluntary base. However, recent research involving

parents of immigrant students from Albania, who constitute the largest migrant group in Greece, in an attempt to ascertain their attitude towards the teaching of their mother tongue revealed that this was not a priority. The parents preferred their children to learn proficiency in Greek and other foreign languages, as they believed this would ensure better prospects for social and career advancement both in Greece and abroad (Kokkali, 2011). Similar findings were also noted during the implementation of the programme 'Education of Returning Greek and Foreign Immigrant Children' at the Secondary School of Intercultural Education of Aharnes in 2000 in an attempt to extend the curriculum with selective afternoon activities such as Russian language lessons. Parents preferred their children to select classes in other foreign languages or computing and technology studies rather than learning Russian as they considered the acquisition of their mother tongue a family issue. In essence, their educational standards and aspirations do not differ from those of native Greek parents.[25]

The Intercultural Approach in Greek Education

The intercultural approach appeared in Greece in the early 1980s, coinciding with the return of a large number of Greek migrants from western traditional countries of emigration, mainly Germany. The mass and unregulated influx of immigrants in the years which followed – from neighboring countries and the former Soviet Union initially, and later from Asia, Africa and the Middle East – shaped and continues to shape the circumstances of multiculturalism in Greek society. As a result, Greece is confronted for the first time in its modern history with the issue of the inclusion of people born and raised in other countries with different language and cultural backgrounds. For Greek education, the challenge is particularly significant as this involves the adoption of major changes deemed necessary to meet the new and developing needs.

The 'Education of Returning Greek and Foreign Migrant Students' programme has played an important role in shaping the theoretical framework of intercultural education and intercultural interventions both at the level of the school and at the level of scientific research.

Intercultural Education Framework: Policy Formulation and Implementation

Between the Scientific Director and the members of the Scientific Committee of the Centre for Intercultural Studies at the University of Athens there has been a shared understanding that the philosophy and objectives of the intercultural policies

---

25   Programme for the 'Education of Returning Ethnic Greeks and Foreign Immigrant Students', University of Athens, KEDA 2001–04. Perhaps this is the main reason why, apart from a few cases, there has been up till now no teaching of the migrant children's mother tongue.

adopted, both at the level of scientific discourse and implementation, should neither create nor reproduce minorities but rather foster intercultural understanding and constructive cooperation between native-born Greeks and people from migrant backgrounds. Throughout all the intercultural educational programmes and interventions implemented by the Centre, there have been concerted efforts towards the establishment of a 'rule of law' State where all citizens are able to be included and give legitimacy to the State. These types of intercultural educational activities assist all students to acquire knowledge and skills that will enable them to strive for the realisation of basic democratic principles of equality and justice. In essence, the basic objective of these activities is the shaping of intercultural democratic citizens. For this purpose there is an urgent need to redefine the school curriculum and the school subject course of political and social education.

The traditional principles of civic education as a means of acquiring knowledge on governance, democratic institutions, and national constitutional and political history need to be expanded and reinterpreted in light of broader concepts for rights and obligations of citizens who live and work in multicultural environments both at national and supranational levels. The values of collectivity, solidarity, tolerance, mutual understanding and respect for cultural diversity, peace and international cooperation should be cultivated among young people. Young people should realise that the values of individualism, competition and consumerism that promote the expression of neoliberal global capitalism today impoverish large segments of the population and virtually eliminate the middle class that has historically been the pillar and guarantor of democratic institutions. Ultimately, this will lead, sooner or later, to unrestrainable social unrest and conflict with unpredictable consequences, since the 'exceeding the limits' perpetrated by unaccountable markets will follow a Nemesis of punishment. This is the most important lesson learnt through the teachings of the ancient Greek tragedies: exceeding the limits both at an individual and collective level has inevitable Nemesis (punishment). In Greece, the need for the redefinition of the school curriculum and the school subject course of political and civic education is motivated by two emerging factors within Greek society: a) the majority of immigrants who are now able to acquire Greek citizenship, that is, able to become Greek citizens, originate from countries with autocratic or theocratic regimes; b) the rapid rise of the extreme conservative, racist (in the sense of race) Golden Dawn Party and its representation in the Greek Parliament.

Intercultural Education: Scientific Research Activities

At the level of scientific research, the team at the Centre for Intercultural Studies of the University of Athens questions the validity of many studies regarding the social integration of people from linguistic and culturally diverse groups, as all students usually seek to explain the integration deficits into Greek society either through the influence of their ethnocultural backgrounds or due to the approach of social stratification. The majority of these research studies have as a central theme the exclusion of these social groups from the various sectors of the Greek community. They often include rhetoric about racist attitudes, accentuation of differences and a conceptual limitation of interculturalism in the narrow context of culture, through which there is an attempt to interpret social inequalities and social exclusion. Of course, it goes without saying that there is a dominance of studies which limit their research scope to the behaviour and attitudes of foreigners, using, at best, the respective characteristics of Greek nationals as a comparative factor. Studies which take into account simultaneously the two sides of the integration process and which perceive integration as the effective intercultural interaction and cooperation between all social groups are still pending. For the Centre's scientific research team such perceptions and practice cannot by themselves fully illuminate the plurality of relations of the various groups that make up a contemporary multicultural society, let alone their interrelationship interactions.

This becomes particularly evident in studies regarding the Greek Roma community currently conducted by the Centre for Intercultural Studies as part of the Programme for the Education of Roma Children. The differentiation of the Roma communities into many subgroups according to their various living conditions is a key feature of their social and cultural reality. As socio-cultural reality of the Greek Roma, as with non-Roma Greeks, is not static but rather constantly changing, shapes a multiplicity of conditions which, in any attempt at investigation and analysis, requires a search for a broader spectrum (matrix) of factors affecting the process of integration and interaction.

It is hoped that the current studies conducted by the Centre will contribute to a more comprehensive and holistic understanding of the problems arising from the complexity of social conditions, which in turn will be able to contribute to the development of more effective intervention policy measures. Additionally, it is also hoped that the studies will contribute to the quintessence of public debate encompassing issues not only of the causes of the difficult social conditions directly afflicting the Greek Roma, but also of sharing responsibility for the problems related to their social integration and the relationship between Roma and non-Roma Greeks.

In the current public debate, the deficit integration process regarding the Roma community is often presented as a consequence of the specific social relations and cultural situations shaped by this particular social group who, in support of the various State-proposed integration policies, abandon these deficiencies (i.e., their language, interest in schooling) and adopt an instrumental perception of education. As a result, there is a formation of perceptions at the political level, in the media and amongst non-Roma Greek citizens that attribute this social integration deficit to the Roma themselves, who are perceived as having sole responsibility.

Concluding Statements

Research shows that, despite the serious problems associated with residence and work permits, communication (mainly due to language deficiency), housing and employment etc. it is characteristic of the majority of immigrants in Greece of their intention for long-term prospects of remaining in the country. The intention to settle permanently in Greece is also expressed by their children who attend Greek schools (Haliapa, 2009). This has also shown to be a similar experience in traditional European immigration countries in which expectations for temporary stay of immigrants and the theory of a labour rotation system proved to be unsubstantiated. The permanent nature of migration is still the rule of fact.

Other studies show that the process of legalisation contributes significantly to the successful integration of immigrants in host societies, as it facilitates family reunification, regular school attendance of their children, employment opportunities and generally contributing to the total life organisation of immigrants, since they are able to attain a sense of a better life achievement both for themselves and their families. The status of legalisation has particularly reinforcing value on the psychological position of immigrants, as it promotes the feeling of acceptance and belonging as equal members of society. The legalisation of immigrants also seems to work positively on school performance of migrant children (Moisidis and Papadopoulou, 2011: 9–49).

The successful integration of immigrants who have lived and worked in Greece for many years is now a stated objective in Greek migration policy. The recent Law 3838/2010 amends significantly the Greek Citizenship Code, shifting the right to citizenship from the 'right of blood' (*ius sanguinis*) to the 'right of soil' (*ius soli*). In this way, national identity ceases to be constructed exclusively in terms of ethnicity and incorporates political, educational, cultural and social conditions. With this law, there is noted significant progress in securing legal residency, the right to family reunification and employment, but fundamentally securing participation in the civil and civic life of their place of residence (participation in elections for local authorities). With the most recent changes of Law 3852/2010, there is the provision for the establishment and functioning of a Council for the Integration of Immigrants in the country's municipalities, where local government assumes an important role in promoting the social integration of immigrants living in their administrative area. Although the 'nationalist' concept of the nation, expressed by conservative MPs, perceives naturalisation as a result of a successful process of integration and belonging to the nation as a kind of primordial bond, the modifications in the new law refer to the process of naturalisation as a vehicle for integration. The absence of the nationalist concept of the nation and the nation state is evident in the new law, and the definition of citizenship proclaims the citizen as a member of its constitutional order. The naturalised persons must accept the proclamation of this content, taking an oath after the onset of adulthood.

However, despite the enactment of the new law, supporters of the nationalist concept of nation and the nation state are not solely satisfied with confronting arguments, but have proceeded to dispute the law in the Supreme Court, challenging the constitutionality of certain provisions. A society which is experiencing a continuous stream of migration and in need of an ongoing process of integration into European structures is fully supportive of this new law. Although it is still early, the first naturalisation data show an upward trend, although not particularly significant at this stage.

The granting of citizenship is entrenched in the fundamental principles of a democratic government. The democratic nature of modern states has generated many discussions and reflections on citizenship, since it is directly related to its legitimacy derived from all residents. Beyond the common language, all social groups within a democratic society should demonstrate adherence to the democratic principles, the Constitution and the individual rights provided therein, as well as mutual respect and tolerance. In the common political space of the state, individuals develop interrelations and participate in the same legal, administrative and political contexts. The values and common practices of a democratic society cannot be put in dispute. The specific recognition of collective cultural values, traditions and identities cannot be achieved when these lead to practices that militate against the democratic process of dialogue and consensus arising from the adoption of common rules in the public sphere.

Education is the most important institution for the integration of children from linguistic and culturally diverse backgrounds in any host society. For this reason, the successful or non-educational participation constitutes a reliable criterion for assessing the degree of integration of migrant children in Greek society.

There is evidence to suggest that migrant children are still heavily influenced by the difficulties encountered in the Greek educational system. However, given that integration is a continuous process and observing the rising trend in the indicators pertaining to the number of students from a migrant background who complete primary school and those who continue to junior and senior high school, we observe a gradual improvement in their educational situation. In research by Gotovos and Markou (2004: 124–6) it was found that the average school performance of students from a migrant background is a grade of 14 out of 20, with differences noted between first- and second-generation migrant children. The proportion of migrant students in secondary education is increasing, especially in junior high schools and technical and vocational schools. This seems to be attributed to the contribution of teachers, and especially to the structure of the Greek educational system which has a horizontal single-form structure in secondary education without the vertical variations encountered in other systems, such as the German system with three different types of school at secondary level.

The major problem, and the most serious difficulties facing Greek schools today in the period of neoliberal globalised capitalism and economic crisis, is undoubtedly youth unemployment – particularly for those aged 15–24, where in some regions, namely Western Macedonian, youth unemployment has reached a staggering 72.5 per cent (Eurostat, 2013). This is significantly higher than the unemployment level in other states in Southern and Northern Europe and the EU average of 22.9 per cent. The weakness of the labour market to create new jobs for both unskilled and skilled workers will develop a state of high competition and social tension between Greek and migrant background youth. The inability to integrate second and third generation immigrant children in the labour market undermines significantly the schools' task of intercultural integration into Greek society.

References

Banks, J.A. and Banks, C.A.M. (1993). *Multicultural Education: Issues and Perspectives* (2nd edn). Boston, MA: Allyn and Bacon.

Bagavos, X. and Kapsalis, A. (2008). The context of migration policy in Greece, *Series Studies*, 29. Athens: HPC/INE/GSEE–ADEDI–KEKMOKOP.

Brubaker, R. (1992). *Citizenship and Nationhood in France and Germany*. Cambridge, MA: Harvard University Press.

Dretakis, M. (2001). Exceeding 5 per cent of the student population are children of returning Greek and foreign migrants in schools. *Modern Education*, 119.

Eurostat (2013). *Eurostat Database*. http://epp.eurostat.ec.europa.eu/portal/page/portal/eurostat/home [retrieved January 2013].

Gotovos, A. and Markou, G. (2003). *Returning Ethnic Greek and Foreign Immigrant Children in Greek Education*. Athens: Institute for Greek Diaspora Education and Intercultural Studies.

Gotovos, A. and Markou, G. (2004). *Returning Ethnic Greek and Foreign Immigrant Students in Greek Education*. Athens: IPODE/CER.

Greek Parliament, (2010), *Report on the Bill 'Current provisions for Greek citizenship and political participation of Ethnic Greeks and legally residing immigrants and other provisions'* (8 March). Athens: Directorate B Scientific Studies, Department of Legal Drafting and Bill Proposals.

Haliapa, A. (2009). *Integration in Greece. The Problem of the Second Generation*. PhD thesis, Harokopio University.

Harmovitis, D. (2011). For a 'Migrant Integration Policy Index' (pp. 108–17). In Syrri, D. (ed.), *Coexisting with Immigration*. Athens: Ianos.

Kanellopoulos, K. et al. (2011). *Illegal Immigrants in Greece*. Athens: CIF.

Kokkali, I. (2011). Strategic integration and adjustment forms of Albanian immigrants in Greek society. The example of Thessaloniki. In Moisidis, A. and Papadopoulou, D. (eds), *The Social Integration of Immigrants in Greece. Employment, Education, Identities*. Athens Review, 211–65.

Kontis, A. (ed.) (2009). *Social Issues: Immigrant Integration*. Athens: Papazisis.

Krispi-Nikoletopoulou, E. (1965). *Nationality*. Athens: Sakkoulas.

Law 2413/1996

Law 2790/2000

Law 2910/2001

Law 3013/2002

Law 3284/2004

Law 3386/2005

Law 3446/2003

Law 3838/2010, Explanatory Memorandum '*Right of blood (ius sanguinis)*'

Law 3852/2010

Lianos, T. et al. (2008). *Estimate of the Number of Foreigners Residing Illegally in Greece*. Athens: IMEPO.

Markou, G. (2010). *Introduction to Intercultural Education*. Athens: University of Athens.

Maroukis, T. (2011). *Illegal Migration in Greece: Realism, Respect, and 'Smart' Deportations* (pp. 42–50). In Syrri, D. (ed.), *Coexisting with Immigration*. Thessaloniki: Ianos.

Marshall, T.H. (1950). *Citizenship and Social Class and Other Essays*. Cambridge: Cambridge University Press.

Moisidis, A. and Papadopoulou, D. (eds) (2011). *The Social Integration of Immigrants in Greece. Employment, Education, Identities*. Athens Review.

National Statistic Services (2001). *National Census 2001*. Athens: NSS.

Press Office of the New Democracy Party (2010a). Letter by the President, Mr Antonis Samaras, to the Minister of Interior Affairs, Decentralisation and e-Government, Mr John Ragousi (11 January). Athens.

Press Office of the New Democracy Party (2010b). Speech. Reply by the President of New Democracy Party, Antonis Samaras, on the agenda of the parliamentary debate on Citizenship and Migration Policy (8 February). Athens.

Robolis, S. (2008). *Migration in Greece. An Expert Report for SOPEMI–OECD*. Paris.

Robolis, S. (2011). Economic crisis, labour market, migration. In Moisidis, A. and Papadopoulou, D. (eds), *The Social Integration of Immigrants in Greece. Employment, Education, Identities*. Athens Review.

Vermeulen, H. (2001). *Culture and Inequality. Immigrant Cultures and Social Mobility in Long-Term Perspective*. Amsterdam: Institute for Migration and Ethnic Studies (IMES).

Chapter 8

From Intercultural Education to Citizenship Education in the Netherlands: Enhancement of Cultural Values or Development of Critical Democratic Citizenship?

Martha Montero-Sieburth and Hana Alhadi[1]

Introduction

In this chapter, intercultural educational policies are traced against the multicultural[2] backdrop adopted by the Council of Europe[3] and the European Union (EU) during the 1990s and are followed in the Netherlands, where they became a preferred modality for integrating migrants up into 2005 and were replaced by citizenship education from 2006 to the present.[4] Of particular focus is:

1. How do member states interpret and put this policy into practice at the national level?
2. How the Netherlands implemented intercultural education policies and in 2006 shifted towards citizenship education.
3. How intercultural/citizenship education in the Netherlands is closely linked to migrant integration.

---

1 We are particularly grateful for the careful review which Prof. Dr Sabine Severiens – Chair of Education with a focus on diversity at Erasumus University Rotterdam, and also Chair of Education with a focus on vulnerable children at the University of Amsterdam – provided on this chapter from a Dutch perspective.

2 It should be noted from Stephen Vertovec's (2010: 92) comment that 'multiculturalism has never been made up of a single type of piece of policy, institutional framework or programme. Moreover, most multicultural policies were intended not to produce economic outcomes or a sense of separateness among minority communities, but rather a broad social acceptance and recognised inclusion in dominant public spheres.'

3 Contributing to this European vision of interculturalism under multiculturalism was not only the Council of Europe and the European Union, but also UNESCO, the World Bank, OSCE, UNICEF and the Soros Foundation during the 1970s.

4 The term migrant is used throughout the chapter instead of immigrant, because it is more commonly used throughout European literature.

4. How are schooling practices in Dutch non-denominational schools using citizenship education implemented, and what are their strengths and limitations?
5. Where is citizenship education in the Netherlands currently headed: towards the enhancement of values or the development of critical democratic practices?

In order to answer these questions, the methodology used included content analysis of the frameworks used for intercultural education at the EU level; their interpretation through various programmes; the interpretation of policies within the Netherlands addressing intercultural education; and the actual implementation of these within districts and schools. The latter also included interviews conducted with local project managers organising intercultural activities and with primary and secondary teachers in 'black' schools.[5]

The shift from intercultural to the adoption of citizenship and democratic education by several European countries (Portera, 2008) has impacted policies in the Netherlands, where they have been closely related to the integration of migrant populations over several decades.

Research by the senior researcher[6] and that of her Masters students in primary and secondary schools[7] in Rotterdam and Amsterdam[8] highlight some of the intercultural practices used in Dutch schools, and include the junior researcher's[9]

---

5   Some Dutch schools are unofficially characterised as zwarte or 'black' schools, defined either on the basis of having 50 per cent or more minority students or by the proportion of school-aged migrant children in the neighbourhood (Vedder, 2006). The concentration of black schools is higher in urban Amsterdam, The Hague, Rotterdam and Utrecht, where close to half of the schools can be described as black (Stevens et al. 2011). Depending on the source and year, the percentage by which a school is referred to as being black may vary. In 2007, CBS used 50 per cent students from non-Western ethnic origins and reported that one-third of schools had over 80 per cent. The Ministry of Education website however identifies black schools on the basis of having 70 per cent pupils with low-skilled or non-Western parents, citing that black schools are not necessarily ethnically segregated and identifying well over 300 official black schools in the Netherlands.

6   The senior researcher has studied and worked with pluralism in Latin American schools particularly with indigenous populations; multiculturalism and teacher professionalisation and diversity in the United States; interculturalism in Spain, and world citizenship education in Dutch schools and with Dutch-Turkish and European educators in the Netherlands.

7   Only non-denominational public (i.e. state) schools are included as part of the research in this chapter.

8   Students studied world citizenship education; bicultural issues in raising children; disruptive behaviours of young female students with ethnically different teachers (German and Turkish Dutch); native and non-native Dutch teachers' expectation of Turkish and Moroccan students in primary schools; and minority youth identity in secondary schools.

9   The junior researcher completed a research study on the policy implementation of intercultural principles from the European Union intercultural principles to a local Amsterdam district level for her Master's thesis. Her interest in intercultural dialogue,

investigation of how EU intercultural policies are implemented through organised activities in one of Amsterdam's local districts. The researchers are not Dutch, but one lives and works in the Netherlands and the other lived in the Netherlands but now resides in Slovenia. They build on the extensive research of several Dutch and European scholars: Leeman (2006, 2008); Leeman and Ledoux (2003a, 2003b, 2005); Leenders et al. (2008, 2012); Veugelers (2011); Reid (2008); Driessen (2000); Leeman and Pels (2006); Portera (2008); Allemann-Ghionda (2008, 2009); and Duyvendak and Scholten (2012).

The Enactment of Intercultural Education at the European Union Level

In the United States, policies for multicultural education arose out of its historical legacy of race relations moulded during the Civil Rights movement and increasing immigration, and were based on the reality that schools needed to serve a multiplicity of ethnic groups and cultures.[10] In contrast, the majority of European countries, with a history of conflicts and violence stemming from national and cultural differences, adopted intercultural education as a way to ameliorate diversity in schools and encourage integration. Cristina Allemann-Ghionda has brought the social discourse of intercultural education into focus through her international and comparative studies in the late 1990s, and advocated for the modernisation of schools in dealing with migrant diversity. As she states 'intercultural education' is:

> an education aimed at fomenting a tolerant and sensitive approach towards socio-cultural differences between groups with different ethnic, cultural and religious origins, especially when these are controversial and likely to create conflicts. Intercultural education is therefore about improving understanding between different societies and different majority or minority groups in the same society. (Allemann-Ghionda, 2008: 2)

In Europe, the interactive aspects and dialogue necessary for co-existence have been clearly emphasised.

Allemann-Ghionda (2009) argues that with rapid globalisation and the resulting mobility of people during the 1970s, greater numbers of migrants entered Europe, and a variety of languages and cultures needed to be linked to European integration policies. The Council of Europe adopted multiculturalism and multicultural pedagogy to deal with the children of migrant workers and decided upon 'inter' in intercultural education, implying 'breaking down barriers, exchange and reciprocity, rather than merely passively accepting differences in

intercultural experiences and personal family experience perspective as a European, Slovenian and Middle Eastern Yemeni complements this perspective.

10   Multicultural education has been strongly advocated in Canada, Australia and the USA for different historical reasons.

a tolerant manner or even assuming that individuals belong to defined and fixed groups' (Allemann-Ghionda 2008: 2). Yet Portera (2008) considers that because it is impossible to respect all diversities, multicultural pedagogy has become in many European schools pedagogy for minority assimilation.

While there are few official documents or guidelines identifying intercultural education policies at the European level, intercultural competences in education are implied in several of the educational programmes and projects of the Council of Europe and the European Commission, and UNESCO has developed salient curriculum principles and guidelines for intercultural education. Thus, even though multiculturalism was considered an umbrella concept, European educational sciences and European policy documents identified intercultural education and pedagogy as it was closely tied to European integration and migration, and as appropriate responses to globalisation, multilinguism, different religions and cultural behaviours (Portera, 2008). Among the targeted goals were:

- the learning of one language beyond the mother tongue;
- the fostering of bilingual education as a means to create respect for diverse identities;
- the study of different religions in the curriculum;
- value teaching (relativism versus universalism);
- the promotion of teacher training aimed at helping migrant or ethnically different students;
- the successful integration of migrant students through education; and
- 'the diversity dimension in the curricula of subject matters' (Reich et al., 2000 as quoted by Allemann-Ghionda, 2009).

Later guidelines such as that of the 2004 Eurydice survey specified that Europeans needed to: 1) Learn about cultural diversity to develop tolerance and create respect among pupils to fight against racism and xenophobia; 2) Emphasise the social diversity in European history to encourage pupils to develop a sense of European identity (European Commission, 2004 as cited in Duyvendak and Scholten, 2012).

As a consequence, not all countries shared official national policies or followed similar guidelines, but cooperated with UNESCO, the Council of Europe, the European Commission and other supporting institutions in developing projects that included, among many other activities, intercultural competencies,[11] international exchanges, youth peace building, inter-religious dialogue and conflict prevention. Each country determined how to implement intercultural education and develop its practices, yet by 2000 citizenship education became a preferred modality, replacing intercultural education at the EU level because it placed the onus for integration more on the individual than on national level and required a refocusing on diversity.

---

11   Examples of this are the Pestalozzi Programme or the European Diploma in Intercultural Competence sponsored by the EU's Lifelong Learning Programme.

However, the implementation of intercultural/citizenship education is critiqued by Allemann-Ghionda (2009) in that many countries identify the value of including diversity as part of their educational policies; however, they do not necessarily implement social equality practices, allowing educational systems to become highly selective, even segregating their student populations, or neutralising the inclusion of diversity in the curriculum.

Reception and Integration of Migrants in the Netherlands, Implementation of Intercultural Education and Shift to Citizenship Education

One of the oldest immigrant countries in Europe, the Netherlands has witnessed substantial in- and outflows of peoples since the 1500s (Lucassen and Penninx, 1994). During the European wars of the fifteenth and sixteenth centuries the Netherlands experienced the confluence of Spanish, French and German cultural and social influences, and later drew into its borders many migrants such as those fleeing religious intolerance and persecution – the English Pilgrims, French Huguenots and Jews – who settled permanently due to its attitudes of tolerance, liberalness and lack of nationalism (Schama, 1991). Later, Chinese migrants and post-colonial migrants from Surinam, Indonesia,[12] the Moluccas and the Dutch Antilles – who arrived as citizens after their countries became independent from the Netherlands – came and settled, and today make up the growing second and third generations.

However, how migrants have been integrated into the Netherlands is explained through several diverse perspectives. Eldering (1996) asserts that migrants were integrated through two dominant factors: 1) equality of opportunity and 2) the equivalence of cultures based on religion. While the first is based on economic access and accommodation, the second focuses on the culture of minorities. This has led to a focus on culturalism in which members of an ethnic cultural group are associated with the cultural characteristics of that group, and has resulted in the treatment of minorities as monolithic and essentialised groups (Leeman and Ledoux, 2003b; Leeman and Reid, 2006).

Duyvendak and Scholten (2012: 270) discuss the system of 'pillarisation' which prevailed from the 1920s to 1960s and supported the compartmentalisation of schools along religious and sociocultural as well as ideological lines and gave rise to the current pluralistic frameworks. Koopmans' position, they argue, upholds the Dutch approach to integration as being linked to the system of pillarisation 'where ethno-cultural cleavages were stressed in a similar way in multicultural policies', and in which Dutch society was divided into specific religious or socio-cultural pillars responding to the religious, schooling and community needs of Protestants, Catholics, Socialists and Liberals (Lijphart, 1968, in Duyvendak and Scholten, 2012). A fifth pillar, based on the influx of Muslim migrants, was added; and although each

---

12   Indonesians are one of the largest groups that by the second generation are considered to have fully integrated.

pillar was separate, the prevailing policy was for equitable distribution of resources, services and needs as an official expression of Dutch tolerance.

Jan Rath's analysis, on the other hand, shows that the Dutch model is a product of class difference and ideological conflict within Dutch society rather than a consequence of the history of pillarisation. They state:

> whereas the academic modelling of the Dutch approach to migrant integration depicts the Netherlands as a country that values pluralist concepts of citizenship, it is the exact opposite which has occurred. Since the 1990s, Dutch politicians are becoming less willing to make room for cultural differences. In fact, they are very critical about the pluralistic institutional framework that still exists as a consequence of the era of pillarization. (Duyvendak and Scholten, 2012: 280)

Hurenkamp, Tonkens and Duyvendak (2011) attribute the recent return to nationalism in Dutch politics to the demise of multiculturalism. The discourse of citizenship enters the public domain in the Netherlands, they say, through three routes: 1) communitarianism which grows out of an anti-self-centredness and lack of civic engagement; 2) the fear or diversity diluting social cohesion; and 3) the need to debate differences as part of a republican citizenship towards finding shared solutions.

During the 1950s and 1960s, the Netherlands needed to augment its labour force, and migrant workers arrived from Spain, Portugal and other Southern European countries. Some returned home with compensation, but a sizeable group stayed on and is now also into a second and third generation. At the same time, as Duyvendak and Scholten (2012) indicate, because Dutch society had been undergoing de-pillarisation, the focus on culture was more of a discursive influence, like multiculturalism, than an institutional and normative ideal and a more descriptive way to increase social diversity.

By the 1970s, guest workers from Turkey and Morocco contracted for temporary work came with the expectation that they would return to their countries once that work was completed. The policy for intercultural education in the Netherlands became characterised, according to Driessen (2000: 59), as a 'two track approach' emphasising migrant pupils' integration into the Dutch educational system and at the same time preparing for their return home, with home language instruction provided in classrooms. However, many decided to settle permanently in the Netherlands, and during the 1980s through family reunification legislation also brought their families, thereby increasing the numbers of Turkish and Moroccan migrants, particularly in large urban centers, and making them the first and third largest minority groups.[13]

The Dutch government claimed that because a multicultural society had to be reflected through suitable school subjects, intercultural education became a 'starting

---

13   Of the minorities in the Netherlands, the most numerous are Turks, followed by Indonesians and Moroccans.

point for all subjects' in schools (Driessen 2000: 63). By the 1980s, intercultural education was considered by the government an effective two-way integration acculturative process which would not stigmatise ethnic group integration (Driessen, 2000), and schools were required to prepare students for life in a multicultural society through compulsory intercultural education taught in ethnically mixed classrooms (Leeman and Ledoux, 2003b; Leeman and Pels, 2006).

Children were to gain knowledge of each other, live harmoniously and be free of prejudice, discrimination and racism (Leeman and Ledoux, 2003b). Extensive documentation exists during this period which attests to the support of intercultural education, but indications of what schools should do and how to allocate funds for their implementation were wanting.

The Cultural Minority Policy, enacted during the 1980s, allocated additional resources for migrant students who appeared to have greater problems in learning than Dutch working-class pupils.[14] According to Duyvendak and Scholten (2012: 272), this policy 'expressed the idea that an amelioration of the social-cultural position of migrants would also improve their socio-economic position. The objective was to combat discrimination and socio-economic deprivation' and at the same time 'support socio-cultural emancipation'. Disadvantaged children in primary schools were categorised by so-called 'weighting factors': ethnic minority[15] children counted as 1.9, Dutch working-class children 1.25 and 'other' children 1.0 (Eldering, 1996). Such weightings became a form of assessing school scores, with high-scoring schools receiving more funding.

Minorities up to and including the third generation were further distinguished in 1983 by the Netherlands Scientific Council for Government Policy as being *allochtonen*, – meaning foreigner, or migrants from outside the Netherlands – as distinct from *autochtoon*, used for native Dutch.[16] Since then the term *allochtoon* has acquired negative and often derogatory connotations in the media, particularly for the characterisation of Moroccans. Policy-level discussions attempted first to substitute the term with 'bicultural', but this did not receive wide public support. However, in February 2013 the term *allochtoon* was changed by the City Council of Amsterdam to a hyphenated term: Amsterdam-Moroccan or Amsterdam-Turk. Whether this will extend to the national level is yet to be seen, but with the desire to maintain an equitable and fair Dutch society, changes like this are likely to occur in other cities with large minority populations.

---

14   According to Driessen (2000), the national Social Priority Policy (1974), which targeted working-class pupils, was adopted on the basis of the 1960s–1970s educational initiatives and programmes in Dutch cities which attempted to engage parents in their children's schools in working-class neighbourhoods.

15   Driessen (2000) explains that to be a minority child, and be defined as such, the parents needed to be born in a Mediterranean country or a former colony, or be refugees.

16   For children born in the Netherlands, if one parent is born abroad the child is *allochtoon*; only when both parents are born in the Netherlands is the child Dutch.

Adopted in 1985, the Education Priority Policy (EPP) was designed to provide educational opportunities to migrant and Dutch working-class students to equalise disadvantages. Between 1993 and 1998 it focused on improving arithmetic and language achievement levels of target minority groups and reducing absenteeism and school dropout rates (Driessen, 2000). Additionally, bilingual reception and mother tongue instruction (MTI) were implemented under EPP; but in 1991, MTI's focus shifted from integration to developing positive self-concept, diminishing the gap between school and the home environment, and facilitating the learning of Dutch (Driessen, 2000).

By 1990, the content of intercultural instruction for ethnic minority students focusing on language, geography, history and religion gradually became an isolated part of the curriculum. There was little or no contact between ethnic minority teachers who had limited command of Dutch and native Dutch teachers; and interculturalism took a back seat in fostering equality of cultures for the sake of equality of opportunity (Eldering, 1996). Education during this period, stipulates Veugelers (2011), was not to be a tool for social change, but rather the control over secondary education, vocational education and the setting of standards and national curricula as means to tighten the previous notions of collective emancipation.

During this time, signs that the education policies for minorities had not had the desired effect were already evident (Driessen, 2000) and despite some progress, the performance of migrant children, especially of Moroccan and Turkish background, was far behind that of their native Dutch counterparts. Thus, a newer technical-instrumental view of education was combined with what Veugelers (2011) refers to as the 'marketing' ideology of education and self-regulation became the norm. The Committee for Non-Indigenous Pupils in Education critiqued the previous policies for using ethnic identity and socio-economic factors to explain the poor educational and Dutch language performance of migrant children (Driessen, 2000). They recommended that the government should: 1) adopt a perspective on minorities as enrichment to, and not a problem for, Dutch society; 2) reinforce bilingual reception models and mother tongue instruction (MTI); 3) allow minorities to maintain and develop their cultures; and 4) allow municipalities to decide school budgets on the basis of parents' educational levels rather than ethnic origins.

By 1998 and 1999, the EPP became the Educational Disadvantage Policy (EDP) and administrative responsibility of Educational Priority Areas[17] was decentralised to municipalities which allotted resources to schools. As a result, primary schools employed additional staff based on the socio-economic and ethnic composition of the school population, and secondary schools were provided programme resources (such as Dutch as a second language classes and international transition classes) aimed at facilitating entry of students into the Dutch educational system.[18]

---

17   Areas identified as in need of urgent attention regarding educational disadvantages.

18   Cooperation between schools, libraries and day-care nurseries was fostered; and reading, homework, registration and guidance for truants and early school leavers, and preschool level activities with parents and children were implemented.

Driessen's (2000) EDP school evaluations indicate that most schools used resources to form smaller classes with more individualised teacher attention, and committees made decisions about Dutch as a second language and MTI. Such recommendations were readily adopted because intercultural education was no longer seen as a separate policy track but rather as part of general educational policy.

In retrospect, Duyvendak and Scholten (2012: 275) highlight that compared to the 1980s – when the preservation of cultural identity was seen as an 'important condition for the cultural emancipation of minorities in Dutch society' – in the new millennium 'cultural diversity has become increasingly seen as an obstacle for integration'. The unrest brought on by the September 11, 2001 attack in the United States, the London and Madrid bombings, and the murders of Pim Fortuyn in 2002 and Theo Van Gogh in 2004 raised questions about the effectiveness of integration policies. Yet, despite such questioning, findings from the Blok Commission report showed that partial, or in some cases, total success of educational advancement of minorities was evident (Duyvendak and Scholten 2012).

From 1995 to 2005, Hurenkamp et al. (2011) report that the Netherlands underwent an increased public presence of citizenship leaning towards communitarianism, requiring citizens to adopt certain norms, values and respect for others, and to show loyalty to Dutch democracy. In 2006, the Ministry of Education, Culture and Science in the Netherlands introduced the policy of 'active citizenship and social inclusion' (*Actief burgerschap en sociale integratie*)[19] – with 'active citizenship' referring to a person's willingness and ability to be part of a community and actively contributing, and 'social integration' referring to the participation of citizens in institutions[20] and the expressed commitment to Dutch culture irrespective of their ethnic and cultural backgrounds (Bron and Thijs, 2011: 126). The pedagogical task of education thus centred on values and the curriculum, and the goal was to promote 'good' or 'active citizenship' with the expectation that migrants would live up to their civic duties and responsibilities and become economically self-sufficient.

The Ministry of Education, Culture and Science deemed such a policy necessary in fostering social cohesion, which had greatly decreased, and in increasing the engagement of citizens between and amongst each other, the government and with Dutch traditions and customs. Currently, the Dutch Inspectorate of Education requires citizenship instruction to be based on knowing and learning about different cultures and backgrounds of peers as the promotion of active citizenship and social inclusion in the Netherlands.[21]

---

19   This policy was integrated in Article 8 of the Law on Primary Education; Article 11 of the Law on Centers; and Article 17 of the Law of Secondary Education.

20   This includes visits to museums and tours, and immersing oneself in Dutch culture.

21   Source: the official website of the Dutch Inspectorate of Education: http://www. onderwijsinspectie.nl/actueel/nieuwsbrieven/details/Actief+burgerschap+en+sociale+inte gratie.html.

According to Bron and Thijs (2011: 128–9), schools in primary and secondary education teaching citizenship need to not only enable students to 'learn about and get acquainted with the diversity of backgrounds and cultures of peers', but also to help them acquire knowledge about the main characteristics of religious and cultural groups in Dutch society and learn to respectfully handle different cultural views. In primary and secondary schools citizenship education is evaluated on the basis of 'quality' and 'educational indicators'.[22] Quality indicators refer to the school's vision of how it contributes to citizenship and civic competences through learning objectives. Educational indicators are about the social skills, openness to society, diversity, participation, community involvement, basic values,[23] democratic skills and knowledge operant in the learning and working environment where citizenship is visible and students have opportunities to practise.[24]

Schools have the dual tasks of strengthening citizenship and integration through social, moral and religious formation, environmental and human rights education and social training. Taken into account are the local community, student composition, needs of parents and guardians (*verzorgers*) and ideological school principles. Expressions of core ideas, aims of citizenship and integration, awareness of suspicious conditions and student behaviours – as well as the prevention of intolerance, extremism and discrimination – are examples of this conscious effort.[25] Thus what is new in citizenship education, states Veugelers (2011: 2), is the conscious focus on values, the development of identity and the recognition of diversity in identities, hidden by what he calls 'a semblance of uniformity'.

Evaluation of the implementation of a coherent systematic plan for citizenship education in Dutch schools reveals several issues. Using the evaluations of the Dutch Inspectorate of Education (2008–10), Bron and Thijs (2011) report that the core curriculum objectives are loosely formulated[26] and that close to one-third of elementary schools and half of secondary schools are not meeting desired requirements regarding citizenship education, although nearly all schools met the lowest requirements.[27] Projects and activities of citizenship education reflect limited

---

22   The quality of education since October 2006 is monitored by the Dutch Inspectorate of Education based on the interpretations of citizenship that schools provide.

23   Basic values of the democratic constitutional state based on Chapter 1 of the Dutch Constitution and the Universal Declaration of Human Rights refers to some basic values: equivalence, understanding of others, tolerance, autonomy, rejecting intolerance, rejecting discrimination.

24   Source: the official website of the Dutch Inspectorate of Education: http://www.onderwijsinspectie.nl/actueel/nieuwsbrieven/details/Actief+burgerschap+en+sociale+integratie.html .

25   Source: the official website of the Dutch Inspectorate of Education, http://www.onderwijsinspectie.nl.

26   Stated in the Dutch Inspectorate of Education in 2008, 2009, 2010 (Bron and Thijs 2001: 129).

27   Source: the official website of the Ministry of Education, Culture and Science, http://www.government.nl/ministries/ocw.

progress in the development of an explicit curriculum with specific goals. They point out that schools actively engaged in citizenship education tend to prioritise general social competencies over intercultural knowledge and skills (Bron and Thijs, 2011).

These evaluations confirm Thijs, Langberg and Berlet's (2009)[28] assertion that schools with a focus on cultural diversity only rarely implement the vision of cultural diversity in policy guidelines, curriculum or activities. In practice, citizenship education is disseminated through primary school activities and is taught in high schools through civics, history and geography classes and through thematic issues, projects or combined field trips. How citizenship education is evaluated – given varying implementation from one school to another, different approaches by teachers and non-systematisation of the actual learning – presents an elusive picture of its effectiveness.

The Dutch Population, Educational System and Intercultural Practices

In 2012, the population of the Netherlands was 17,730,348 of which 79.1 per cent were native Dutch (CBS, 2012c). Almost 21 per cent were minorities, up from 17 per cent in 1999, due not only to the high birth rates among Moroccans and Turks but also to the arrival of Eastern European migrants and asylum seekers from Afghanistan, Iraq, Iran and Somalia (Bijl et.al, 2012). Turks account for the largest numbers (2.34 per cent), followed by Indonesians (2.26 per cent), Moroccans (2.16 per cent), Surinamese (2.06 per cent) and Antilleans and Arubans (0.86 per cent) (CBS, 2012a, 2012c). Close to 50.6 per cent of minorities are concentrated in Amsterdam, 49.5 per cent in The Hague, 48.4 per cent in Rotterdam and 32.1 per cent.in Utrecht (CBS, 2012d). The Dutch Bureau of Statistics further categorises the migrant population based on country of birth: Europeans, North Americans, Oceaneans, Japanese and Indonesians (including inhabitants of the former Dutch East Indies) are classified as Western;[29] persons of Turkish, African or Latin American background as non-Western (Alders, 2001). Of the total non-Dutch population, 11.6 per cent are classified as non-Western and 9.3 per cent as Western. Poles make up the largest numbers of Westerners (CBS, 2012a).

The Dutch educational system is compulsory until age 16 (*leerplicht*); however, students are required to stay in school until 18, when they can start qualifications (*kwalificatieplicht*). After eight years of primary education, students enter secondary education at 12, once they have taken the CITO test[30] and are

---

28 This refers to a qualitative study of five primary and secondary schools.

29 Japanese and Indonesians are included on the basis of their social and economic position in the Netherlands: Indonesians with parent(s) originating from the former Dutch East Indies, and Japanese mostly because they are employees of Japanese companies (CBS).

30 CITO is a nationwide test at the end of primary school, and students are advised on the basis of their scores as to which higher education track they should enrol in (Traag, 2012: 9).

tracked into different programmes based on achievement scores, ability and teacher recommendations (Traag, 2012; Alberts 2001). Students can enter:

VWO – six-year preparation for university
HAVO – five-year preparation for higher vocational college; or
VMBO – four-year preparation for vocational education (Figure 8.1).

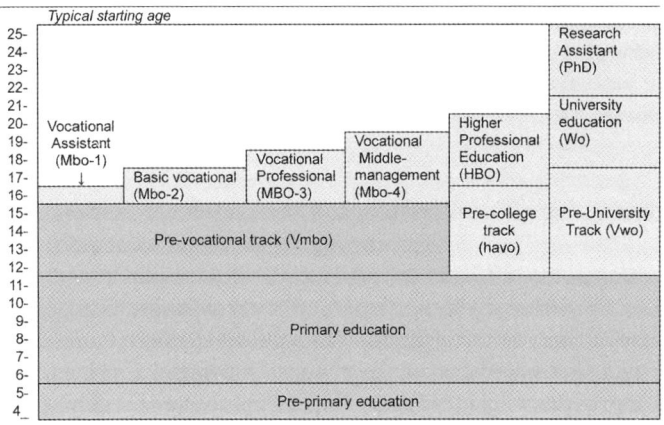

Figure 8.1   The Dutch education system

Source: Traag (2012). The majority of Dutch schools use CITO or a comparable test to determine track placement, but schools are not obliged to use such tests.

In 2012, 1,517,476 pupils were in Dutch primary education (including special primary education[31] and special schools);[32] 948,949 in secondary education; 423,719 in higher professional education; and 245,322 enrolled in universities (CBS, 2012e).

All schools in the Netherlands are government funded, follow a common curriculum with prescribed subjects, and test students through uniform national exams at the end of primary school (CITO exam) and at the end of each track in secondary schools until they receive a diploma (Fraser, 2003; Alberts et al., 2008). Schools are differentiated as denominational (*bijzondere*) or non-denominational

---

31   Special primary education caters to children with learning and educational problems in remedial schools.

32   Special education and the Act on Expertise cover primary and secondary education and offer services to children with learning problems. This includes children who are deaf or hard of hearing, visually handicapped, physically handicapped, multiply handicapped, chronically ill, who have serious speech impediments, and children in schools linked to pedagogical institutions.

(*openbare*);[33] the former include Roman Catholic, Protestant, Orthodox Jewish and Islamic schools (CBS, 2012b), while the latter are governmental/public. The majority of Dutch schools are denominational: over a half are primary and close to three-quarters are secondary schools.

While 'black schools' vary widely in terms of curriculum and programmes, some are quite successful despite the negativity with which they are often characterised, and provide opportunities for high achievers through quality education in science, mathematics, languages and the humanities, and through national and international competitive scientific competitions.[34] These schools are, however, chosen by word of mouth, so much of their success is predicated on how parents respond to the information they receive during open days/fairs and school visits and the decisions they make.

As part of the educational freedom established by the Constitution of 1848, Dutch communities have the right to establish and organise schools, and determine their religious or ideological orientation based on parental choice (Vedder, 2006). Dutch parents prefer schools with no or low levels of ethnic mixing because they believe that migrant students degrade the quality of their children's academic experience and future careers. Vedder (2006) suggests that parental choice is one of the reasons for segregated schools. This causes the phenomenon of 'white flight' – parents leaving the schools and going to other neighbourhoods. Meanwhile, on the other hand migrant parents find better schooling for their children as they experience the phenomenon of 'black flight', where migrant parents seek ethnically mixed or integrated schools with lower concentrations of migrant children. To prevent segregation and white flight, the 'postcode policy' allows schools to admit primary school students from areas in the school's vicinity based on their postcode (catchment areas).

In the past 15 years, the autonomy of Dutch schools has increased, according to Veugelers (2011). Parental choice has become closely linked to the socio-economic and ethnic segregation of principally primary schools (Stevens et al., 2011). Parental choice, along with contextual and demographic factors such as residential segregation in school neighbourhoods, can lead to 'progressive ethnicisation' of certain schools, increasing the number of 'black school' states (Vedder, 2006). In some non-public schools, families receive notification of early calls for enrolment, which are often overbooked, and are also required to pay unaffordable special fees, allowing for constraints to be used by some schools to maintain predominantly white students (Gramberg, 2000, as quoted by Vedder,

---

33   Included here are a series of interconfessional, extraordinary, anthroposophic and evangelical, orthodox-Jewish schools. Many have specific orientations: Dalton, Montessori, Freinet, Rudolf Steiner or Jena Plan (Fulbright Center, http:///www.Fulbright.nl).

34   The black schools in which the senior researcher conducts studies from primary to secondary levels tend to score high in the Inspectorate Evaluations (scoring 3 or 4 out of 4), and the results of the CITO exam in primary schools is 536.1 (when the national average is 535 and the inspection standard is 532).

2006: 39). Some specialised schools such as Montessori or Rudolf Steiner cater to white parents – and minority parents, who do not know about their offerings, do not apply.

Trends in the Schooling of Minority Students

During the past two decades, research on the schooling of minority students in the Netherlands has presented a rather bleak picture of their educational advancement. Moroccans and students of Turkish background are often cited as problems within the educational system because they:

1. stay on the lower rungs of education, mainly in vocational classes from which they often take the long route to access HAVO and VWO;
2. have lower enrolment rates in the high-status educational tracks of HAVO and VWO;
3. are cognitively behind their Dutch counterparts;
4. score lower in the CITO exams;
5. have poor Dutch language skills;
6. have high dropout rates (although these have been diminishing).

Close to 67 per cent of all students in 2011 were enrolled in VMBO, according to Severiens (2013).[35] In 2011/12, of the native Dutch students in secondary education, 31.6 per cent attended VWO, 29 per cent HAVO and 35.6 per cent VMBO. Furthermore, of those classified as having Western immigrant backgrounds 34.2 per cent attended VWO, 27.8 per cent HAVO and 33.2 per cent VMBO (CBS, 2013). Of the non-Western immigrant background secondary education students, 19.2 per cent were in VWO, 22.1 per cent in HAVO and 48.1 per cent in VMBO.[36] These figures reflect the difference between students of non-Western origin, having the largest share in lower secondary education, and native Dutch and Western migrant students having the largest share in higher secondary education (around 60 per cent).

Vedder (2006) reports that four-year-old children of migrants from Morocco, Turkey, Suriname or the Dutch Antilles are two years behind in conceptual knowledge, which leads to learning problems in mathematics, reading and writing persisting into secondary schooling. Meanwhile Stevens et al. (2011) state that non-Western ethnic minority students start and finish primary education in considerable arrears in mathematics and the use of Dutch compared to native Dutch students.

---

35   Written communication via email provided by Sabine Severiens, 17 May 2013.

36   Because in the first two years of secondary education students can also combine programmes, the data considers only the 3rd and 4th years of VMBO, years 3–5 of HAVO and 3–6 of VWO.

Crul and Doomernik (2003) point to other factors: parents' low socio-economic status and poor educational attainment; close-knit networks that value early marriage, thereby excluding girls from education; and difficulties with the Dutch language. Moreover, they maintain that Dutch institutional systems do not address early school leaving, lack of preparation for the CITO exam, poor Dutch language training and insufficient professional teacher training of intercultural education. Traag (2012: 26) also reports that, compared with their peers, minority students have 'fewer cultural resources from their peers' as the majority come from lower social and economic backgrounds.

On average, the four largest non-Western ethnic minority groups – Turkish, Moroccan, Surinamese and Antillean – score lower on CITO tests compared to native Dutch students. While over the years this gap has been reduced, research by Amsterdam's Department of Development in Society finds that even Turkish and Moroccan pupils who scored high in CITO were more likely to receive less counselling regarding further enrolment in secondary schools then their Dutch peers (Stevens et al., 2011).

Quantitative reports and studies of Dutch schools conclude that there is 'a clear relationship between a school's racial mix and the educational performance of its students' (Traag, 2012: 26). Turkish and Moroccan students tend to have higher drop-out rates in 'black' schools than in 'white' schools, and a 10 per cent decrease in the share of minority students in schools results in a 13 per cent decrease in the drop-out risk (Traag, 2012: 33).

These downward trends are nevertheless changing. Moroccan and Turkish students can be found at both extremes of the educational system, a process known as polarisation, whereby some have advanced, moved up the ladder and entered the labour market, while others stagnate in vocational educational placements and take more time to move to a higher tier (Crul and Doomernik, 2003). Crul and Doomernik (2003: 1039) attribute the success of those who move up to 'mutual help and support they have received from family and community networks' as well as peer mentoring, afterschool tutoring, extended day classes and parental involvement in schools. Studies of new arrivals of refugees and asylum seekers[37] show they perform better in schools than traditional minority groups, which has led to a statistical increase in migrant performance (Bijl et al., 2012). In general, minority pupils are reaching higher scores, have better attendance in pre-university programmes (the share of pupils with non-Western background in university increased from 6 per cent in 1995/96 to 14 per cent in 2011/12) and show lower drop-outs (down from 15 per cent in 2001 to 10 per cent in 2010) (Bijl et al., 2012).

---

37   During the last two decades the Netherlands has attracted refugees from Eastern Europe, Africa and the Middle East – in particular from the former Yugoslavia, Iraq, Iran, Afghanistan and Somalia (Driessen, 2000).

Teachers and Intercultural to Citizenship Educational Practices[38]

In the Netherlands, teachers are links to intercultural/citizenship learning[39] and are viewed as role models who stimulate the development of certain values and help students confront different perspectives (Leenders et al., 2008: 156). Yet, because teachers in the Netherlands are predominantly white, they are not likely to have cultural awareness about the minority students they teach. Leeman and Ledoux's studies of teachers show they may not have 'the theoretical background to move beyond the discourse of cultural difference' to intercultural practices they develop, and can offer only pragmatic solutions for the dilemmas they confront in ethnically diverse classrooms (2005: 576). For many teachers, it is a challenge to introduce topics of intercultural and citizenship education into a classroom environment which politically does not favour multiculturalism, and in schools where maths and language are priorities.

Furthermore, Leeman and Ledoux point out that 'specific knowledge-oriented, attitudes-oriented or skills-oriented approaches to intercultural education do not exist' (2005: 586), and concur that 'intercultural education appears to be a container concept for teachers' (2005: 587). Teachers chose, they state, 'a social relations approach' with which they maintain peace and harmony in the classroom following the policy guidelines of reducing violence and using cooperative learning. Teachers educate and prepare pupils for a multicultural life by establishing 'a *good society* inside the classrooms' (2005: 587) and choosing examples of diversity that would 'create little commotion such as discussing age differences and different tastes in music and lifestyles' (2005: 588).

Depending on the type of school and the pupils' age group, teachers strive for different educational goals in citizenship education. Research by Leenders et al. (2008), covering more than 150 secondary schools, identified three types of citizenship practice:

1. individualistic citizenship, which focuses on communication skills, critical reflection, rational discussion, identity, independence and personal autonomy;

---

38   Among the scholars who has written extensively on intercultural and citizenship education in Dutch schools is Yvonne Leeman, who has addressed new forms of intercultural education (Leeman and Ledoux, 2003a); policy shifts of intercultural to citizenship education through classroom interactions and pedagogy (Leeman and Pels, 2006); national policies and teacher educators addressing cultural and religious diversity (Leeman, 2008); teacher opinions of intercultural education (Leeman and Ledoux, 2005); intercultural dilemmas in secondary schools (Leeman, 2006); and the operationalisation of intercultural education in pre-service teacher education (Leeman and Ledoux, 2003b).

39   It should be noted that while intercultural education is no longer extensively practised, except for activities within the core content of education, it has become infused in primary school teaching; but at the high school level it is taught as citizenship education.

2. adaptive citizenship, which focuses on value transmission, discipline, obedience, hard work, integrity, respect, responsibility and teacher transmittal of right and wrong values;

3. critical democratic citizenship, which emphasises critical thinking, care, solidarity, democratic values, active participation, value communication, teacher mediation of democratic values and dialogue participation where students give meanings to value.

Of the surveyed secondary school teachers: 18 per cent followed 'individualistic citizenship' practices; close to 29 per cent followed 'adapting citizenship'; yet 53 per cent followed 'critical-democratic citizenship', demonstrating a deeper commitment to student 'meaning-making', where students make sense of the meaning of experiences Leenders et al. (2008). Teachers in vocational schools emphasised social commitment and discipline, which might be necessary to 'facilitate the learning process in vocational education and to solve students' behavioural problems', whereas almost all of the teachers who practised individualistic citizenship taught in academic schools. While older teachers were oriented towards critical-democratic citizenship, younger teachers followed individualistic citizenship (Leenders et al., 2008: 167–8).

Another study by Leenders et al. (2012: 9) in vocational schools with a dominant proportion of foreign students revealed that more attention is given to cultural and ideological diversity in learning to deal with difficulties and students in major cities are more familiar with diversity themes than those in rural schools, white schools or multi-ethnic schools in medium-sized towns. Students in minority schools felt that 'teachers tend to be reluctant to raise strongly value-laden themes', although these students want to form political opinions. All students, however, agreed that they learn to get along with each other mainly outside of the school and not within their classrooms. Their research concluded that teachers avoid being too political and prefer to focus on social development, autonomy and discipline rather than social involvement and political engagement (2012). An earlier study also showed student expressions of citizenship education (Leenders et al., 2008). On the one hand, students believe it is the teacher's task to discipline students, but on the other hand they want more the autonomy granted through citizenship education and less the social involvement and development of a critical democratic citizenship.

Veugelers argues that the global free-market ideology is prevalent in Dutch political discourse tends to focus on furthering a competitive knowledge-based society as well as nationalist ideology. However, he considers that 'citizenship education in its global, and especially in its nationalist perspective is important in Dutch national policy, but subsidiary to the *knowledge society*' (2011: 216). Hurenkamp et al. (2011: 207) go further in declaring:

> the current transformation of citizenship is directed toward the reinstatement of a dutiful, communitarian and at the same time, national republican idea of citizenship […]. Citizens must acknowledge their duties, which consist of both

loyalty and self sufficiency. They need to identity with the nation-state and be as independent as possible at the same time.

Becoming a citizen, as Benedicto and Morán (2007: 618) point out, is a progressive learning process of social interactions, that helps youth identify 'social representations of what citizenship means and involves'.

In short, intercultural education has shifted to citizenship education in the Netherlands and has currently moved, as Leeman and Pels point out, 'from diversity to civilization' – becoming more of a disciplining and assimilationist approach in which teachers find themselves having to find the 'balance in communality and diversity' (2006: 341). As Leeman and Reid (2006: 68) express: 'Teachers saw intercultural education mainly as education for tolerance, emphasizing the necessity of a safe atmosphere in the classroom and competencies to promote this. According to these teachers, these competencies include empathy and communication skills.' Yet today teacher training in intercultural education is not encouraged and is no longer actively promoted (Leeman and Pels, 2006).

Implementation of Citizenship Education Practices

Over the past 30 years, some of the intercultural educational practices which have become absorbed by citizenship education include curriculum programmes and activities[40] such as:

- cooperative learning, introduced by Pieter Batelaan and Ieva Gundare (2000) during the late 1970s and now institutionalised, wherein students develop skills and attitudes using creativity, critical thinking, imagination, communication and cooperation for decision making dealing with conflicts;[41]
- project-based cooperative learning which promotes team work and democratic decision making;
- thematic interdisciplinary learning through history, art and music or science, maths and languages;
- moral education linked to the teaching of values and which has resurfaced in citizenship education;
- tutoring and peer mentoring by highly successful Moroccan and Turkish students in higher education to provide 'direct assistance with career and

---

40   The Netherlands Institute for Curriculum Development (SLO) has been a forerunner in the development of curricula, curriculum models and core objectives – resources that stimulate citizenship educational learning

41   Further promoting cooperative learning as part of intercultural education has been the International Association of Intercultural Education, which has been at the helm of publishing research in this field.

professional development, emotional and psychological support and role modelling' for other students (Crul 2002: 276).

Evaluations of such mentoring show positive results in cognitive and non-cognitive fields.

Many of these former strategies and practices have now been integrated into the curriculum structure and are no longer distinguishable as intercultural practices, but as citizenship education requiring dialogue and discussion. Research conducted by Irene Giolitti (2009) in a Dutch black high school demonstrated that cooperative learning was highly stressed by teachers because it provided opportunities for their students to learn new skills. For the students, working in groups, developing projects and being responsible for results helped them learn how to cope, work and better understand each other.

The strengths of the intercultural education approach previously used in the Netherlands can be found in its intent to create harmonious spaces of interaction and cultural learning through dialogue processes. Teachers may practise intercultural education through unstated or unspecified interpretations of the type of dialogue being taught, but such practices may not be totally contextualised in schools. Furthermore, the notion of diversity for its own sake as a foundation for intercultural education practice has taken a back seat to the pragmatic concept that unity with national, social and economic goals is a personal responsibility and can best be realised through citizenship education. Assessment of the effectiveness of such policies in practice requires a more systematised evaluation system. Yet, as has been shown by some of the studies presented here, while citizenship education may be highly regarded, how it is taught in classrooms remains diffuse and elusive; and in spite of a strong national policy there tends to be duplicity and lack of consistent implementation and evaluation.

Another weakness is that much of the responsibility for implementation of citizenship education is in the hands of individual teachers who do not know what is expected, and have little guidance and training in citizenship competences, resulting in a potpourri of teaching strategies which may or may not lead to the desired behavioural citizenship outcomes.[42] In some cases, teachers revert to viewing the cultures of minorities as culturalistic and hence essentialistic, as static and non-organic in their evolution.[43] What occurs then is the stratification of minorities, with frequent displays of their exotica and without identifying similarities – a

---

42   In 2008 the 'SBL' competences requiring the development of citizenship competencies in the Netherlands were supplemented by a publication entitled *Burgerschapscompetenties voor leraren: Servicedocument bij de SBL-competenties (Citizenship Competences for* Teachers*).* Citizenship development in this supplement does not address specific subjects but can be used by all, including non-teaching staff.

43   Such a process is known in the multicultural literature as the product or artefact approach to culture, where customs, festivals and given holidays are celebrated as cultural understanding.

process which leads to stereotyping, generalisations and marginalising. Teachers teach respect but avoid the risks of more open discussion of values and cultural differences, playing it safe and being 'politically correct'.

Noticeable from research conducted in black schools by the senior researcher and Masters' students dealing with global citizenship education was the hesitancy on the part of teachers to openly discuss topics such as religion, genocide, race and discrimination. Jokes and comments such as the following among high school peers targeted fellow Moroccan students, ridiculing them: 'Where is Ali? 'We know where he is, he's most likely robbing the Rabobank'. Such incidents were not discussed as worthwhile topics by teachers and students, which led to their being avoided, swept under the rug and not confronted. At the primary school level, how teachers view the home culture of their minority students in terms of norms to be met and schooling preparation indicates a level of frustration on how to deal with cultural differences (Pham, 2012) and results in lost opportunities for engaged critical democratic citizenship education.

At the local district level, migrant integration and social cohesion are expressed through citizenship and diversity policies. *No Citizenship without Civility* (Geemente Amsterdam, 2011) is deemed to represent active citizenship and active participation in society, with solidarity, responsibility and the rule of law. These principles become implemented through active local organisations and associations in the Netherlands. They are organised in districts with activities and projects such as gallery talks and barbecues as a means to overcome the conflictual behaviour of residents, encourage interaction and build tolerance. However, research conducted at district level in one area of Amsterdam shows that intercultural principles are not openly voiced and ethnic-based conflicts are rarely discussed.

On the other hand, activities such as those organised by Inkr8 provide residents with training and workshops that address and resolve conflict issues through an appreciative inquiry method and role play.[44] These are in demand and are carried out by *buurtkrachters*, youngsters who are trained to deliver such workshops and who are good conflict mediators. Youth network with other youth to encourage successful dialogue, and some of the migrant youngsters with troubled backgrounds in schools voluntarily join Inkr8.

---

44   Inkr8, an organisation founded in Amsterdam's Nieuw-West district, offers training and workshops in schools, municipalities, housing associations and other local institutions. Training and workshops are based on addressing conflicts and conflict resolution through role play of concrete conflicting situations using an appreciative inquiry method. They believe that successful dialogue and conflict resolution demand awareness and deeper understanding of the needs of self and others.

Where is Citizenship Education in the Netherlands Headed: Towards Value Enhancement or Critical Democratic Citizenship?

It is clear from the research conducted and the literature covered herein that the Netherlands is headed towards the consolidation of citizenship education as a way to encourage migrants and their offspring to take personal responsibility to become integrated. Decentralised citizenship education is, so to speak, the Dutch way of passing the baton directly to migrants to learn Dutch civic behaviours, moral values and the Dutch language, with the hope that they become fully integrated and productive citizens.[45]

At stake is the migrants' willingness to embrace the notion of a Dutch national identity. As Ghorashi (2003: 167) has stated: 'the Dutch notion of national identity is exclusive and *thick* going back to common understanding of Dutchness based on colour, roots, and certain codes of behaviour that exclude difference'. To gain such an identity requires more than simply breaking down barriers by learning about other cultures; it demands a deeper meaning of dialogue and instilling of a critical democratic citizenship within the curriculum and schools based on our research. Yet, we have found that the means for the migrant to attain such a mind-set are somewhat unclear. Leeman (2006) advocates that teachers have the responsibility to develop students' moral values by creating moral dialogues; but this implies that the individual's perspective of social and moral values such as 'justice', 'autonomy' and 'social and moral commitment' is already connected to those concepts in society at large. Closing this gap for some migrant groups is the challenge.

We found that while schools in the Netherlands may be focusing on moral enhancement, making students feel safe and comfortable in their classrooms, what is needed is more focus on citizenship education which is closely connected to moral development and, vice versa, to citizenship development. Leenders et al. (2012: 2) state that:

> morally founded citizenship education may encourage young people to actually apply their knowledge and skills, and to act morally and socially. Citizenship education may by improving moral reasoning and action also become more reflective and dialogical and therefore susceptible to changing attitudes.

In conclusion, given the Netherlands' history of migrant reception and integration, the current assimilative measures, the rise of nationalism and growing racialisation throughout Europe, heeding May (2009) and Leeman and Reid's (2006) admonitions to refocus on post-modern conceptions of culture and identity while using emancipatory politics may prove useful in the Netherlands. This requires that critical discussions take place on questions such as: What is meant by 'feeling

---

45   The senior researcher has been collecting data on her own *inburgering* process, the civic and language learning that is required to acquire Dutch nationality, and a reflective article of what this has entailed will be forthcoming.

Dutch?' How do migrants achieve such an identity? How they can be loyal while being self-sufficient? How are spaces for dialogue being created?

A migrant's path to becoming a Dutch citizen demands more than the legal acquisition of citizenship. Benedicto and Morán (2007) stress that young people integrate into a social and political community through being involved and belonging, two important processes that lead to the existence of a common national 'us'. Such a process needs to take place amidst an understanding of European or national identity which Aman (2012) recognises is often represented as 'us' still linked to colonialist thinking which distinguishes the 'them' as the 'other'.

While teaching moral, active and critical democratic citizenship principles in Dutch schools is designed to promote better integration of migrant students, the implementation of these policies and practices will need to be ideologically standardised and consistent and, more importantly, able to confront how effectively will teaching of citizenship create a new notion of 'we' that does not perpetuate the distinction between Dutch as 'us' and migrants as 'them'?

References

Alders, M. (2001). *Classification of the Population with a Foreign Background in the Netherlands*. Statistics Netherlands.

Allemann-Ghionda, C. (2008). *Intercultural Education in Schools*. Brussels: European Parliament.

Allemann-Ghionda, C. (2009). From intercultural education to the inclusion of diversity. Theories and policies in Europe (pp. 134–45). In J. Banks (ed.), *The Routledge International Companion to Multicultural Education*. London: Routledge.

Alberts, R.V.J. (2001). Equating exams as a prerequisite for maintaining standards: experience with Dutch centralised secondary examinations. *Assessment in Education: Principles, Policy and Practice*, 8 (3), 353–67.

Alberts, R., Kremers E. and Béguin, A. (2008). National examinations in the Netherlands: Standard setting procedures and the effects of innovations. Cito, National Institute for Educational Measurement – Paper presented at the IAEA Conference. Cambridge.

Aman, R. (2012). The EU and the recycling of colonialism: Formation of Europeans through intercultural dialogue. *Educational Philosophy and Theory*, 44 (9), 1010–22.

Batelaan, P. and Gundare, I. (2000). Intercultural education, cooperative learning and the changing society. *Intercultural Education*, 11 (3), 31–4.

Benedicto, J. and Morán, M. L. (2007). Becoming a citizen. *European Societies*, 9 (4), 601–22.

Bijl, R., Boelhouwer, J., Cloïn M. and Pommer, E. (eds) (2012). *The Social State of the Netherlands 2011 – Summary. A Translated Summary of 'De sociale staat van Nederland 2011'*. The Hague: The Netherlands Institute for Social Research SCP.

Bron, J. and Thijs, A. (2011). Leaving it to the schools: Citizenship, diversity and human rights education in the Netherlands. *Educational Research*, 53 (2), 123–36.

CBS-Centraal Bureau voor de Statistiek (2012a). *Bevolking. Generatie, geslacht, leeftijd en herkomstgroepering*, 1 January.

CBS (2012b), *Denominatie (onderwijs)*. http://www.cbs.nl/nl-NL/menu/methoden/begrippen/default.htm?ConceptID=3616.

CBS (2012c). *Population. Sex, Age, Origin and Generation.* 1 January.

CBS (2012d). *Regionale Kerncijfers Nederland.*

CBS (2012e). *School Size by Type of Education and Ideological Basis.*

CBS (2013). *Voortgezet onderwijs; deelname leerlingen naar onderwijssoort.*

Crul, M. (2002). Success breeds success. Moroccan and Turkish student mentors in the Netherlands. *International Journal for the Advancement of Counselling*, 24, 275–87.

Crul, M. and Doomernik, J. (2003). The Turkish and the Moroccan second generation in the Netherlands: Divergent trends between and polarization within the two groups. *International Migration Review*, 37 (4), 1039–65.

Driessen, G. (2000). The limits of educational policy and practice? The case of ethnic minorities in the Netherlands. *Comparative Education*, 36 (1), 55–72.

Duyvendak, J.W. and Scholten, P. (2012). Deconstructing the Dutch multicultural model. A frame perspective on Dutch immigrant integration policymaking. *Comparative European Politics*, 10 (3), 266–82.

Eldering, L. (1996). Multiculturalism and multicultural education in an international perspective. *Anthropology and Education Quarterly*, 27 (3), 315–30.

Fraser, C. (2003). *The Public School Market in the Netherlands*. Winnipeg: Frontier Centre for Public Policy.

Geemente Amsterdam (2011). *Burgerschap en diversiteit, geen burgerschap zonder hoffelijkheid/Citizenship and Diversity, No Citizenship without Civility*. Amsterdam.

Ghorashi, H. (2003). Ayaan Hirsi Ali: Daring or dogmatic? Debates on multiculturalism and emancipation in the Netherlands. *Focaal: European Journal of Anthropology*, 42, 163–73.

Giolitti, I. (2009). Proving myself, continuing to study, getting an honest job, and being an example. An ethnography of the perspectives of second generation Dutch high school students of Turkish and Moroccan backgrounds who are overcoming the negative and making their way in the Netherlands. Unpublished masters thesis, University of Amsterdam.

Hurenkamp, M., Tonkens, E. and Duyvendak, J.W. (2011). Citizenship in Netherlands. Locally produced, nationally contested. *Citizenship Studies*, 15 (2), 205–25.

Leeman, Y. (2006). Teaching in ethnically diverse schools. Teachers' professionalism. *European Journal of Teacher Education*, 29 (3), 341–56.

Leeman, Y. (2008). Education and diversity in the Netherlands. *European Educational Research Journal*, 7 (1), 50–59.

Leeman, Y. and Ledoux, G. (2003a). Preparing teachers for intercultural education. *Teaching Education*, 14 (3), 279–91.

Leeman, Y. and Ledoux, G. (2003b). Intercultural education in Dutch schools. *Curriculum Inquiry*, 33 (4), 385–99.

Leemann, Y. and Ledoux, G. (2005). Teachers on intercultural education. *Teachers and Teaching: Theory and Practice*, 11 (6), 575–89.

Leeman, Y. and Pels, T. (2006). Citizenship education in the Dutch multiethnic context. *European Education*, 38 (2), 64–75.

Leeman, Y. and Reid, C. (2006). Multi/intercultural education in Australia and the Netherlands. *Compare*, 36 (1), 57–72.

Leenders, H., Veugelers W. and de Kat, E. (2008). Teachers' views on citizenship education in secondary education in the Netherlands. *Cambridge Journal of Education*, 38 (2), 155–70.

Leenders, H., Veugelers, W. and de Kat, E. (2012). *Moral Development and Citizenship Education in Vocational Schools*. Amsterdam: Department of Child Development and Education, University of Amsterdam.

Lucassen, J. and Penninx, R. (1994). *Newcomers: Immigrants and Their Descendants in the Netherlands 1550–1995*. Amsterdam: Het Spinhuis.

May, S. (2009). Critical multiculturalism and education (pp. 33–48). In J. Banks (ed.), *The Routledge International Companion to Multicultural Education*. London: Routledge.

Pham, K. (2012). 'The Kid in Front'. A study of implicit knowledge of teachers in diverse Dutch primary schools. Unpublished masters thesis, University of Amsterdam.

Portera, A. (2008). Intercultural education in Europe. Epistemological and semantic aspects. *Intercultural Education*, 19 (6), 481–91.

Schama, S. (1991). *The Embarrassment of Riches. An Interpretation of Dutch Culture in the Golden Age*. London: Fontana.

Stevens, P.A.J., Clycq, N., Timmerman, C. and Van Houtte, M. (2011). Researching race/ethnicity and educational inequality in the Netherlands. A critical review of the research literature between 1980 and 2008. *British Educational Research Journal*, 37 (1), 5–43.

Thijs, A., Langberg, M. and Berlet, I. (2009). *Leren omgaan met culturele diversiteit Aandachtspunten voor een kansrijke aanpak*. Enschede: Stichting leerplanontwikkeling (SLO).

Tonkens, E., Duyvendak, J.W. and Hurenkamp, M. (2010). Culturalization of citizenship in the Netherlands (pp. 233–52). In d'Appollonia, A.C. and Reich S. (eds), *Managing Ethnic Diversity After 9/11. Integration, Security, and Civil Liberties in Transatlantic Perspective*. London: Rutgers University Press.

Traag, T. (2012). *A Multidisciplinary Study of Risk and Protective Factors Explaining Early School-Leaving in the Netherlands*. The Hague/Heerlen: Statistics Netherlands.

Vedder, P. (2006). Black and white schools in the Netherlands. *European Education*, 38 (2), 36–49.

Vertovec, S. (2010). Towards post-multiculturalism? Changing communities, conditions and contexts of diversity. *UNESCO International Social Science Journal*, 61 (199), 83–95.

Veugelers, W.M. (2011). Theory and practice of citizenship education. The case of policy, science and education in the Netherlands. *Revista de Educación*. Special Issue, 209–24.

Chapter 9

An Equitable Education System's Achilles Heel? Intercultural Education in the Swedish Context

Guadalupe Francia

Introduction

Sweden has one of the most equitable education systems in OECD countries (Dupriez and Dumay, 2004; Mons, 2007). At the same time '[g]rowing ethnic inequalities are probably the Achilles heel of the present-day Swedish education system' (OECD, 2005: 47).

These inequalities are self-evident in the percentage of students eligible to attend upper-secondary school. In 2011 only 76 per cent of girls and 74 per cent of boys with a foreign background were eligible for upper-secondary studies, compared to 92 per cent of girls and 90 per cent of boys with a Swedish ethnic background (Folkhälsoinstitutet, 2013: 56). Families with a foreign background are overrepresented in statistics in the groups at risk of poverty and poor health in Sweden (Folkhälsoinstitut, 2013; Salonen, 2012).

However, students with a foreign background are not a homogeneous group. The intersectional relation between students' ethnicity and other factors such as gender, social class, parent education level, time of residence in Sweden – as well as the country in which the students were born – are important to avoid generalisations about the foreign students' situation in Sweden.

This contribution aims to discuss the impacts of historical, cultural, socioeconomic and educational factors on the situation of students with a foreign background in the current Swedish educational system. In addition, it analyses curricular differentiations as a political and educational strategy to increase equity in education for children with a foreign background in the Swedish educational system.

Immigrant Groups in Swedish Society

A Long Tradition of Cultural Continuity and Structural Segregation

Swedish society has a long tradition of cultural and linguistic homogeneity. Swedish history has been characterised by a cultural continuity from the former ideology of Lutheranism to the modern ideal of social democracy. Therefore, striving for homogeneity became the normal and rational Swedish cultural path (Sjögren, 1995, 2010).

According to a report on structural discrimination in Sweden, discrimination against ethnic minorities such as the Sami and Roma are examples of a failure to develop cultural diversity in Swedish history (SOU, 2005: 56). This report points to the existence of a negative representation of people from Africa and Asia in Swedish popular culture. It also considers the existing denial of ethnic discrimination has contributed as the fact that 'Sweden, along with most other European countries, was very slow in developing effective laws against ethnic discrimination' (SOU, 2005: 42). It has even contributed to the current discrimination against people of foreign background in employment as well as in other areas of society. The report considered the following factors as central reasons for ethnic discrimination in Swedish society:

- media and politicians' negative portrayal of migrants as a threat and a problem;
- media representation of migrant men as 'criminals' and migrant women as 'passive and repressed';
- the media tendency to describe socioeconomic problems as cultural and ethnic problems;
- legal participation of migrants in Swedish political organs and voting;
- the dominant ideology of 'Swedishness as the norm' in the school system;
- negative attitudes of school staff with regard to students and parents with a foreign background;
- legitimisation of the exclusion of immigrants from the labour market or their concentration in low-wage jobs in terms of lack of understanding of 'Swedish codes' or lack of competence in the Swedish language;
- racial segregation (racification) in cities, creating ethnically segregated areas and making it more difficult for people with a foreign background to compete in the housing market;
- discrimination in welfare services and the legal system;
- discrimination in health services, in particular for women with a foreign background;
- ideological division of the population into 'Swedes' and 'immigrants' and the existence of an ethnic hierarchy;
- reproduction of ethnic segregation in order to protect underlying interests of privileged individuals/groups in maintaining the status quo;
- short-term labour and educational strategies policies targeting people with a foreign background instead of re-examining the structural discrimination mechanism in working life and education;
- the discrimination spiral that spreads and reinforces discrimination impacts from one area to another;

- earlier research focuses on 'immigrants' more than on the structures in Swedish society that reproduce structural ethnic segregation.

A report by the National Integration Agency shows that foreigners of African and Asian origin are greatly affected by structural discrimination in their working life (Integrationsverket, 2004). Employment rates of these groups are lower than those of other ethnic groups, irrespective of time spent in Sweden, education, marital status and gender.

At the end of May 2013 riots spread for several days in the poor suburbs largely inhabited by migrants of African and Asian background. Young people, most of them boys, set fire to cars and buildings. This disorder forced then Prime Minister Fredrik Reinfeldt to hold an emergency meeting. Parents and community leaders were asked to pacify the young people and put an end to the trouble in these neighbourhoods. This commotion was similar to other disturbances in European cities such as Paris (2005), Athens (2008) and London (2011). According to a article presented by Swedish and international researchers in the Swedish and international press these riots were a response to discrimination and relatively high unemployment among young people in these areas, as well as increased polarisation of rich and poor in Swedish society (Svenska Dagbladet, 2013; Mediapart, 2013). At the same time, increase in free choice and the state's retreat from its responsibility for the school system have especially reduced access to quality welfare services for the inhabitants of the most socially and segregated areas where those riots took place.

A Short Tradition of Immigration in Swedish Society

Migration *to* Sweden is a relatively new phenomenon. Before the Second World War Sweden was a country *from* which a high rate of the population emigrated because of poverty and unemployment. In 1930, foreigners in Sweden amounted to only 1 per cent of the population, or 61,700 people (Nilsson, 2004: 15, 18). However, after the war Sweden became an immigration country. Immigration increased considerably during the Second World War with refugees from other Nordic countries and from the Baltic countries. These refugees were never registered in the Swedish population statistics during the war, the majority of them returning to their own countries after the war (Nilsson, 2004).

After the war the immigration increase was characterised by work immigration due to the need of labour in Sweden. In the 1950s and 1960s migrant workers were directly integrated to the work market because the Swedish population could not provide enough workers to the developing industry sector. Most of these work migrants came from Europe, especially Italy, Belgium, Austria, Netherlands, West Germany, Greece and Hungary by the end of the 1940s and the 1950s and from the former Yugoslavia during the 1960s. This work migration resulted in a considerable increase of foreign people from 198,000 in 1950 to 538,000 in 1970. By the end of the 1960s restrictions were introduced to reduce the number of migrant workers from non-Nordic countries, but these regulations did not impact on the considerable migration from the former Yugoslavia, which continues to be high. At the same time, immigration from other Nordic countries, particularly Finland, was considerable. Work migration was concentrated in the municipalities with high levels of industries and factories. On the other hand, there was very little immigration from countries outside Europe during the period 1945–70 (Nilsson, 2004).

In the 1970s, work migration decreased as a result of changes in the labour market. The number of immigrants was stable and relatively low during the period 1970–85. However, migration changed its characteristics, the majority of migrants now being political refugees from Latin America and Asia. About 30,000 Chilean refugees arrived in Sweden in 1973–90, and the number of political migrants from Turkey, Iran, Lebanon and Syria was also significant. Moreover, this political migration includes European countries such as Poland at the beginning of the 1980s (Nilsson, 2004).

After 1985 political refugees and family migrations increased again. Refugees came from the former Yugoslavia as well as from Asia, thus being the most important immigrant groups to Sweden. This migration resulted in a significant number of foreign people: about 20,000 new immigrants arrived in Sweden every year during the period 1985–2000. The most important groups arrived between 1985 and 2003 for family reasons. Only 36 per cent of immigrants were political refugees during this period. Sweden's entry in the European Union in 1995 resulted in an increased migration of citizens from other EU countries (Nilsson, 2004).

Labour migrants in the 1950s and 1960s were characterised by an overrepresentation of men and young people. The children of these immigrants were often of preschool age. Conversely, later immigrants due to political or family reasons were older, as were their children. A restrictive immigration policy in the 1990s reduced the possibility of migrants bringing their older parents to Sweden (Nilsson, 2004). Migrant workers chose to live in industrial areas, while political refugees and migrant families chose the big cities and their neighbourhoods (Nilsson, 2004).

The immigration rate is relatively high in Sweden. In 2011 96,467 migrants came to Sweden (45,643 women and 50,824 men). However, the most important migrant group is Swedish citizens returning to Sweden (21.4 per cent). In second place are migrants from Iraq and Poland (4.6 per cent), followed by Afghanistan (3.5 per cent), Denmark (3.3 per cent), Somalia (3.2 per cent), China (2.7 per cent), Thailand (2.6 per cent), Finland (2.4 per cent) and Germany (2.3 per cent). The remainder (49 per cent) come from other countries (SCB, 2012a).

In 2010 the migration ministry introduced considerable restrictions on immigration from Somalia for family reasons. At the same time, Sweden again implemented policies to develop labour migration that considerably increases the number of workers coming to Sweden. This policy has resulted in an increase in migrants from countries outside the EU and the European Economic Area (EEA) (SCB, 2012b).

Depending on how migrants are defined, the number of foreign people living in Sweden will be reflected in different ways in statistics. By the end of 2003, Sweden had 476,000 foreign citizens and just over 1 million foreign inhabitants: 880,000 with a foreign background born in Sweden, 560,000 with one Swedish and one foreign parent, and 320,000 with two foreign parents. These statistics show that 16 per cent of inhabitants in Sweden had a foreign background in 2003 (Nilsson, 2004).

At the same time, the considerable increase in migration after the Second World War transformed Sweden into a migration country with an important ethnic diversity among its citizens and inhabitants. This diversity is also present in the Swedish education system. According to statistics from the National Agency for Education (Skolverket, 2011) 1 in 5 students has a foreign background, with students from Iraq being the most numerous in compulsory schools, upper secondary schools and in adult education. The second most prominent group is Somalia. Almost half of the students in the Swedish school system (compulsory and upper secondary schools and adult education) are from Asia.

Students with a Foreign Background in the Swedish School System

The National Agency for Education includes in the category 'students with a foreign background' either those born abroad or those born in Sweden of two parents with a foreign background. Conversely, Swedish-born children with at least one parent of Swedish background are considered to have a Swedish ethnic background. A child with a foreign background involves two different categories: students coming to Sweden before and after school entry.

Statistics concerning the preschool system in Sweden report the students' mother tongue as a statistical variable for foreign background. Statistics for 2010 show that 19 per cent of preschool students had a mother tongue other than Swedish. These statistics show an increase of this group from 12 per cent to 19 per cent since 2000. Statistics show that 18 per cent of all students attending the compulsory school level had a foreign background in the academic year 2010/11. This group includes 10 per cent of students born in Sweden with two parents with a foreign background and 8 per cent of students born abroad (Skolverket, 2011).

The category of students born abroad and migrated to Sweden after school entry is larger than the group who migrated to Sweden before starting school: 66 per cent and 34 per cent respectively in the academic year 2009/10 (Skolverket, 2011). The considerable number of students migrating to Sweden after school entry is related to the relatively high percentage of political refugees among its migrants in recent years. This kind of migration has a higher percentage of older migrants with school-age children than earlier labour migration in Sweden (see Nilsson, 2004).

These statistics showed as well that students born in 180 different countries outside Sweden attended the compulsory school systems in the year 2010. They also showed that 45 per cent were born in Asia and 14 per cent in Africa. The percentage of students born in Europe was 33 per cent (18 per cent were born in EU countries not including Nordic countries; 7 per cent in Nordic countries not including Sweden and 8 per cent in other European countries not including EU or Nordic countries). The majority of students born in EU countries were from Germany and Poland (Nordic countries not included), while 9 per cent of students were born in North or South America or in Oceania (Skolverket, 2011).

Sweden lacks official statistics about the percentage of students with a foreign background attending the special school system. However, different reports have pointed out the overrepresentation of this group in special schools. This overrepresentation is not easy to explain and must be carefully followed to discover its reasons (Skolverket 2011).

The number of pupils with a foreign background was 18 per cent in upper secondary schools during the academic year 2010/11 – 10 per cent born abroad and 8 per cent born in Sweden with both parents of foreign background (Skolverket, 2011).

The statistics for adult education for 2010 show 194,000 students with a foreign background. This includes 34,000 in compulsory adult schools and 160,000 in upper secondary adult schools. These statistics show an overrepresentation of foreign students in compulsory adult schools: 9 out of 10 belonging to this group as compared to 3 out of 10 at upper secondary adult school level (Skolverket, 2011).

Academic Results of Students with a Foreign Background

Statistics of the Swedish National Agency for Education showed that students with a foreign background have lower academic results than students of Swedish ethnic background (Skolverket, 2011). However, as pointed out before, students with a foreign background are not a homogeneous group. The interrelation between students' ethnicity and other factors – such as gender, social class, parents' education level, time of residence in Sweden – must be taken into account to understand national and international statistics concerning these students' academics result in the Swedish school system.

The overrepresentation of foreign background students in school failure statistics can be explained by the social differences found in families of foreign background as it may also be explained by worse socio-economic situations, higher unemployment levels and a higher percentage of single-parent families. According to the Swedish National Agency for Education (Skolverket, 2011), the effect of foreign background on students' school results is negligible compared to the effect of social background. However, length of residence in Sweden does affect students' academic results. The foreign background effect is obvious in foreign-born students who arrived in Sweden after school entry. For these groups, academic differences remain and can increase at secondary upper school. These students need continuous pedagogical support during compulsory school and secondary upper school. Statistics show that foreign students living in disadvantaged neighbourhoods have the worst academic school results because of the concentration of social problems in ethnic and social ghettos.

Parents' educational level and length of residence are the factors with most impact on pupils' academic results. For example, statistics show that foreign students with a background in North America and Nordic countries outside Sweden have the best academic results at compulsory and upper secondary level, whereas those from Africa showed the lowest academic results. However, these differences are in relation to parents' educational background rather than place of birth and length of residence. Students from African countries have in Sweden both a lower percentage of parents with higher education levels and a shorter time of residence in relation to the other two groups (Skolverket, 2011).

Reports from the organisation Save the Children (Salonen,2012) show the overrepresentation of children from families with a foreign background in the group at risk of poverty. The families'time of residence as well as the parents' access to the labour market have important impacts on these families' socio-economic level in Sweden.

Parents' educational level is an important factor to be considered when analysing the differences in students' results and ethnic background. According to the Swedish National Agency for Education (Skolverket, 2011) most of the students with a Swedish ethnic background have one parent with at least upper secondary level education. On the other hand, students of foreign background born abroad have a higher percentage of parents with only compulsory level schooling.

Students' place of birth also has a relevant impact on their academic results. For example, migrant students from North America showed better results than those born in Africa. Students' time of residence also has a considerable impact on this area. Students having migrated to Sweden before starting school show similar results as students of Swedish ethnic background. Gender is also a relevant factor to be considered when analysing academic results, girls with a foreign background having better results than boys with a foreign background (Skolverket, 2011).

It is important to point out that even if students with a foreign background have worse results than students of Swedish ethnic background in all school areas, this situation is the opposite in relation to access to university level. Students with a foreign background follow university studies more often than students with Swedish ethnic background: 38 per cent of students with a foreign background in comparison with 23 per cent of students with Swedish ethnic background in spring 2009 (Skolverket, 2011).

Swedish Compulsory and Upper Secondary School Systems

Statistics of the Swedish National Agency for Education show that students with a foreign background have lower academic results than students of Swedish ethnic background. However, girls with a foreign background show better academic results than boys with Swedish ethnic background if these girls have immigrated to Sweden before school entry. Girls with a foreign background who have migrated after school entry have lower academic results than students of Swedish ethnic background, but little better results than boys with a foreign background entering Sweden after school entry (Skolverket, 2012a).

Statistics concerning students having finished the last year at compulsory school showed the following differences in eligibility for the sciences programmes at upper secondary level. Foreign background shows to be one of the main factors having negative impacts on students' eligibility for upper secondary school. Statistics from the National Agency for Education show considerable differences in relation to students' ethnic background and the eligibility for most scientific programmes at upper secondary school level. These programmes are considered the most renowned in the Swedish education system (Skolverket, 2012a). At the same time, the category foreign background involves different groups with different results (Tables 9.1 and 9.2).

Table 9.1   Eligibility for the national programme at upper secondary school level according to ethnic background and gender.

Students' Ethnic Background	Girls	Boys	Total
Swedish background	89	84,9	86,9
Foreign background (total)	71,4	66,1	68,7

Excerpt from Skolverket (2012a) *Grundskolan- Betyg och Prov – Riksnivå Tabell 1 C: Elever som avslutat årskurs 9 läsåret 2011/12 och har behörighet till nationellt program* http://www.skolverket.se

Table 9.2   Eligibility for the national programme at upper secondary school level according to ethnic background, time of residence and gender.

Students' Ethnic Background	Total	Girls	Boys
Swedish background	86,9	89	84,9
Foreign background born in Sweden	79,3	81,1	77,6
Foreign background arrived at Sweden before 2003	79,5	81,3	77,5
Foreign background arrived at Sweden year 2003 or later	47,2	50,3	44,5

Excerpt from Skoverket (2012b) *Grundskolan- Betyg och Prov – Riksnivå Tabell 1 C: Elever som avslutat årskurs 9 läsåret 2011/12 och har behörighet till nationellt program* http://www.skolverket.se

These tables show that foreign background has important impacts on students' eligibility for the most highly regarded programme in upper schools. Having access to this programme gives students better chances to attend to the most renowned university programmes. They show significant differences in relation to student's time of residence in Sweden. Gender is also a relevant factor to consider, even if it is not as relevant as time of residence (Skolverket, 2012a).

Next, similar differences are presented in statistics concerning students' eligibility for social sciences, economics, humanities and aesthetic programmes that also give eligibility for university studies. In addition, statistics show similar differences for eligibility to professional programmes that do not offer eligibility for higher education (Skolverket, 2012a).

Statistics from the National Agency for Education (Skolverket, 2012b) show that students with a foreign background drop out or take a break from upper secondary school more often than students of Swedish ethnic background (6 per cent in comparison with 2 per cent). A lower percentage of students with a foreign background finished upper secondary school with a diploma than students of Swedish background (51 per cent compared to 72 per cent) after three years. These considerable differences still apply if we include statistics four or five years after students start secondary upper school (62 per cent compared to 80 per cent) (Skolverket, 2012b).

International Assessment

Trends in International Mathematics and Science Study (TIMSS)

TIMSS is an international test to follow up students' knowledge in maths and sciences in year 4 (at about 10 years old) and 8 of the compulsory school system, and 50 different countries took part in TIMSS 2011.[1] In Sweden, this involved 52 schools and more than 4,600 students in year 4 and 153 schools and 5,500 students in year 8 (Skolverket, 2012c).

Swedish year 4 and 8 students show lower than average academic results in maths for EU/OECD countries. If we compare different groups' results, we can see that students of Swedish ethnic background have higher academic results in TIMSS than students with a foreign background. Students with a foreign background with one Swedish parent have better results in maths and sciences than students born in Sweden with two parents with a foreign background, and then come students born outside Sweden. These ethnic differences remain when we consider other factors such as social class both for year 4 and 8. TIMSS also shows that a considerable percentage of students born outside Sweden lack basic knowledge in maths and

---

1   This is part of the International Association for the Evaluation of Educational Achievement (IEA). Unless stated otherwise, all references are to TIMSS 2011, the latest at the time of writing.

science:[2] 17 per cent in this group for maths in year 4 and 23 per cent for year 8. In addition, other sources show 17 per cent of students in year 4 and 27 per cent in year 8 (Skolverket, 2012c).

This international test shows better results in maths than in sciences. The National Agency for Education explained a language problem in understanding the science test for students who do not have Swedish as their mother tongue. At the same time TIMSS showed that 35 per cent of students with a foreign background born outside Sweden had better maths results in year 4 than students with a Swedish ethnic background (at least one Swedish parent) (Skolverket, 2012c).

Progress in International Reading Literacy Study (PIRLS)

PIRLS is an international test to compare children's literacy in year 4 in 49 countries. In PIRLS 2011 Sweden shows results above overage for EU/OECD countries.[3] However, 14 countries have better results than Sweden. Furthermore, PIRLS 2011 shows that reading levels for Swedish students is lower than in PIRLS 2006 and 2001 (Skolverket, 2012d). At the same time, the results of PIRLS 2006 and 2011 show considerable differences between students of Swedish background and students of foreign background. This last group of students shows worse reading levels than students with a foreign background in multicultural countries such as Singapore and Canada. The National Agency for Education gives as a possible reason for these differences the varying of groups of migrants that these countries receive, Sweden traditionally receiving more political refugees than Canada for example (Skolverket, 2007a, 2012d).

Programme for International Student Assessment (PISA)

PISA is an international test that evaluates 15-year-old students in different countries in three knowledge areas: reading, maths and science. The results of PISA 2009 in 65 participating countries show that Swedish levels in maths and reading have fallen since PISA 2000. Although Swedish students show scores on an average level in comparison with other OECD countries for these two knowledge areas, the gap between the best and the worst student groups increased considerably. In addition, the scores of Swedish students in the science test were below the OECD average. Sweden's position in equity is now on the average level because the level of equity has decreased. This deterioration in equity levels is due to the increased gap between high- and low-performing students' scores as well as the increased impacts of the students' social background on their test results.

---

2   In TIMMS this means that if a student has all scores below 400 points, he/she lacks basic knowledge.

3   Unless stated otherwise, all references are to PIRLS 2011, the latest at the time of writing.

Sweden shows a high level of students with a foreign background with low scores in reading in comparison with other countries. The differences in reading for students with a foreign background amount to 65.5 points compared with 43.1 points at the OECD level. However, if the students' social background is taken into account, this gap decreases by 25.5 points in relation to 16 points at the OECD level. Furthermore, the gap in reading level between students ethnic Swedes and foreign students is higher than the OECD level. Paradoxically, however, those students with the highest position in the PISA reading tests have a foreign background (Skolverket, 2010).

On the other hand, there are considerable differences regarding the time of residence in Sweden in relation to students' scores in literacy. Swedish-born students with a foreign background or students who move to Sweden before they are 6 years old show better results than students moving to Sweden after this age. Students of foreign background speaking Swedish at home have better results than those using their mother tongues at home (Skolverket, 2010).

Differentiation Strategies as Political and Pedagogical Measures for Equity

The long tradition of cultural homogeneity in Sweden has characterised the standardised equality vision of the post-war welfare education reforms. These reforms, aimed at reducing educational differences between the various social classes as well as between genders, hampered the progress of ethnic minorities. Based on cultural and social homogeneity as a norm, these reforms considered the pupils belonging to these minorities and the diversity in education to be a problem. The standardised equality vision failed to take into account pupils' cultural and individual differences and to provide real equal education for all pupils (Sjögren, 1995; Francia, 2011).

However, this uniform and standardised equality policy was interrupted by neoliberal reform at the end of the 1980s. The replacement of the concept of equality with the concept of equity in the legal texts introduced by this reform can be seen as a measure to guarantee diversity in the Swedish education system (Francia, 1999, 2011). This reform radically changed Sweden's highly centralised and homogeneous school system. By transferring power to the individual, this reform introduced free choice, decentralisation, privatisation and individualisation. This neoliberal reform aimed to develop equity by increasing diversity in the school system. Furthermore, it emphasised the development of individualisation as a strategy for respect for diversity and equity. Focusing on diversity, this neoliberal education policy emphasised the adjusting of teaching to the students' interest and needs in order to guarantee academic success for all children (Francia and Moreno Herrera, 2008).

As an equity policy measure the national steering documents for Swedish compulsory schools stipulate diversity strategies in order to individualise and adjust curricula to suit students' ethnic and language background. The schools' claims for individualisation and adaptation of education to students' backgrounds and needs have resulted in the emphasising of differentiated curricular strategies targeted at students of foreign background in order to increase their academic results and to guarantee their rights to equal education in the Swedish system. In this section I will discuss some of the differentiated curriculum strategies in relation to these aims and their implementation in school practice:

Mother Tongue Education

An example of this vision of equity by diversity is the subject of 'mother tongue'. Students with a mother tongue other than Swedish have the right to study their language in compulsory and upper secondary school and the right to pedagogical support in their original language when learning other subjects, if they need it. Studying the language of origin is voluntary, but municipalities are obliged by law to organise such education (Skolverket, 2007b).

According to statistics from the Swedish National Agency for Education (Skolverket, 2007b), the mother tongue tuition included 15 per cent of all students in Sweden during the academic year 2005/06. The three largest cities, Stockholm, Gothenburg and Malmö, have the majority of the students participating in this programme. In the group of students entitled to education in their language of origin, the Somali-speaking students show the highest participation (72.8 per cent), followed by the Albanian-speaking group (67.6 per cent), the Arabic group (66.5 per cent), the Persian (64 per cent), the Turkish (58.7) and the Kurdish group (55.9). Those having the lowest participation are the English-speaking students (49.8 per cent) and the Finnish students (42.5 per cent).

Swedish as a Second Language

Another example of this differentiated curricular strategy was the introduction in 1995 of Swedish as a second language (SSL) as a subject for pupils with a foreign background whose mother tongue is not Swedish. The introduction of SSL as differentiated curricular strategies was legitimised in the name of recognition of differences in the Swedish language learning process for students with Swedish as a second language. SSL aimed to help foreign background children achieve the proficiency required to study their other school subjects in Swedish. According to the Swedish National Agency for Education, SSL has similar achievement goals and proficiency requirements to 'Swedish' (as a first language). SSL is equivalent to the curricular subject 'Swedish' as regards eligibility for university or other post-secondary study. The differences between these two curricular subjects are based on the first- versus the second-language acquisition perspective used when teaching them. The right and opportunity to study SSL is guaranteed both in compulsory and upper secondary schools (Francia, 2012).

Among students entitled to receive instruction in 'Swedish as a second language', Somali speakers show the highest participation (70.8 per cent), followed by those speaking Turkish (63.4 per cent), Kurdish (62.2 per cent), Arabic (60.5 per cent), Albanian (57.7 per cent) and Persian (41.9 per cent). Those having the lowest participation are English- and Finnish-speaking students (22.8 per cent and 22.3 per cent respectively) (Skolverket, 2007b).

Can Increased Differentiation Assure Students' Right to Equitable Education?

It is interesting to observe that the migrant groups having the higher participation in differentiated curricular subjects such as mother tongue tuition and Swedish as a second language are also the most affected by socio-economic segregation in Sweden. For example, migrants speaking Somali, Arabic, Kurdish, Turkish and Persian are more affected by segregation. On the other hand, the Finnish and English minorities who are more integrated in Swedish society show at the same time the lowest level of participation in these subjects.

An analysis of the Education Priority Strategies for Equity[4] implemented in Sweden by the National Agency for School Development in the period 2003–07 shows that the strategies targeting children from socially disadvantaged neighbourhoods focused only on strategies against ethnic segregation. Therefore, these policies tend to implement educational actions that are mainly concentrated on the development of Swedish as a second language, mother tongue tuition, the teaching of school subjects in origin languages or bilingual education. These improvement strategies are legitimated by research showing that mother tongue education and Swedish as a second language teaching provide effective pedagogical support for students with foreign backgrounds. However, analysis of students' academic results shows that achievement continues to be low in the majority of municipalities where these education priority actions have been implemented. Furthermore, these strategies lack a problematisation of the negative effects of implementing different syllabuses and evaluation criteria for different pupil groups at school level (Francia and Moreno Herrera, 2008).

In addition, an evaluation of the curricular subject Swedish as a second language puts in question the existence of this kind of differentiated curricular strategy for the teaching of Swedish (Myndigheten för Skolutveckling, 2004). This evaluation shows that students of foreign origin who follow Swedish as a second language are more affected by school failure than those who study Swedish as first language. It also showed that only a small proportion of those students have recently arrived in Sweden. This report also registered negative attitudes

---

4   This equity priority policies were motivated by the poor academic outcome of students living in social and ethnic segregated neighbourhoods, as well as the unfavourable economic situation of the schools located there. These strategies mainly targeted students born outside Sweden or children born in Sweden but whose parents were born abroad were implemented in order to increase the pupils' academic results in these school areas.

among students and parents towards Swedish as a second language, which is often associated with discrimination and stigma for this category of pupils.

According to OECD (2010) Swedish as a second Language (SSL) education is not integrated in other pedagogical strategies targeted at pupils with a foreign background in school practice. The OECD suggested the need to develop intercultural guidelines to support SSL teachers to focus more and more on integrating the teaching of subjects in their classes rather than the Swedish language. Since international research and experiences from school practice in Sweden show that cognitive skills and language proficiency develop hand in hand and that students might learn a language more effectively when taught for a specific purpose, it is recommended to increase the teaching quality of Swedish, English, maths and new technologies for these students in Swedish schools.

Measures to develop the teaching of mother tongue and SSL pay attention to the first- versus the second-language acquisition perspective in learning process. They are implemented as a strategy to improve student's learning of school subjects (OECD, 2010). However, mother tongue and Swedish as a second language are strategy targets in practice for the more disadvantaged social ethnic groups, for example children with Somali, Albanian and Arabic mother tongues. Conversely, the minorities more integrated into Swedish society do not take part in these differentiated curricular strategies in the same manner. It is therefore necessary to make a deeper political, educational research analysis about the impacts of these differentiated curricular strategies, starting by analysing pupils' social class and native tongues before extending the teaching of different curricular subjects in those languages (Francia and Moreno Herrera, 2008).

Education priority policies implemented by the Swedish National Agency for School Development in 2003–07 mainly focused on the reduction of academic failure as a result of ethnic segregation (Francia and Moreno Herrera, 2008). This reduction of ethnic segregation has consequently resulted in the lack of questioning of the existence of a differentiated syllabus in Swedish for Swedish citizens belonging to second- and third-generation immigrant groups. In these cases, the role played by students' social class, birthplace and mother tongue in foreign students' academic results has often been neglected. Consequently, this limitation on ethnic and language segregation implies a risk of increased social segregation. In this way, these education priority policies may work more as *ethnification of socio-economic inequalities* than as equity strategies.

Educational and social research also shows that several kinds of reduced curriculum practices are implemented in the teaching of physical education and health, music, religion and sex education in the Swedish multicultural school system (Gustafsson, 2004; Högdin, 2007). This research shows the existence of curriculum reduction practices according to gender and religious background that tend to decrease and reshape the national compulsory education knowledge standards at the school level. In particular, it is necessary to develop policies that guarantee girls from minority cultures the right to equal education when reduced and differentiated curriculum practices are implemented in the name of recognition of cultural and religious differences at the school level.

Parental Involvement in Migrant Children's Schooling

In 2010 a commission for a *Socially Sustainable Malmö* (Malmö Commission) was created to develop strategies to reduce health inequality in Malmö, one of the three most important cities in Sweden. Malmö has been in the media in recent years because of its relatively high degree of ethnic and social segregation as well as its relatively high degree of violence in comparison with other Swedish cities (Kommission för ett socialt hållbart Malmö, 2013).

The Malmö Commission included active participation of organisations and citizens who can share their experiences and contribute to the analysis of strategies to develop equality standards in the city. This commission recommended increasing economic and social investment in social segregated areas, increasing cooperation between different actors at the university, at national and municipal levels as well as private organisations, and a continuous follow-up of inequalities in the city.

Furthermore, a report from the Commission pointed out the need to increase parents' involvement in children's schooling in ethnic and social segregated areas (Bouakaz, 2012). One example of this kind of involvement is the development of complementary schools in Malmö that offer parents a possibility to support their children's education. The schools created by parent initiatives offer migrant children homework help as well as cultural heritage, language and religious education. Complementary schools seem to be a phenomenon that engages migrant parents from different ethnicities and religions. According to Bouakaz (2012) these schools are an example of good practice that counteracts the negative effects of marginalisation and stigmatisation of migrant families. The parents' involvement in these schools contributes towards showing them as active participants in their children's schooling. They contribute as well to support migrant children in their academic studies and identity development.

However, complementary schools, particularly those with religious and cultural heritage profiles, are not always accepted by Swedish society. Swedish school staff show have a negative attitude to this kind of parental involvement, sometimes recommending that pupils abandon complementary schools in order to achieve better academic results in mainstream schools.

However, the Malmö Commission recommends developing better cooperation between this 'informal' complementary school system and the formal municipal school system (Bouakaz, 2012). Therefore, the Commission suggests the following strategies to develop migrant parents' involvement in their children's schooling:

- spread information about complementary schools activities to migrant groups and to Swedish society as a whole;
- offer complementary schools access to municipal building;

- develop cooperation between complementary and municipal schools by way of staff visits to complementary schools;
- develop intercultural dialogue between different actors involved in immigrant children's education;
- include visits to complementary schools in the programmes of teacher training schools.

Conclusion

The current Swedish education system is characterised by the ethnic diversity of its students. With more than 18 per cent of students with a foreign background at compulsory and upper secondary level, cultural homogeneity is no longer possible in Sweden. National and international statistics show that students with a foreign background are still the Achilles heel of the Swedish education system, often having lower academic results at secondary schools in relation to students of ethnic Swedish background.

However, students with a foreign background are not a homogeneous group. Therefore, interrelation between students' ethnicity and other factors such as gender, social class, parental education level, time of residence is necessary to avoid generalisation concerning foreign students' school situation. The intersectional analysis of different variables can also explain why students of foreign background can achieve both the highest and the lowest scores in international tests such as PISA.

Curricular strategies such as mother tongue support or Swedish as a second language as a differentiated methodological support can contribute to developing the right to equal education of students with foreign backgrounds. However, these strategies must include measures assuring at the same time a fair distribution of academic standards and intellectual skills for all students. Therefore, I will point out the need to carefully follow up the negative impacts of the following differentiation strategies on equity for students with a foreign background:

- strategies that legitimate reduced curricular and lower knowledge standards for children of minorities and socially marginalised groups;
- strategies that do not take into account the impact of the interaction of ethnicity, social class and gender;
- strategies that do not include the development of academic standards and intellectual skills for all children.

Therefore, the existence of a differentiated syllabus for Swedish as a second language or reduced curricular practices according to students' gender, mother tongue, religion or culture must be questioned in order to guarantee minority children's right to equitable education.

In order to develop equity in diversity it is necessary to individualise and adapt educational content to students' backgrounds and needs. However, a deeper questioning of the impacts of decentralisation and privatisation of the Swedish schools system on schools in social and ethnic segregated areas is needed. This re-examination will put in doubt equity policies for students with a foreign background based on a culturalisation of socioeconomic differences to stop the growthe of ethnic inequalities in the Swedish education system and society. Experiences from the riots in migrant neighbourhoods as well as the results of the Malmö Commission show the need to develop strategies to support migrant parents' involvement in their children's schooling. Strategies showing migrant parents as active participants contribute to counteract the negative attitudes towards immigrant families present in the Swedish school system and society in general.

Only with more comprehensive equity priority policies that pay attention to the interrelation of ethnic and socioeconomic inequalities as well as structural discrimination mechanism will students with a foreign background no longer be considered the Swedish education system's Achilles heel.

References

Bouakaz, L. (2012). *'Att behålla mitt och lära mig något nytt' Föräldraengagemang i mångkulturella miljöer. Ett diskussionsunderlag framtaget för Kommission för ett socialt hållbart Malmö.* http://www.malmo.se/download/18.1558e15e13973 eeaa0e800011507/Att+beh%C3%A5lla+mitt+och+l%C3%A4ra+mig+n%C3 %A5got+nytt_Laid+Bouakaz.pdf [retrieved 23 June 2013].

Dupriez, V.Y. and Dumay, X. (2004). L'égalité dans les systèmes scolaries: effect école ou effet société? *Les Cahiers de Recherche en education et Formation*, 31 (October). Girsef: CPU.

Folkhälsoinstitutet (2013). *Barn och unga 2013. Utvecklingen av faktorer som påverkar hälsan och genomförda åtgärder.* http://www.fhi.se/Publikationer/ Alla-publikationer/Barn-och-unga-2013-Utvecklingen-av-faktorer-som-paverkar-halsan-och-genomforda-atgarder [retrieved 2 June 2013].

Francia, G. (1999). *Policy som text och praktik. En analys av likvärdighetsbegreppet i 1990-talets utbildningsreform för det obligatoriska skolväsendet.* Serie Doktorsavhandlingar från Pedagogiska institutionen, Stockholms universitet, 94, 1104–625.

Francia, G. (2011). Dilemmas in the implementation of the children's right equity in education in the Swedish compulsory school. *European Education Research Journal.* http://www.wwwords.eu/eerj/content/pdfs/10/issue10_1. asp [retrieved 21 May 2013].

Francia, G. (2012). *Swedish as Second Language. Literacy Practice for Equity or for Social Reproduction?* Contribution to Symposium Literacy and Didactics: Perspectives Practices and Consequences I Network 27. Didactics – Learning and Teaching. ECER Cadiz, September.

Francia, G. and Moreno Herrera, L. (2008). Suède (pp. 217–36). In Frandji, I.D. et al. (eds), *Pour une comparaison des politiques d'Éducation prioritaire en Europe EUROPEP. December 2007*. Lyon: INRP.

Fraser, N. (1997). *Justice Interruptus. Critical Reflections on the 'Postsocialist' Condition*. London: Routledge.

Gustafsson, K. (2004). *Muslimsk skola, svenska villkor. Akademisk avhandling*. Umeå: Bokförlag.

Högdin, S. (2007). *Utbildning på (o)lika villkor: om kön och etnisk bakgrund i grundskolan*. Stockholm: Institutionen för socialt arbete, Stockholms universitet.

Integrationsverket (2004). *Integrationsverkets årsredovisningen 2004*. http://www. temaasyl.se/Documents/Offentliga%20utredningar%20och%20rapporter%20 (sv)/Integrationsverkets%20arsredovisning%202004.pdf [retrieved 1 June 2010].

Lahdenperä, P. (1997). *Invandrarbakgrund eller skolsvårigheter? En textanalytisk studie av åtgärdsprogram för elever med invandrarbakgrund*. Stockholm: HLS.

Kommission för ett socialt hållbart Malmö (2013). *Malmös väg mot en hållbar framtid. Hälsa, välfärd och rättvisa. Slutrapport*. http://www.malmo.se/ download/18.31ab534713cd4aa921357ef/malm%C3%B6kommissionen_ slutrapport_digital_130312.pdf [retrieved 13 June 2013].

Mediapart (2013). *Pourquoi les banlieues de Stockholm se sont-elles enflammées?* http://blogs.mediapart.fr/edition/les-invites-de-mediapart/article/130613/ pourquoi-les- banlieues-de-stockholm-se-sont-elles-enflammees [retrieved 13 June 2013].

Mons, N. (2007). *Les nouvelles politiques éducatives. La France fait-elle les bons choix?* Paris: Presses Universitaires de France.

Myndigheten för skolutveckling (2004). *Kartläggning av svenska som andraspråk*. Dnr 2003:757

Nilsson, Å. (2004). *Immigration and Emigration in the Postwar Period*. Demographic Reports, 2004, 5. Stockholm: Statistics Sweden. http://www.scb. se/statistik/_publikationer/BE0701_1950I02_BR_BE51ST0405.pdf [retrieved 21 May 2013].

OECD (2005). *Equity in Education Thematic Review. Sweden*. http://www.oecd. org/dataoecd/10/5/35892546.pdf [retrieved 21 May 2013].

OECD (2010). *Review of Migrant Education Sweden*. March 2010. http://www. oecd.org/dataoecd/45/40/44862803.pdf [retrieved 21 May 2013].

Salonen, T. (2012). *Barns ekonomiska utsatthet. Årsrapport 2012:2*. Stockholm: Rädda barnen. http://www.svt.se/nyheter/regionalt/sydnytt/article894776.svt/ BINARY/Barnfattigdomsrapporten_2012_2_Helhet.pdf [retrieved 23 June 2013].

SCB (2012a). *Invandring och utvandring 2011: Var femte invandrare är svensk medborgare*. http://www.scb.se/pages/article____333969.aspx [retrieved 21 May 2013].

SCB (2012b). *Befolkningsframskrivningar*. http://www.scb.se/Pages/TableAndChart 91832.aspx [retrieved 21 May 2013].

Sjögren, A. (1995). *En 'bra' svenska, från rimligt krav till försvarsmekanism.* Paper presented at the IMER congress, 'Det mångkulturella Sverige efter år 2000. Forskning och framtidsvisioner', Lund 26–27 October 1995.

Sjögren, D. (2010). Riktade utbildningssatsningar för inhemska minoriteter. Några motivoch kategoriseringsproblem i historisk belysning. In Larsson, E. and Westberg, J. (eds). *Utbildningens sociala och kulturella historia.* Meddelanden från den fjärde nordiska utbildningshistoriska konferensen. Uppsala; SEC, Uppsala University.

Skolverket (2007a). *PIRLS 2006. Rapport 305.* Stockholm. http://www.skolverket. se/publikationer?id=1756 [retrieved 26 June 2013].

Skolverket (2007b). *Descriptive Data on Pre-School Activities, School-Age Childcare, Schools and Adult Education in Sweden 2006. Report 283.* http:// www.skolverket.se/om- skolverket/publicerat/visa-enskild-publikation?_ xurl_=http%3A%2F%2Fwww5.skolverket.se%2Fwtpub%2Fws%2Fskolb ok%2Fwpubext%2Ftrycksak%2FRecord%3 Fk%3D1651 [retrieved 21 May 2013].

Skolverket (2010). *Rustad att möta framtiden? PISA 2009 om 15-åringars läsförståelse och kunskaper i matematik och naturvetenskap. Internationella Studier Rapport 352.* Stockholm. http://www.skolverket.se/ publikationer?id=2473 [retrieved 21 May 2013].

Skolverket (2011). *Utdrag: Barn och elever med utländsk bakgrund. Skolverkets lägesbedömning 2011 Del 1 – Beskrivande data – Rapport 363.* http://www. skolverket.se/publikationer?id=2692 [retrieved 21 May 2013].

Skolverket (2012a). *Grundskolan- Betyg och Prov – Riksnivå Tabell 1 C: Elever som avslutat årskurs 9 läsåret 2011/12 och har behörighet till nationellt program.* http://www.skolverket.se [retrieved 21 May 2013].

Skolverket (2012b). *Beskrivande data 2012. Förskola, skola och vuxenutbildning. Rapport 383.* Stockholm. http://www.skolverket.se/publikationer?id=2994 [retrieved 21 May 2013].

Skolverket (2012c). *TIMSS 2011 Rapport 380.* http://www.skolverket.se/ publikationer?id=2942 [retrieved 21 May 2013].

Skolverket (2012d). *PIRLS 2011. Läsförmågan hos svenska elever i årskurs 4 i ett internationellt perspektiv. Fortsatt nedåtgående resultat. Rapport 381.* Stockholm: Skolverket http://www.skolverket.se/publikationer?id=2941 [retrieved 21 May 2013].

SOU (2005). *Det blågula glashuset – strukturell diskriminering i Sverige. Strukturell diskriminering i Sverige: betänkande / av Utredningen om strukturell diskriminering på grund av etnisk eller religiös tillhörighet.* Arbetsmarknadsdepartementet. Statens offentliga utredningar. Stockholm: Fritzes offentliga publikationer.

Svenska Dagbladet (2013). *Husby- kommissionen krävs för djup analys.* http:// www.svd.se/opinion/brannpunkt/husby-kommission-kravs-for-djup-analys_8230682.svd 1 June 2013 [retrieved 21 June 2013].

Concluding Remarks

Marco Catarci

This study provides a comparative analysis of intercultural theories and practices in the primary 'old immigration countries' (the United Kingdom, France and Germany), 'new immigration countries' (Italy, Spain and Greece) and some Northern European countries (Netherlands and Sweden) where specific approaches to intercultural education have been established. A broad spectrum of intercultural approaches to intercultural education in the European context has been developed in accordance with national histories (including the colonial past of many European countries), educational politics and migration flows. With regard to these approaches, some remarks can be formulated about the results of this study, based on an analysis of the work of the various contributors.

First of all, a *framework of the presence of immigrants and immigrant students in European societies* shows that there are 32.5 million non-nationals living in Europe today, over three-quarters of whom are spread across five countries: Germany (7.1 million), Spain (5.7 million), the United Kingdom (4.4 million), Italy (4.2 million) and France (3.8 million). Three main migration waves have taken place in Europe since the Second World War. The first consisted of primary labour migration between the 1950s and the oil crisis of 1973–74, driven by the needs of economic reconstruction in Western Europe. The second was related to secondary-family migration between the mid-1970s and the end of the Cold War in 1989–90, consisting mainly of high-skilled immigrants. The third wave consisted of asylum-seeking and illegal flows after 1989–90 (Geddes, 2003: 17–18).

These waves of migration have directly affected European education systems. There are now many students from different cultural and social backgrounds in various European countries. For instance, in the United Kingdom there are 1,992,600 non-national students (24.3 per cent of the academic population), in Spain 781,446 (9.9 per cent), in Italy 755,939 (8.4 per cent) and in Germany 665,960 (7.7 per cent). In France, however, this category is no longer given in official statistics. These figures undoubtedly call for effective and consistent responses to the cultural and educational needs of students with immigrant cultural backgrounds in European education systems.

Several scholars have remarked on the *structural segregation of students with immigrant backgrounds in European schools*. The long tradition of cultural and linguistic homogeneity in several European education systems has in many cases led to the isolation of immigrant students in a context of lower social and economic opportunities. This has often resulted in certain schools having a high concentration of immigrant students. This double ethnic and socio-economic segregation can mean that formulating any realistic perspective on interculturalism simply becomes impracticable. For instance, in the Dutch context (as in many other European countries), schools with a ratio of 50 per cent or more minority students in relation to school-aged migrant children in the neighbourhood are unofficially characterised as *zwarte* (black) and are often widespread in urban contexts. It is not always true that a high incidence of immigrant students is linked to poor-quality education, but such segregation can create a dangerous segmentation within society in terms of opportunities for higher education, employment and citizenship for students. Furthermore, the moving of native students (and also of some students with immigrant backgrounds) to schools with lower numbers of immigrant students indicates the possibly inaccurate perceptions of some parents that a multicultural environment is related to poor school achievement.

Another issue highlighted by this study relates to *social equity as a major challenge for intercultural education*. Inequalities between immigrant students and their native peers must be addressed by an intercultural approach that is able to promote not only cultural understanding but also effective opportunities for immigrant students. Several authors have remarked that in many contexts a gap in achievement by immigrant students can still be observed, even in the more equitable education systems of countries belonging to the Organisation for Economic Cooperation and Development (OECD) such as Sweden, where 76 per cent of immigrant girls and 74 per cent of immigrant boys are eligible for upper-secondary studies, compared to 92 per cent and 90 per cent of native girls and boys.

The OECD (2010) has stated that, although education has expanded over recent decades in many countries, inequalities in outcomes continue to hinder social mobility. Its reports show that native-born children of immigrants generally tend to perform better than their immigrant counterparts of the same age, and that significant gaps are registered between the children of natives and the native-born children of immigrants (Liebig and Widmaier, 2010). In this regard, achievement gaps between immigrant and native students can be largely explained by language barriers and socio-economic differences (OECD, 2010, 2012a, 2012b). Moreover, in European education systems, students with immigrant backgrounds are generally more likely to drop out, especially from secondary education, and to choose secondary schools marked by vocational priorities. These aspects appear to be especially rooted in highly selective and segregated educational systems, and indicate the need for a more accurate understanding of the dynamics of social marginalisation and inequality of opportunities in education and within the overall social system.

A *gap between statements of intercultural principles and assimilationist practices* also emerged from the study. The principles of intercultural perspectives in Europe often appear to be highly innovative and to exist on a progressive and democratic level. However, real practices are often implemented from 'assimilationist' and 'compensatory' viewpoints which can entrench education in a linguistic and cultural homogeneity. For instance, in its White

Paper on Intercultural Dialogue – which was intended to provide policy makers and practitioners with guidelines for the promotion of intercultural dialogue – the Council of Europe (2008: 17) stated that it intends to create a 'process that comprises an open and respectful exchange of views between individuals and groups with different ethnic, cultural, religious and linguistic backgrounds and heritage, on the basis of mutual understanding and respect'. This double perspective concerning both immigrants and nationals is seldom taken into account. As a matter of fact, education systems generally are responding to the challenge of multiculturalism with an assimilationist and compensatory approach. This confirms previous research findings (Allemann-Ghionda, 2008: 41) and highlights the need for policies that promote specific continuing education opportunities in which teachers and educators can reflect on those principles and plan strategies to translate them into their daily professional practice.

Another topic that was transversally present in several analyses of the study concerns the *critical revision of the project of European society*. The riots by youth with immigrant backgrounds – which first occurred in the *banlieus* of Paris in October 2005, then in the suburbs of London in August 2011, and even in the periphery of Stockholm in May 2013 – put the whole project of European society into question. Indeed, the protests of these young people, often second- or third-generation immigrants born in Europe, show that their being formally acknowledged as national citizens in a European state does not necessarily mean that they have the same social opportunities as their peers. Thus, is European society really able to assure equal opportunities for young people, regardless of their cultural origin, and to combat social inequalities through an efficient educational system? From this perspective, students must be considered as agents of change who can overcome their traditional roles of reproducing the social structure.

Dramatic cases like the murders in the Netherlands of the politician Pim Fortuyn in 2002 and of the film director Theo Van Gogh in 2004, and of the British Army drummer Lee Rigby in London in 2013 have also raised serious questions about the effectiveness of the integration policies adopted towards immigrants within European society. In particular, 'integration' cannot be intended only as a process of including immigrants in the European context, as it implies a dynamic two-way process of mutual accommodation by both immigrants and national residents. Therefore, measures addressed not only at immigrants but also at nationals must be implemented in order to provide them with the necessary skills to interact appropriately with people of various cultural backgrounds. In this sense, a remark by Amin Maloouf appears particularly evocative: 'While most of the European nations have been built on the platform of their language of identity, the European Union can only build on a platform of linguistic diversity' (Maloouf, 2008: 5).

Finally, this study highlights *the role of the best practices across European countries* in promoting the development of an effective intercultural approach to education. Among the practices described by the contributors are:

- The Centre Académique pour la Scolarisation des élèves allophones Nouvellement Arrivés et des enfants issus de familles itinérantes et de Voyageurs (CASNAV), which is an academic centre for the education of newly arrived allophones, children from migrant families and traveller pupils. This agency has considerable expertise in the education of newly arrived students at a regional level in France, with regard to the tasks of information, training, creation and dissemination of educational tools, on behalf of teachers, school principals, inspectors, parents, associations or social workers;
- ADRIC (Agence de développement des relations interculturelles pour la citoyenneté or the Agency for the Development of Intercultural Relations Citizenship) is a French organisation which offers continuing educational opportunities on behalf of institutional actors (such as public officials, social workers and members of local authorities), socio-economic actors (personal business, unions etc.) or associative actors (employees, volunteers, civil society, neighbourhood residents etc.) in order to enhance awareness and build a common culture in terms of modes of communication, knowledge of cultural diversity and citizen involvement. It promotes teaching methods which involve the participants in the description of the situations they are encountering, in changing their perceptions and behaviour and in the construction of new knowledge;
- The 'Aula Intercultural' (Intercultural Classroom) is a project developed in 2003 by the education department of the Spanish Union UGT with the collaboration of the Spanish Ministry of Education, the Ministry of Employment and Social Security and the European Fund for Integration. It aims to create a website offering information on immigration and intercultural education, in order to provide teaching professionals with intercultural teaching and informative materials. It also hopes to provide the educational community with a space to exchange information, reflections and experiences on intercultural strategies.

All of these approaches highlight the importance of investigating intercultural practices, reflecting on them and putting them into circulation from the perspective of social innovation.

This study raises fundamental questions about what projects of social education contribute to Europe. The notion of 'Fortress Europe' has been adopted to identify the closure of European politics to immigrants, particularly restricting their access from outside European borders. However, this notion also requires a deep understanding of the cultural and educational dynamics supporting such a closure. Jagdish Gundara has remarked that while nationals living in Europe have a range of cultural backgrounds, the educational systems of the Member States are still designed as though people belong to a single national culture, tying education to a 'hegemonic canon' that recognises only its own 'Eurocentric' tradition. Even when it recognises different traditions it evaluates them according to its point of view and values (Gundara 2000: 116).

Only through a critical analysis of the excluding dimensions of the curriculum, and of how humanities, the social sciences and the sciences are constructed, can a broader universalistic and human dimension of knowledge be restored. Thus, overcoming Eurocentrism (i.e. a tendency to interpret the world in terms of western and especially European values and experiences) in education is an essential task of intercultural education. In this sense, Eurocentrism has replaced rational explanations of history with partial 'pseudo-theories' involving the contradiction of generating a dominant capitalist culture and of denying the universalist aspiration on which that culture claims to be founded. This paradigm, which works naturally in the so-called 'grey areas of common sense', originated in the nineteenth century. It is thus a strictly modern phenomenon which constitutes a dimension of culture and ideology of the capitalist world (Said, 1978: 7; Amin, 1989: 104).

In conclusion, among the major current challenges facing European education systems are those of overcoming a persistent Eurocentric setting, building effective responses for all students – including those from different cultural backgrounds, – and providing them all with skills that are indispensable for full, active citizenship in an interdependent and pluralistic Europe.

References

Allemann-Ghionda, C. (2008). *Intercultural Education in Schools: A Comparative Study*. Brussels: European Parliament.

Amin, S. (1989). *Eurocentrism*. London: Zed books.

Council of Europe (2008). *White Paper on Intercultural Dialogue: Living Together as Equals in Dignity*. Strasbourg: Council of Europe.

Geddes, A. (2003). *The Politics of Migration and Immigration in Europe*. London: Sage.

Gundara, J.S. (2000). *Interculturalism, Education and Inclusion*. London: Chapman.

Liebig, T. and Widmaier, S. (2010). Overview: Children of immigrants in the labour markets of OECD and EU Countries. In OECD, *Equal Opportunities? The Labour Market Integration of the Children of Immigrants* (pp. 15–52). Paris: OECD.

Maalouf, A. (ed.) (2008). *A Rewarding Challenge: How the Multiplicity of Languages Could Strengthen Europe*. Luxembourg: EUR-OP.

OECD (2010). *Closing the Gap for Immigrant Students: Policies, Practice and Performance*. Paris: OECD.

OECD (2012a). *How Do Immigrant Students Fare in Disadvantaged Schools?* Paris: OECD.

OECD (2012b). *Untapped Skills: Realising the Potential of Immigrant Students*. Paris: OECD.

Said, E.W. (1978). *Orientalism*. London: Routledge and Kegan Paul.

Index

Note: italic page numbers indicate figures and tables; numbers in brackets preceded by *n* are footnote numbers.

Research in Migration and Ethnic Relations Series

Full Series List